The Act of the Mind

Roy Harvey Pearce is chairman of the Department of Literature at the University of California, San Diego. J. Hillis Miller is chairman of the Department of English at The Johns Hopkins University.

THE ACT
OF THE MIND

Essays on the Poetry of Wallace Stevens

Edited by
Roy Harvey Pearce and J. Hillis Miller

The Johns Hopkins Press, Baltimore, Maryland

"Of Modern Poetry" is reprinted, by permission of Alfred A. Knopf, Inc., from *The Collected Poems of Wallace Stevens.* Copyright 1942, 1954 by Wallace Stevens.

"The Region November," "As You Leave the Room," and "The Course of a Particular" are reprinted, by permission of Alfred A. Knopf, Inc., from *Opus Posthumous,* by Wallace Stevens. Copyright 1957 by Elsie Stevens and Holly Stevens.

"The Snow Man" is reprinted, by permission of Alfred A. Knopf, Inc., from *The Collected Poems of Wallace Stevens.* Copyright 1923, 1931, 1954 by Wallace Stevens.

"Not Ideas about the Thing but the Thing Itself" is reprinted, by permission of Alfred A. Knopf, Inc., from *The Collected Poems of Wallace Stevens.* Copyright 1954 by Wallace Stevens.

Other quotations from *The Collected Poems of Wallace Stevens, Opus Posthumous,* and *The Necessary Angel* are printed with the permission of Alfred A. Knopf, Inc.

Of Modern Poetry

The poem of the mind in the act of finding
What will suffice. It has not always had
To find: the scene was set; it repeated what
Was in the script.
                    Then the theatre was changed
To something else. Its past was a souvenir.
It has to be living, to learn the speech of the place.
It has to face the men of the time and to meet
The women of the time. It has to think about war
And it has to find what will suffice. It has
To construct a new stage. It has to be on that stage
And, like an insatiable actor, slowly and
With meditation, speak words that in the ear,
In the delicatest ear of the mind, repeat,
Exactly, that which it wants to hear, at the sound
Of which, an invisible audience listens,
Not to the play, but to itself, expressed
In an emotion as of two people, as of two
Emotions becoming one. The actor is
A metaphysician in the dark, twanging
An instrument, twanging a wiry string that gives
Sounds passing through sudden rightnesses, wholly
Containing the mind, below which it cannot descend,
Beyond which it has no will to rise.
                              It must
Be the finding of a satisfaction, and may
Be of a man skating, a woman dancing, a woman
Combing. The poem of the act of the mind.

                              Wallace Stevens

for Don Cameron Allen

Preface

The essays published here, however different in point of view and method, have in common a general intention: to take seriously Wallace Stevens' claims as a philosophical poet, and to study the implications, the range, and the import of those claims. The majority of these essays have been published in *ELH* over the past few years. We have added to them four hitherto unpublished essays, which are consonant in intention with those previously published. The "style" of the volume may well testify to the fact that *ELH* is edited at an institution where the study of the relations of literature and ideas constitutes a major discipline; so that it was not by chance that a number of scholar-critics happened to think of *ELH* as an appropriate journal in which to publish their interpretations of Stevens' life-long attempts to justify the ways of art to men. For Stevens' work surely constitutes its own kind of an intellectual history. Thus the rationale of this volume: to take that work on its own terms and to inquire both into the conditions under which the terms are made operative and into the mode of operation itself. The conditions are those of a world, Stevens' and ours, which obliges him to give his poems their particular force and direction. The mode of operation is one expressive of that genesis and movement of ideas which only the art of poetry makes possible. Reading the poems, studying the acts of the poet's mind, we may discover the ideas which could, or should, become ours.

R. H. P.

J. H. M.

Summer, 1964

Contents

The Act of the Mind

I

WALLACE STEVENS: THE USE OF POETRY

BY BERNARD HERINGMAN

The world of Wallace Stevens' poetry has always been two, "things as they are" and "things imagined." The dichotomy has been so constant that certain terms are stock symbols of the two realms. The moon, blue, the polar north, winter, music, poetry and all art: these consistently refer to the realm of imagination, order, the ideal. The sun, yellow, the tropic south, summer, physical nature: these refer to, or symbolize, the realm of reality, disorder, the actual. And just as Crispin, "the poetic hero" of "The Comedian as the Letter C," alternates between the two in his search for a valid aesthetic, so Stevens, in his poetry, has

> . . . conceived his voyaging to be
> An up and down between two elements,
> A fluctuating between sun and moon.

From *Harmonium* to "Notes toward a Supreme Fiction," the poetry is concerned with these two worlds, separately and in varying relation. The concern is made explicit in dust-jacket statements by Stevens: about *Ideas of Order*, which "attempts to illustrate the role of the imagination in me, and particularly in [the realistic] life at present"; about "The Man with the Blue Guitar," which "deals with the incessant conjunctioning between things as they are and things imagined."

The concept of the *fiction* becomes a key to Stevens' developing projection of a synthesis of imagination and reality and thus to his concern (in both his poetry and his occasional criticism) with the use of poetry. At first the *fiction* is roughly equivalent to *poetry*, as a manifestation, or a voice, of imagination. In "A High-Toned Old Christian Woman" (*Harmonium*),

> Poetry is the supreme fiction, madame.

In "The Comedian as the Letter C," in the course of Crispin's search, "The moonlight fiction disappeared" in favor of "the essential prose," or reality. But Stevens carefully reminds us that

1

the prose may " wear a poem's guise at last," suggesting a possible synthesis. It is suggested again in " Another Weeping Woman " (*Harmonium*) , with

> The magnificent cause of being,
> The imagination, the one reality
> In this imagined world.

" To the One of Fictive Music " (*Harmonium*) is an invocation to the poetic muse, saying that poetry must work from imme- diate reality, yet asking that it be endowed with " the strange unlike," with the unreal imagination.

Stevens also makes use of the *fiction* in *Parts of a World*, in terms of a problem of belief. Here, in " Asides on the Oboe " he poses " a question . . ./ Of final belief," a question of choosing the fiction in which to place our final belief. " If . . . man is not enough " to believe in, the poem says, we can still believe in an " impossible possible philosophers' man," a man who sums up the world and us. This man is like the inhabitant of the heaven or ideal realm pictured in " The Greenest Continent " (" Owl's Clover ") , in being " the transparence of the place in which/He is." He is a creator of reality in his own supreme imagination. He is a poet, " and in his poems we find peace." The poem suggests a fusion of reality and imagination by means of a *fiction*.

Stevens has mentioned the *supreme fiction* in his prose as well as in his poetry, in a way that encourages interpretation of a developing use of the concept as connected with the fusion or synthesis of his dichotomy.

There is, in fact, a world of poetry indistinguishable from the world in which we live, or, I ought to say, no doubt, from the world in which we shall come to live, since what makes the poet the potent figure he is, or was, or ought to be, is that he creates the world to which we turn incessantly and without knowing it and that he gives to life the supreme fictions without which we are unable to conceive of it.[1]

It is not likely that Stevens means that the two " indistinguish- able " worlds are in all respects the same. But the passage has double relevance to his theme of the intersection of imagination and reality: socially, in that the poet thereby helps men to live

---

[1] " The Noble Rider and the Sound of Words," in *The Language of Poetry*, ed. Allen Tate (Princeton, 1942), pp. 120-21.

their lives; aesthetically, and ontologically, in that poetry thereby constitutes a greater reality.

Both aspects of the theory find major development in " Notes toward a Supreme Fiction." The two aspects—the social and the aesthetic—cannot, of course, be mutually exclusive, but this paper is primarily concerned with the aesthetic. In this consideration, an examination of the function and location of poetry (as subject or referent *in the poems*) in terms of Stevens' dichotomy is an illuminating guide. Poetry has generally in his work been a symbol of the whole realm of imagination, and a special manifestation of that realm. It has been a means of escape from reality, a means of ordering the chaos of reality, a means of finding the good in reality, and, simply, a means of describing reality. At times the last two functions have been carried to the point where poetry has been relocated as a subordinate part of reality, usually as the voice of that realm. The relation of the two realms has naturally varied with the variation in the place of poetry, chiefly in an alteration between conflict and conjunction, sometimes with a separation so nearly complete that no systematic relation could be traced.

For an estimate of the final development of the fictive synthesis of imagination and reality, the location and function of poetry are again guiding factors. The shifting process of these factors reaches a kind of finality in the " Notes," corresponding to the final development of the synthesis. Although in most of Stevens' work, poetry is located either in the realm of imagination or, less frequently, in reality, another tendency makes itself felt almost from the beginning, always in connection with the development toward the idea of synthesis. There has been a shift toward the center, toward the balancing point between the two members of the dichotomy. This became fairly evident in " Owl's Clover " and " The Man with the Blue Guitar." It culminates in the " Notes," where the central location of poetry is not only an implicit necessity but a symbolically explicit fact and theme. For example, in a section (VII) of " It Must Give Pleasure," the third book of the " Notes ":

> . . . It must be that in time
> The real will from its crude compoundings come,
>
> Seeming, at first, a beast disgorged, unlike,
> Warmed by a desperate milk. To find the real,
> To be stripped of every fiction except one,

> The fiction of an absolute—Angel,
> Be silent in your luminous cloud and hear
> The luminous melody of proper sound.

Here poetry is the supreme fiction, central between the *real* and the *absolute* or ideal, central between men and *Angel*, between *crude compoundings* and refined reality. The fiction is agent of synthesis and, in *luminous melody*, product of synthesis. This development parallels the poet's remark that "It is not only that the imagination adheres to reality, but, also, that reality adheres to the imagination and that the interdependence is essential"; a corollary also of his remark on the poet's intenser "realization" of "resemblance": his "sense of reality keen enough to be in excess of the normal sense of reality creates a reality of its own." [2] Starting from an intersection of imagination and reality, poetry creates a synthesis, and thus creates a new world of transcendent reality.

Stevens adds evidence of his interest in the poetry of intersection and synthesis by finding similar transcendence in the poems of Marianne Moore and William Carlos Williams. He sees it, as Miss Moore sees it, in her "conjunction of imaginary gardens and real toads"; and in his preface to one of Williams' books: ". . . how often the essential poetry is the result of the conjunction of the unreal and the real, the sentimental and the anti-poetic, the constant interaction of the two opposites." [3]

"Notes toward a Supreme Fiction" is no formalized philosophic discourse, logically constructing this metaphysics of intersection and consequent synthesis. It is well to consider the title, which establishes a tentative tone and a feeling, common in reading Stevens, of the poet's deprecatory attitude toward himself and his art. Still, the "toward" indicates approach to a goal, and three sub-titles suggest a definition and possible construction of the supreme fiction. "It Must Be Abstract"; "It Must Change"; "It Must Give Pleasure."

The brief prologue sums up Stevens' dedication to poetry. He meets it in a light of "living changingness," finds "the uncertain light of single, certain truth," and makes his affirmation:

---

[2] *Ibid.*, p. 122; and "The Realm of Resemblance," *Partisan Review*, XIV (1947), 247.

[3] "A Poet that Matters," *Life and Letters Today* (London), XIII, No. 2 (Dec., 1935), 65; W. C. Williams, *Collected Poems 1921-1931* (New York, 1934), p. 3.

> For a moment in the central of our being,
> The vivid transparence that you bring is peace.

Here is another crucial mention of the *transparence* which brings peace and is a quality of "heaven." This sublime state comes *in the central of our being*. The phrase conveys more than a sense of intense feeling. *Central,* used as a noun, carries a sense of relation which *center* would lack, as well as making the statement more striking. In other words, it locates the situation at the intersection of the two realms. The use of *our* supports this interpretation with both of its main possible readings. If *our being* means that of Stevens and the muse he addresses, then the *vivid transparence* is between them. If *our,* in contrast with the first person singular of the rest of the poem, refers him to his fellows, then the poet becomes representative of the reality-world of mankind in that intersection with imagination which results in the sublime situation he describes.

The idea of the poet as representative of humanity-reality is borne out, in turn, by a theme to which Stevens has given considerable attention. It is especially noteworthy here because of its relevance to the theme of intersection in the dichotomy. For Stevens the poet is a microcosm, summing up in himself the whole universe of the dichotomy and, in himself, constituting an intersection which results in poetry. Stevens states a credo for a projected ideal poet:

I am the truth, since I am part of what is real, but neither more nor less than those around me. And I am imagination, in a leaden time and in a world that does not move for the weight of its own heaviness.[4]

The development of this theme also traces back through the whole of Stevens' work. It begins with such early examples as "I was the world in which I walked," from "Tea at the Palaz of Hoon" (*Harmonium*), where it is related to the location of the poet *in* reality. It develops through a stage represented by "Re-Statement of Romance" (*Ideas of Order*), where a poet-lover is true to his "separate self," which he best perceives against a background of night, by perceiving that night "is what it is as I am what I am." The final stage appears in "Chocorua to Its Neigh-

---

[4] "The Figure of the Youth as Virile Poet," *Sewanee Review*, LII (1944), 526.

bor" (*Transport to Summer*), where the man on top of the mountain says:

> . . . My solitaria
> Are the meditations of a central mind.
> I hear the motions of the spirit and the sound
> Of what is secret becomes, for me, a voice
> That is my own voice speaking in my ear.

The entire poem describes this man as a fusion of the two realms of imagination and reality, making him the microcosm and the voice of the synthesized world.

The whole of the "Notes" works toward and around the idea of the intersection as a locus for the supreme fiction, intersection as producing the fictive synthesis. As the poet embodies the synthesis, he will know the supreme fiction by knowing himself. But Stevens must work toward knowing it, by taking notes on its definition, new notes which will incorporate some of his earlier ones.

"IT MUST BE ABSTRACT"

To Stevens, starlight has always been a "Good light for . . . poets," and "for those / That know the ultimate Plato," those who can find tranquillity with the star in "The torments of confusion" ("Homunculus et la Belle Etoile," *Harmonium*). He has always been interested, Platonically, in "The abstract . . . The premise from which all things were conclusions" ("Contrary Theses II," *Parts of a World*). He has stressed in his prose the importance of the poet's power to abstract himself and to take reality into the abstraction with him, by putting it into his imagination, which, in turn, he must recognize is inseparable from reality.

Thus the "Notes" begins with the symbolic abstraction of reality:

> You must become an ignorant man again
> And see the sun again with an ignorant eye
> And see it clearly in the idea of it.

This Platonic *idea*, in Stevens usually the *first idea*, recurs in eight of the ten sections of this first book of the "Notes." In several cases there is an approach to synthesis by way of specific relation of the *idea* to the reality of which it is an abstract. This is particularly true in section III, where "The poem refreshes life," making it possible for us to return to "the first idea," which is "an immaculate beginning," and to move between "that ever-early candor" and "its late plural," between the idea and its descendant manifestations. From this movement begun by "the poem" we feel "an excitation, a pure power." Finally, in III the nonsense of life "pierces us with strange relation." *Nonsense* refers to some nonsense syllables in previous lines, to the nonsense sounds of the rise and fall of the ocean, an old symbol of life-reality, and to the non-sense which is the first idea of life, or poetry, which relates the first idea and life.

Section IV attempts definition of the source of poetry: "From this the poem springs: that we live in a place that is not our own and . . . not ourselves." And this is hard. The implications are that the poem springs from desire to escape the place, to soften its hardness, or to make it our own. The last seems most likely in the context, particularly as the poem is, in the last line of the section, "the sweeping meanings that we add." This is another note toward the intersection of two worlds.

Section VI refers back to the place we live in, which is not our own, where it was hard "in spite of blazoned days." Now the sun (which blazoned the days) has changed the poet's house, and magnolia fragrance comes close, "False flick, false form, but false-ness close to kin." This is a prefiguration of "the unreal of what is real" of "Holiday in Reality" (*Transport to Summer*), another hint of fusion in the dichotomy, of the merging of false and true, real and imagined. The hint is supported in succeeding lines of the section, which state "It must be" one or both in a series of opposites, symbolizing fusion quite clearly in the concluding paradox which "It" must be: "An abstraction blooded, as a man by thought." Since "It" has no distinguishable antecedent in the section, this "It" is probably the same one which "Must Be Abstract," that is, the supreme fiction.

Section VII supplies another note toward the same goal, with an alternation of symbols of the two realms on which "the truth" is said to depend. The dependence seems to be not so much on the "lake" of one realm (reality) or on the "composing" of the other (imagination) as on the presence of both, on the "balances that happen," with "moments of awakening."

Section VIII tells of *the first idea* in terms of the "major man," another of Stevens' related figures, who is not man but an abstract

of man, who lounges by the sea and reads about the thinker of
the first idea (God?). He is another point of intersection for
the symbolic dichotomy; he is given the possibility of expressing
the synthesis in a sudden new language. This major man is an
extension partly of the figure of the poet and partly of the earlier
hero-figure in Stevens, thus linking two realms again, microcosm-
fashion.[5]

The final section modifies and clarifies:

> The major abstraction is the idea of man
> And major man is its exponent, abler
> In the abstract than in his singular,
>
> More fecund as principle than particle,
> Happy fecundity, flor-abundant force,
> In being more than an exception, part,
>
> Though an heroic part, of the commonal.
>
> . . . .
>
> It is of him, ephebe, to make, to confect
> The final elegance . . . .

The ambiguous genitive of *idea of man,* both subjective and objective, conveys in itself the basic intersection which culminates in
the *final elegance.* We are given in one phrase the abstraction
about common man and the abstraction which is a force in the
mind of man, the two merging to become the source of creation.

" IT MUST CHANGE "

Section I relates the idea of change to the idea of abstraction.
Because of change, there is the perpetual cyclical flux which we
notice in particular objects in nature. Thus " The constant /
Violets, doves, girls . . ." are also " inconstant objects . . ./ In a
universe of inconstancy." The *constant* violets in this world of
change, of living and dying, can only be the abstractions of these
objects. This is another example of the " ever-early candor " and
" its late plural " given in section III of " It Must Be Abstract."

Section IV figures forth the whole essence of Stevens.

> Two things of opposite natures seem to depend
> On one another, as a man depends
> On a woman, day on night, the imagined

---

[5] The poet, of course, regularly epitomizes imagination; the hero, in Stevens, epitomizes
society and environment, i. e., reality.

On the real. This is the origin of change.
Winter and spring, cold copulars, embrace
And forth the particulars of rapture come.

The rest of the section elaborates on this in some of Stevens' most beautiful lines. From this passage Hi Simons drew his relation of " It Must Change " to " the law of inherent opposites " of " Connoisseur of Chaos," (*Parts of a World*), the law which in the "Notes " he found " expanded into a sort of dialectical principle of universal movement." [6] This is not merely an expansion, however, because here the opposites embrace and the embrace produces rapture. This is a note on the relation of change to the supreme fiction. The passage epitomizes the dichotomy, synthesis, and at least an aspect of the supreme fiction which arises in synthesis.

This book of the " Notes " is also a development of some of Stevens' uses of *change* in " Owl's Clover" (II, v): " It is only enough to live incessantly in change," and " So great a change/Is constant," and " But change composes, too." One significant example of change in the earlier passage shows summer, which is a symbol of nature-reality, changing with a sudden falling of the leaves. This would correspond to abstraction. Later in " Owl's Clover " (V, i), change makes a meaningful reappearance in relation to the poet, who is the cause of " rhapsodies of change " but is not changed by them.

Other sections of " It Must Change " suggest various processes of change, in the realms of both reality and imagination, and synthesis of the poles or opposites which produce change. Thus, in VIII, the spouse, the stripped women who is elemental, physical reality is not naked, not stripped of the " final filament," because

. . . A fictive covering
Weaves always glistening from the heart and mind.

Similarly in IX the poem is spoken of as alternating between " the poet's gibberish " and " The gibberish of the vulgate," with a question as to whether it moves " to and fro " or is " of both at once." The question is answered in the closing lines, where the poet is said to try " by a peculiar speech " to compound the two.

The last section echoes one of the hints of synthesis in " It Must Be Abstract," (VII) with a " lake . . . full of artificial things,"

[6] " Wallace Stevens and Mallarmé," *Modern Philology*, XLIII (1946), 244.

a complete metaphor for the synthesis of reality (the lake) and imagination, the synthesis which has now been given a source in a corresponding pair of principles of the supreme fiction, change and abstraction. The final couplet refers to both, to abstraction again in "beginnings" and to change in the process recorded by time, writing down the particulars of "The suitable amours" which are proposed "Of these beginnings."

"IT MUST GIVE PLEASURE"

The place of pleasure in the fictive synthesis is less clearly described than the place of the abstract or of change, but "pleasure" surely resides in "The luminous melody" which is sounded by finding "the fiction of an absolute." This comes with the intersection of the real and the ideal, with poetry at the center of the two realms, as I have already indicated in reference to this passage of section VII.

Again a passage of Stevens' prose illuminates his poetry:

It is the *mundo* of the imagination in which the imaginative man delights and not the gaunt world of the reason. The pleasure is the pleasure of powers that create a truth that cannot be arrived at by the reason alone, a truth that the poet recognizes by sensation.[7]

This later definition of pleasure is a direct echo of a passage in section I, where, after mentioning the "facile exercise" of speaking and singing the joy in the heart of the multitude, Stevens writes:

> But the difficultest rigor is forthwith,
> On the image of what we see, to catch from that
>
> Irrational moment its unreasoning,
> As when the sun comes rising, when the sea
> Clears deeply, when the moon hangs on the wall
> . . . .
> We reason about them with a later reason.

The concluding line is almost verbatim the first line of section IV, which continues:

> And we make of what we see, what we see clearly
> And have seen, a place dependent on ourselves.

---

[7] *Sewanee Review*, LII (1944), 522.

The place is the *mundo* of the passage from Stevens' essay, made of our vision, which consists of the ideal abstraction (what we see clearly) crossed with the real (what we have seen, experience). This would seem over-reading except that it is exactly what is symbolized in the following lines, as a " mystic marriage " between two who before had loved but would not marry. Then they took one another and married, and it was well because " the marriage-place was what they loved," and " They were love's characters come face to face." Here the pleasure is the pleasure of love. In section I, as glossed by the prose, it appeared as the pleasure of a perception which is a creation of truth beyond reason. But marriage is, after all, a creation of truth beyond reason, particularly if the partners, like these, are the characters of love, the paradigms of pleasure, the symbols of real and ideal.

Section VI indicates synthesis again, when the protagonist makes a choice beyond thought, which can again be glossed from the prose passage and thus indicate the pleasure in creation of truth beyond reason. The Canon (who has been punned on as humming a fugue in section V) chooses

> . . . to include the things
> That in each other are included, the whole,
> The complicate, the amassing harmony.

Stevens has shown us the pleasure of music before, as well as written about the pleasure of music. Harmony as pleasure is supported by the "luminous melody " of section VII. And this pleasure is also related, in VII, to the discovery of " an order as of / A season," as of summer and winter, symbols of the two worlds, as *order* is a symbol of their intersection.

THE IDEAL POETRY

The supreme fiction is the ideal poetry, the poetry which fixes the balance of the real and ideal realms, the synthesis which induces moments of illumination, like "Pure coruscations . . . beyond / The imagination " (" Late Hymn from the Myrrh-Mountain," *Transport to Summer*). The last section of the " Notes " offers an appropriately consummate example, even to the touch of irony which so often accompanies instances of special intensity in Stevens' poetry.

> That's it: the more than rational distortion,
> The fiction that results from feeling. Yes, that.
>
> They will get it straight one day at the Sorbonne.
> We shall return at twilight from the lecture
> Pleased that the irrational is rational,
>
> Until flicked by feeling, in a gildered street,
> I call you by name, my green, my fluent mundo.
> You will have stopped revolving except in crystal.

Mundo, the world he is in and the world he *is*, the world beyond reason, will be fixed and illuminated in a supreme fiction. In a moment of epiphany, knowing the world, knowing himself, knowing reality and imagination in intersection, he knows the supreme reality. It is the reality of poetry.

II

THIS INVENTED WORLD:
STEVENS' "NOTES TOWARD A SUPREME FICTION"

BY FRANK DOGGETT

> . . . the whole perceptual and sensible world is
> the primordial poem of mankind. — NIETZSCHE

Intent on his personifications, Stevens addresses from time to time the nature of the self within him as it conceives the world from moment to moment. "Who, then, beheld the rising of the clouds," he asks while considering the transformations of "A Sea Surface Full of Clouds." His reply personifies his inner being: "C'etait mon frère du ciel, ma vie, mon or." This heavenly brother, the self within him, who realizes a certain integration of consciousness, at another moment and with another conception of the world becomes for him another self and is to him "Mon enfant, mon bijou, mon âme." The self which he regards is capable of an infinite variety of transformations, capable at any moment of becoming a new self apt for a new knowledge of the appearance of things. This is the imagination, the poet within him, the conceiving self within any man. For Stevens, who is always ready for the instant expansions of synecdoche, poetry is the quintessence of all concept, and the poet therefore "has had to do with whatever the imagination and the senses have made of the world."

THE INANIMATE, DIFFICULT VISAGE

To conceive the world, as we do in our precise realizations of it, is (in this expanded sense) a kind of poetry. And thus (holding to that sense) the first poem of "Notes toward a Supreme Fiction" can be understood to be an address to a young poet. "Begin, ephebe," the poem opens and continues in this style in so much of its first section that the youth (ephebe) is the probable audience of all the rest, even of the poem's apostrophes. The ephebe seems to be a version of the youth in "The Figure of the Youth as Virile Poet," one of two essays that must have shared with the poem

13

the mind of the poet. The ephebe has the guise of a poet in the
fifth poem where he is put in his traditional pose and setting.
In this metaphor of the imaginative self as poet looking from the
attic window, the mansard room with its rented piano, or turning
on the bed in the pains of composition, the poet represents for
anyone the rigours of adequate realization and expression.

> . . . You clutch the corner
> Of the pillow in your hand. You writhe and press
> A bitter utterance from your writhing, dumb,
>
> Yet voluble dumb violence. . . .

This utterance of the ephebe, his " voluble dumb violence," is
the violence described in the other of the two essays that are so
closely related to the poem, " The Noble Rider and the Sound of
Words," and it is described there as the inner violence of the
imagination pressing against the violence of reality without. " It
is a violence from within that protects us from a violence without.
It is the imagination pressing back against the pressure of reality."
This is " the war between mind and sky " stated in the epilogue
of the poem as the work of the poet. The youth as virile poet in
the essay by that name is identified as a personification of the
poetic intelligence. " It is the spirit out of its own self," the
essay says, " not out of some surrounding myth, delineating with
accurate speech the complication of which it is composed." And,
just as the youth of the essay is presented as that part of one that
is the poet within, " the spirit out of its own self," the ephebe of
the poem seems to be also an aspect of the mind, a kind of intelligence within the self, and the one who is addressed (along with
the muse) as both self and fellow in the last lines of poem IV of
the second section (" Two things of opposite nature ") .

> Follow after, O my companion, my fellow, my self,
> Sister and solace, brother and delight.

Personification (the ephebe as the poetic intelligence for instance) is the staple rhetorical device of " Notes toward a Supreme
Fiction," and, in its use, Stevens gains for his large abstractions
something of the urgency and poignancy belonging to individual
lives. Each personification is a kind of man and at the same time
a kind of idea. Stevens uses the term major man for an idea of
man expressed in a personification. Many poems of " Notes toward

a Supreme Fiction " are constructed of major men like the one in which he represents man in his world as the planter "On a blue island in a sky-wide water." Blue symbolizes the imagination, and the poet is indicating here that man's world is an imagined thing. The planter is generic man, but he is also single individual man and as such leaves after death the continual effect of his existence. The sexual basis of human life is indicated by the symbols of pineapple and banana tree; and its origin in the womb, by the melon. This is plain allegory brought to intensity by the poet's skill in giving a feeling of a life lived and a sense of the reality of place.

> These were his beaches, his sea-myrtles in
> White sand, his patter of the long sea-slushes.

Man in a general sense (like the planter), man considered as an idea, is one of the more important themes of "Notes toward a Supreme Fiction," especially of the first section, "It Must Be Abstract," whose concluding poem opens with "The major abstraction is the idea of man." Man with his "voluble dumb violence" (as in the fifth poem), resisting the violence of outer fact through his will and the bitter inner violence of the imagination—man lives within his own constructions, within the things and ideas his mind has made, like the social order he has created, and the constructs of his intellect. In the fourth poem (beginning "The first idea was not our own") man in the abstract is considered as extraneous to the real world in one of the rare passages of direct statement in "Notes toward a Supreme Fiction." Here Stevens indicates that the physical geography that seems to hold us is really a metaphysical geography, a "non-geography" formed by the elaborations on reality of the human imagination. These elaborations are based on the scene, the place of our lives, but yet that scene, its weather, the mere air even, is no more than blank matter. "The air is not a mirror but bare board," he says, and again,

> Abysmal instruments make sounds like pips
> Of the sweeping meanings that we add to them.

Thus the reality of this world in which we live is that of a world that is made partly of our concept of it. But its existence as at least "a muddy centre," even before man conceived it—that is one of our certainties.

A PLACE DEPENDENT ON OURSELVES

The idea that place is made of an integration of human concept
and external reality and that man's familiar scenes are dependent
on his imagination—this idea is basic to an understanding of the
supreme fiction. "Sight / Is a museum of things seen," he remarks
in another poem, indicating that the world we see is predetermined
for us by the concepts and interpretations we receive from art and
memory. Another aspect of this idea appears in the poem beginning, "We reason of these things with later reason." Ostensibly, Stevens presents here an allegory of the marriage of the male
and female principle, personified as the great captain and the
maiden Bawda, "love's characters come face to face." The heavy
tone of the allegory is contradicted by the light touch of its puns,
its sexual humor.

> Each must the other take not for his high,
> His puissant front nor for her subtle sound,
>
> The shoo-shoo-shoo of secret cymbals round.

In this marriage poem, as in most allegory, there is an underlying didacticism that gives point to its mere arrangement of
allegorical surrogates. The point made in the poem is an aspect
of the major theme of "Notes toward a Supreme Fiction." This
theme can be summarized as the mind's share in creating reality.

The point he makes is that there is first the simple act of perception ("What we see clearly"). And, then, by conceiving it
and imagining it (by reasoning, he says), by abstracting our
perceptions, we create place through the idea we form of it. In
this way the world becomes a sort of fiction, a mental construction
based on perception and elaborated by thought. The point is
expressed thus in the opening lines of the marriage poem.

> We reason of these things with later reason
> And we make of what we see, what we see clearly
> And have seen, a place dependent on ourselves.

The first line of this stanza is repeated from the last line of
poem one in this section, a poem that assumes that our experience
of the world is, in a sense, self-determined. Thus to know the
world in accordance with the accepted understanding of it is to

form part of the human chorus, is "to feel the heart / That is
the common, the bravest fundament" and to experience reality
in common with other men. But to see the world in immediate
experience, without transforming it into conventional human
terms is the difficult vision. This direct experience is an approach
to what he calls "the first idea," and it is "irrational" because
it is close to the non-human external world. It is later and through
conception that we abstract experiences, that "we reason about
them," and understand them in reflection.

> But the difficultest rigor is forthwith,
> On the image of what we see, to catch from that
>
> Irrational moment its unreasoning,
> As when the sun comes rising, when the sea
> Clears deeply, when the moon hangs on the wall
>
> Of heaven-haven. These are not things transformed.
> Yet we are shaken by them as if they were.
> We reason about them with a later reason.

This is the mind striving to attain to that which is not itself
and without imposing human modification, the mind wishing the
perceived to be no more than what it is in itself. It is the blue
woman at her window of the next poem, the mind looking out,
and without reflection, identifying phenomena, naming,

> The chorals of the dogwood, cold and clear,
> Cold, coldly delineating, being real,
> Clear and, except for the eye, without intrusion.

Although our immediate experiences unfold within us as though
independent of our will, we consciously conceive them, we regard
them according to our idea of what they are, "we reason about
them with a later reason." Thus the world in experience is continually transformed; it is something that seems to be according
to what we consider it is. The character of experience could either
be determined within the self and be a product of will or the will
itself could be a product of the reality that encloses us, as he
indicates in another marriage poem (published the same year as
"Notes toward a Supreme Fiction"), "Desire and the Object."

> It could be that the sun shines
> Because I desire it to shine or else
> That I desire it to shine because it shines.

The sun given here as instance of reality is the same sun that symbolizes the world in the first poem of "Notes toward a Supreme Fiction." Here, with this image, he presents the supreme fiction of his poem in its opening lines and posits as exordium the idea of the world as both perceived and conceived, as given and invented.

> Begin, ephebe, by perceiving the idea
> Of this invention, this invented world,
> The inconceivable idea of the sun.

Stevens defines this invented world, the world of human conception and abstraction, as a supreme fiction in "The Noble Rider and the Sound of Words."

> There is, in fact, a world of poetry indistinguishable from the world in which we live, or, I ought to say, no doubt, from the world in which we shall come to live, since what makes the poet the potent figure that he is, or was, or ought to be, is that he creates the world to which we turn incessantly and without knowing it and that he gives to life the supreme fictions without which we are unable to conceive of it.

This is the world that is composed when we reason with a later reason, that world devised by conception, abstracted from immediate perception. From this passage we can understand the nature of the "war between the mind / And sky, between thought and day and night" in the epilogue. It is waged by the poet who resolves the actual into the fictive, who creates the imagined world of our human conceptions. Realizing the nature and existence of that world, now we can understand, "How simply the fictive hero becomes the real."

True, in his early "A High-Toned Old Christian Woman," he says "Poetry is the supreme fiction," but he means that poetry *creates* a supreme fiction. The term is used again in a letter to Renato Poggioli in connection with a translation of certain poems into Italian, and its use shows that by the term he means any important human abstraction or conception. "If we are to think of a supreme fiction, instead of creating it, as the Greeks did for example, in the form of a mythology, we might choose to create it in the image of a man: an agreed on superman."

The fictions given by the imagination to life and without which we could not conceive of it are part of man and part of his real existence. "I am myself a part of what is real," the youth as poet

says. Therefore, Stevens finds the real to be truly imagined and
the imagined to be truly real. Defining the real as the truly
imagined he says in " The Figure of the Youth as Virile Poet ":

It is easy to suppose that few people realize on that occasion, which
comes to all of us, when we look at the blue sky for the first time,
that is to say: not merely see it, but look at it and experience it
and for the first time have a sense that we live in the center of a
physical poetry, a geography that would be intolerable except for
the non-geography that exists there—few people realize that they are
looking at the world of their own thoughts and the world of their
own feelings.

But the world that is the not-self—to conceive it as it is and
not transform it in our human consciousness—that would be the
impossible first image of reality. For this, the sun, its image, must
not be named (or humanized) he says—naming it, that instant,
" gold flourisher." It must be realized only as that which exists.

> . . . The sun
> Must bear no name, gold flourisher, but be
> In the difficulty of what it is to be.

The real as it is in its simple existence—this is " the quick,"
the basis " of this invention, this invented world." Stevens uses
the term, " the first idea," for such a notion. " The first idea "
is related to other concepts of a reality as it might be in its existence apart from a conceiving mind (to the platonic idea or perhaps Kant's thing-in-itself) . The idea of something solely in terms
of its simple existence and apart from the human conception of
it must be an abstraction, a fictive thing, because to assume the
existence of reality is a subjective act in itself. This is one of the
supreme fictions without which we are unable to conceive our life,
for it is the way we normally think of reality. Stevens says, " The
first idea is an imagined thing." He indicates this again in the
poem that celebrates the pleasures of intuitive, instinctive living,
" It feels good as it is without the giant, / A thinker of the first
idea." There, the first idea is something to be known by a fictive
and generic creature, a giant, personifying the abstract idea
of man.

Major man, or the idea of man—that is another of the fictions
by which we are able to conceive life. As stated earlier in dis-
cussing Stevens' use of personification, the poem is full of instances

of major man. Mention of one or two are all space allows. In the
MacCullough of the eighth poem, "the pensive giant prone in
violet space," major man is given form as idealized man. The
conclusion of the first section presents major man in the image of
the common man with his old coat, his sagging pantaloons, seeking
the fugitive items of experience that vanish in the flux, "Looking
for what was where it used to be."

THOUGHT BEATING IN THE HEART

The poet of "Notes toward a Supreme Fiction" shares with the
youth as virile poet of the essay the hazards that go with philosophical import of one kind or another in poetry. He is pictured
(in the essay) as surrounded by a cloud of those that resemble
him, poetic philosophers and philosophical poets, and is warned
that his speech and thought must be his and not like theirs.

In the most propitious climate and in the midst of life's virtues, the
simple figure of the youth as virile poet is always surrounded by a
cloud of double characters, against whose thought and speech it is
imperative that he should remain on constant guard. These are the
poetic philosophers and the philosophical poets.

It must be admitted that at times the thought of the poem is
like a wisp of this cloud of double characters, even though the
speech is certainly the poet's own. As is often mentioned, Stevens
uses the poetic ideas of philosophers, but almost always the kind
that cannot be identified with a particular system of conjecture
or belief. In fact many of these ideas consider the involvement
of mind and world with such incipience that some version of them
may be found in almost any general philosophical work of the last
two centuries. When something specific does creep into a poem,
usually it is only some novelty like the lion and his red-colored
noise in the fifth poem of "It Must Be Abstract" that has a
possible source in Viollet-le-Duc's *Discourses on Architecture*;
here the lion himself is red and a page or two later the red-colored
noise is the blare of a trumpet. However, if one is searching for
influences, *The Philosophy of 'As If'* by Hans Vaihinger would
seem to be the best place to look. In this book may be found
parallels for many terms and propositions of "Notes toward a
Supreme Fiction" and its two companion essays, like "the fiction
of an absolute" or the phrase, "the invented world." In spite

of Stevens' interest in the use of philosophic concepts in poetry, we should remember that the poet in him always subordinates ideas to the uses of poetry. "La vie est plus belle que les idées," he says lightly, using French to separate himself in mood from the philosophers who, as he remarks, think of the world as an enormous pastiche.

To see how he turns his ideas to the uses of poetry we must examine some of the individual poems of " Notes toward a Supreme Fiction." But first, it should be said that although my discussion of the development of thought in some of these poems will lean heavily on his ideas, one should never suppose that these poems lack intensity or fail to give the dramatic quality of an individual view of the world. They have the poet's sense of the eternal tragedy of being, of the bubble of human conception and desire reflecting for its instant the iron world of fact. This sense of the frailty and inadequacy of life in a world that is non-human is the basis of his poetry; for poetry is always a striving to engage that real world that holds us and whose existence is so completely other than ours.

> From this the poem springs: that we live in a place
> That is not our own and, much more, not ourselves
> And hard it is in spite of blazoned days.

And yet this place that is not our own becomes what it is only through the human conception of it. Remember, the real world is also "this invented world" and that it is composed in that it is conceived. The world in which we live, then, is an alien world and at the same time has its only known existence in human realization. Here we have the paradox that has given rise to so many of the fictions of philosophy. One of these fictions is the idea of the possible. As possibility, reality would have a sort of existence apart from or anterior to experience, even if an existence that is no more than potential. Reality, if it existed in potentiality, would be something we find in experience of it, something we come across. The order (or disorder) we find in the real world, then, would not be a human order, an order imposed by the mind, but would be something we discover.

Poem VII of the third section considers experience to be the discovery of reality. The seasons and their weather in such a conception are something emerging from mere potentiality, something we come upon, a discovery out of nothing.

> . . . To discover an order as of
> A season, to discover summer and know it,
>
> To discover winter and know it well, to find,
> Not to impose, not to have reasoned at all,
> Out of nothing to have come on major weather,
>
> It is possible, possible, possible.

"Out of nothing to have come on major weather"—this is the weather, the mere air that is our environment and the scene of our lives; and, also, as he says in the essay on the youth as poet, this weather, the blue sky, for instance, is a particular of life as well as a physical geography in the midst of which we live. This is "the effortless weather turning blue" of the second poem, this physical geography that out of nothing becomes the world of our own thoughts and our own feelings.

The blue weather, the physical geography emerging out of nothing and becoming real in human experience, the idea of that which is unrealized and enters the life of man through realization, is made by Stevens into one of the most beautiful and subtle poems of "Notes toward a Supreme Fiction," the poem that begins "Not to be realized." Here his thought closely resembles that of those double characters, the philosophic poets or the poetic philosophers, and yet we can see how he keeps himself apart, making his poem something that is plainly poetry and by no means a philosophic substitute for poetry or a poetic substitute for philosophy. Of those double characters, the poetic philosophers, Bergson is one who resembles in his imagery certain aspects of "Notes toward a Supreme Fiction." Like Stevens, Bergson writes (in *The Creative Mind*) of the possible and the realized, and he uses a metaphor very similar to the basic metaphor of Stevens' poem. Bergson believes that the possible is nothing more than an image of the real displaced in time. It is an afterthought, he says, projected back into a purely imagined past. For the possible to become the real, he maintains that it would be necessary to imagine it as a sort of semi-reality that becomes real only through the addition of human thought. Thus, he maintains, "the possible would have been there from all time, a phantom awaiting its hour; it would therefore have become reality by the addition of something, by some transfusion of life or blood."

The transfusion by life or blood takes place in Stevens' poem where our environment, our weather, our mere air becomes what it is in our human realization of it. Therefore the scene of our lives is "an abstraction blooded as a man by thought." In the living mind of a man this vast abstraction and collective possibility becomes what we see and part of the very self. It composes in our experience of it the items of our consciousness. Unrealized, it can only be characterized by separateness from the warm various human life it enters when part of an experience. The method of the poem is an alternating presentation of such characterization of the unrealized followed each time by a certain experience of an environment, an experience that is something seen.

> Not to be realized because not to
> Be seen, not to be loved nor hated because
> Not to be realized. Weather by Franz Hals,
>
> Brushed up by brushy winds in brushy clouds,
> Wetted by blue, colder for white. Not to
> Be spoken to, without a roof, without
>
> First fruits, without the virginal of birds,
> The dark-blown ceinture loosened, not relinquished.
> Gay is, gay was, the gay forsythia
>
> And yellow, yellow thins the Northern blue.

The weather by Franz Hals and the weather of the gay forsythia are realizations of place. The alternating passages "not to be realized" and "not to be spoken to" personify that which is no more than possible of realization.

With another realization of place, the poet turns to his own house among the magnolias; there he observes the creeping change of time in the visible. Time, we know, is an interposition between realization and that which is realized. But not only does realization fail to grasp truly what it realizes because of time and change, but also because the image of what is realized is no more than "close to kin" to the actual scene, no more than an idea or "false form" of it.

Knowing that realization is not presence, the poet understands that what he is looking at is only an image and the world of his own thought and the world of his own feelings. Thus,

> My house has changed a little in the sun.
> The fragrance of the magnolias comes close,
> False flick, false form, but falseness close to kin.

The mind's image of the real—false flick that it is—just the same is a way of seeing that reality. Therefore reality is visible. But as the mind can hold nothing but its own image, and, as vision, in that sense, is only the sight of one's own thought, reality is invisible. Invisible or visible, he considers, trying to resolve the paradox; it is there and not here in my consciousness; it is both a seeing and unseeing in the eye. The passage seems heavy in this exposition of its sense, but, in the language of the poem, it is light and fleeting and accords with the spirit of the paradox.

> It must be visible or invisible,
> Invisible or visible or both:
> A seeing and unseeing in the eye.

Schopenhauer, in the opening of *The World as Will and Idea* (a work once quoted by Stevens), expresses the mystery in language and imagery that resembles Stevens' characteristic phrasing. He is speaking of anyone who attains the philosophic view. "It then becomes clear and certain to him that what he knows is not a sun and an earth, but only an eye that sees a sun, a hand that feels an earth; that the world which surrounds him is there only as idea, i. e., only in relation to something else, the consciousness which is himself." In this view (and one very common to thought and to poetry), the world is truly "a seeing and unseeing in the eye."

A different view (sometimes given in the early poetry) is that of the solipsist, the one who says, "what I saw / Or heard or felt came not but from myself." Another image from his first book, an image of night and of the darkness of inner vision parallels that of the solipsist.

> The body is no body to be seen
> But is an eye that studies its black lid.

For the solipsist not even the eye sees the sun. There is only the idea of a sun. The closed eye is all mind and even the objective reality of its own body has vanished and become blind perception that perceives only its own conceivings. The pure solipsist would be one for whom sight was only an unseeing in the eye. But for the Stevens of "Notes toward a Supreme Fiction" the seeing and unseeing converge into a single perception of the world. "It is important," he says in his essay on the youth as poet "to believe that the visible is the equivalent of the invisible."

Thus, when the poet sits on his bench in the park in the last poem of " It Must Change " and watches the water of the lake, the surface of the water becomes a metaphor for the consciousness, and by means of the idea of the two lakes, the real lake and the metaphorical one (the consciousness) superimposed on it by the poetry, the metaphor expresses the relation of mind and reality and illustrates in this relationship the poet's idea when he speaks of the seeing and unseeing in the eye. The flux, the changes of time and experience, symbolized by the west wind, conjoin the two constituents, mind and world.

> The west wind was the music, the motion, the force
> To which the swans curveted, a will to change,
> A will to make iris frettings on the blank.
>
> There was a will to change, a necessitous
> And present way, a presentation, a kind
> Of volatile world, too constant to be denied,
>
> The eye of a vagabond in metaphor
> That catches our own.

Mind is united to world in the identical transformations of world and mind. The external changes are also the internal ones. The flow of consciousness is our own version of the outer flux of reality. Thus he says of the transformations of the world and mind:

> . . . The freshness of transformation is
>
> The freshness of a world. It is our own,
> It is ourselves, the freshness of ourselves,
> And that necessity and that presentation
>
> Are rubbings of a glass in which we peer.

When Stevens peers into that glass he is peering both within his mind and into the world that holds him. This is why the transformations, the changes of the world, are also transformations within the self. And these changes are changes that affect perception, what is brought by eye and ear, and that spread into the parts of the mind that are pure imagination and beyond perception.

ONE OF THE VAST REPETITIONS
FINAL IN THEMSELVES

The eye and ear stand for all perception in the poetry of
Stevens, and he is a poet who believes that perception is the very
material of the mind. Beneath perception (but dependent on it)
and beyond the world of fact, the mind holds the infinite spaces
of the purely imagined. He says in the essay on the youth as poet
that "our nature is an illimitable space through which the intelligence moves without coming to an end." These are the spaces
ascended by Canon Aspirin

> Beneath, far underneath, the surface of
> His eye and audible in the mountain of
> His ear, the very material of his mind.

In Canon Aspirin's flight Stevens adapts an old cliché (a flight
of imagination) to imagery resembling that of the flight of Milton's Satan. The Canon meets two kinds of nothingness; first
the nothingness of sleep, that ultimate barrier of reality "beyond
which fact could not progress as fact," and where the self lives
solely in its own imaginings. The other nothingness, "the utmost
crown of night," is the nothingness of death, "beyond which
thought could not progress as thought." This is the ultimate
barrier of the imagination and Canon Aspirin seeks it straightway,
"with huge pathetic force," representing in that pathetic flight
the human struggle to transcend one's self and one's mortality by
the efforts of the religious imagination.

The spaces of the mind ascended by Canon Aspirin are the same
vast spaces of the imagination through which the angel of the
next two poems descends. In those spaces the poet can assume
the experience of his imagined angel, forget his image of reality,
the sun, that gold centre and golden destiny, as he calls it. The
mind creating its fictions, its divinities, its angels, becomes the
ascending and descending wings it imagines. The imagined experiences of the fictive are part of the real experience of the live
creature, the poet. Thus the poet who imagines them can do all
that angels can, can enjoy like them, "Like men besides, like men
in light secluded, / Enjoying angels."

Here is another instance that the fictive is part of the real, and it is in the creation of the fictive that the poet engages in his work, a work (as implied in the next to the last poem) that is a pure activity and an expression of simple existence, " a thing final in itself and therefore good." Simple existence as a thing final in itself comprises all the vast repetitions of nature, the seasons, the movement of stars, the leaf spinning in the wind, even the constantly repeated cry of the life principle, the cry of " bethou me " repeated and repeated, " a single text, granite monotony," the cry of the mind that would transform reality into its own image. This is life seen as a continual recurrence by the old seraph of the first poem in the last section, life that remains, that is a vast repetition. And the self that continually cries, " Bethou me," repeating and repeating its cry (" Bethou me, said sparrow, to the crackled blade ") —that self, that life is repeated over and over until the individuality of mind and will are lost in the vast perspective of continual repetition, and the eye that studies its black lid has now become no more than an open eye, reflecting the real on the blank surface of the collective mind.

Eye without lid, mind without any dream.

The eye that shuts and the mind that dreams is always the individual mind that perishes, never the collective one that continues in repetition. It is the individual that is the living thing; the generic is only automatic and hugely mechanistic.

Turning again to the next to the last poem we are reassured that the poet finds existence to be a thing final in itself and therefore good. This he asserts in one of the most famous and most plainly didactic passages of " Notes toward a Supreme Fiction," a passage in which the poet finds the occupation of song to be

A thing final in itself and, therefore, good:
One of the vast repetitions final in
Themselves and, therefore, good, the going round

And round and round, the merely going round,
Until merely going round is a final good,
The way wine comes at a table in a wood.

And we enjoy like men, the way a leaf
Above the table spins its constant spin,
So that we look at it with pleasure, look

At it spinning its eccentric measure.

If Stevens ever has a moral, it is the one that he indicates here and that he repeats in many versions throughout his productive life in poetry. He emphasizes his moral with his singing hidden rhymes and illustrates it with his symbolic picture of wine coming to men in a wood who enjoy the good that comes to them, just as they do the contemplation of the simple activity of that which exists, of the leaf spinning, paradigm of the spinning world. To put his moral in paraphrase: experience is a good in itself.

But "Notes toward a Supreme Fiction" does not end with a moral. In the concluding poem he creates his final personification in the guise of a sort of spouse or muse. The flowing reality that is made into poetry, into "the imagination of life," as he calls it in the essay on the youth as poet—this is his soft-footed phantom, familiar yet an aberration, that he sees as in a moving contour, as in a change not quite completed. Woman is the common image of world or reality in Stevens. "Fat girl," he says, with the lightness and warmth he feels for his conception, "my summer, my night." The world in idea, the invented world is the fiction that results from feeling; it is the more than rational, the irrational distortion. Momentarily in agreement with the academic trust in the rational while returning at twilight from a lecture, he is "pleased that the irrational is rational" (he says ironically), until the flick of feeling, the touch of the irrational turns the world into the subject of poetry. Then the street is gildered. The world becomes word or (as he says) "I call you by name."

He is expressing in his conclusion, then, the genesis of a poem, from the imagination of it pictured in procreant terms ("Fat girl, terrestrial, my summer, my night"), through the evasions and transformations of its conception, with the arduous work of composition ("Bent over work, anxious, content, alone"), until realizing his conception in language (calling it by name), it is fixed in the crystal of a poem.

> Until flicked by feeling, in a gildered street,
> I call you by name, my green, my fluent mundo.
> You will have stopped revolving except in crystal.

The going round and round of his imagination of life set in the crystal of a poem, is (like the spinning leaf) a paradigm for the invented world, and another image of what he calls later (speaking of his book of poems) "the planet on the table."

III

WALLACE STEVENS AT HARVARD:
SOME ORIGINS OF HIS THEME AND STYLE

BY ROBERT BUTTEL

That Wallace Stevens wrote verse as an undergraduate has been known at least since the appearance of the Wallace Stevens number of the *Harvard Advocate* in December, 1940, but perhaps because of the obvious immaturities in the *Advocate* selections, his early poetry has not been seriously considered. The Harvard work is worth examining, however, since it shows the genesis of Stevens' preoccupation with the conflicting yet interdependent worlds of imagination and reality and the early stylistic development which resulted from this preoccupation.

Stevens wrote his undergraduate verse at a time (1898-1900) when as he said on a later visit to Harvard, "it was a commonplace to say that all the poetry had been written and all the paintings painted" ("The Irrational Element in Poetry," *ca.* 1937, from *Opus Posthumous*, ed. S. F. Morse, [New York, 1957], p. 218). This commonplace does not seem to have taken into account Yeats' mastery of his early style or the poetry of Hardy or Housman, but perhaps their voices were obscured by such Decadents as Dowson, Symonds, and Wilde, whose celebration of art for art's sake — the ivory tower Tennyson had warned against in "The Palace of Art"—seemed to mark the end of an era, even though they contributed to the poetry of the era to come when they did much to introduce French symbolism into English poetry. In America, the sweeping innovations of Whitman and the incisive wit and suggestiveness of Emily Dickinson were largely ignored. Edmund Clarence Stedman, the well-known poet, critic, and editor of his day, spoke of the hour in which his *An American Anthology* appeared (Dec., 1900) as a "twilight interval" (see Horace Gregory and Marya Zaturenska, *A History of American Poetry, 1900-1940* [New York, 1952], p. 10). Poetry seemed less and less significant in a world of science, industrialism, and middle-class culture. The Decadents' response was to establish a cult of isolated beauty, while at the opposite extreme the realistic and naturalistic novelists were making a determined effort to deal with the actual world, as sordid as it might be.

The French poet, Henri Regnier, in a series of lectures on the French Symbolist poets given in the spring term of 1900 at Harvard, stressed the conflict between the two literary extremes, which he put in terms of idealism and realism or naturalism:

In the early eighties followed the reaction of idealism against realism. The new movement was headed by Paul Verlaine, Mallarmé, and others. With them slowly arose the new school of poets called " decadents " or Symbolists.

Villiers d'Isle Adam was held in great respect by the young school, who considered him as a living protest against the naturalistic tendencies of the time, and as a living incarnation of idealism.

Poetry in France had been in great peril from the ever-rising wave of naturalism and realism, to which all poets were making concessions.

(From summaries in the *Harvard Crimson*, XXXVII, 15 [Fri., March 2, 1900], 1; 17 [Mon., March 5, 1900], 1; and 23 [Mon., March 12, 1900], 1.) But even before Regnier's visit Stevens had become sensitive to this conflict; in several prose pieces antedating the lectures he had developed his plots in terms of the conflict between ideal beauty, art or imagination, and coarseness, disorder, or reality. In these stories Stevens emphasized both the lifelessness of beauty and art detached from the actual world and the futility of the actual world ungraced by the imagination. More and more his Harvard work juxtaposed the world of imagination and the world of reality, and thus began his life-long meditation on their interrelationship. Out of this general but central theme arose all the later, more specific variations of his theme and his experiments with style and technique that were refined and developed into the mature poetry of *Harmonium*.

Between the fall of 1898 and the spring of 1900, fifteen Stevens poems appeared in the *Harvard Advocate*, two in the *Harvard Monthly*, and one in *East and West*, a short-lived New York periodical. Further, ten short stories and sketches appeared in the *Advocate*, not to mention many editorials when Stevens became its president.[1] As one might expect, most of the Harvard

[1] I am grateful to Mrs. Holly Stevens Stephenson, Samuel French Morse, and the *Harvard Advocate* for their permission to quote extensively from the undergraduate

poems are in the manner of the undergraduate and popular verse of the era, verse in the ebbing Romantic and Victorian tradition. But following the developments in his prose, in which Stevens worked out a more distinctive point of view and displayed some elements of style which look forward to the later poet, there are three of his later undergraduate poems which, in exploring in various ways the relationships of imagination and reality, include a new wit, irony, sophistication and forcefulness.

In the early more conventional poems, Stevens showed a fondness for the sonnet and quatrain forms. Although the speakers tend to be over-wrought, these poems do not erupt from a frenzy

---

material. Following is a chronological list of the poems and stories Stevens published as an undergraduate. The reader may wish to refer to it from time to time, since I have not followed a strict chronology in my discussion. For most of this list I am indebted to Samuel French Morse, *Wallace Stevens, A Preliminary Checklist of his Published Writings: 1898-1954* (New Haven, 1954), pp. 40-41. Below, the unstarred titles are poems, the starred are stories. Those marked with a dagger are not discussed in this article. Unless otherwise noted, the works below are from the *Harvard Advocate*.

"Who Lies Dead?," Nov. 28, 1898.
"Vita Mea," Dec. 12, 1898.
* "Her First Escapade," Jan. 16, 1899.
* "A Day in February," Mar. 6, 1899 (not in *Checklist*).
"Song" ("She loves me . . ."), Mar. 13, 1899.
"Sonnet" ("If we are leaves . . ."), *Harvard Monthly*, Mar., 1899 (not in *Checklist*).
"Sonnet" ("There shines the morning . . ."), Apr. 10, 1899.
* "Part of His Education," Apr. 24, 1899 (not in *Checklist*).
* "The Higher Life," June 12, 1899 (not in *Checklist*).
† "Sonnet" ("I strode along . . ."), *Harvard Monthly*, July, 1899, pseud. John Morris, 2nd (courtesy S. F. Morse; not in *Checklist*).
* "Pursuit," Oct. 18, 1899.
"Quatrain" ("Go not, young cloud, . . ."), Nov. 13, 1899.
* "The Revelation," Nov. 13, 1899.
* "The Nymph," Dec. 6, 1899, pseud. John Fiske Towne.
"Song" ("Ah, yes! beyond . . ."), Mar. 10, 1900.
* "Hawkins of Cold Cape," Mar. 10, 1900, pseud. Carol More.
"Outside the Hospital," Mar. 24, 1900, pseud. R. Jerries.
"Street Songs," Apr. 3, 1900.
† "Night Song," May 10, 1900, pseud. Kenneth Malone.
"Ballade of the Pink Parasol," May 23, 1900, pseud. Carol More (sic).
* "In the Dead of Night," May 23, 1900.
"Sonnet" ("Lo, even as I passed . . ."), May 23, 1900, pseud. R. Jerries.
† "Sonnet" ("Come said the word, . . ."), *East and West*, I, 7 (May, 1900), 201. *East and West* was founded in New York and lasted just a year, Nov. 1899 to Oct., 1900, according to S. F. Morse (not in *Checklist*).
† "Quatrain" ("He sought the music . . ."), June 2, 1900, pseud. Henry Marshall.
* "Four Characters," June 16, 1900.

of youthful passion which forces from the poet insights that demand new rhythms and radical language. The reader is hardly reminded of a Rimbaud, or a Dylan Thomas, and would search in vain for anything approaching the force of Eliot's "The Love-Song of J. Alfred Prufrock," which was begun at Harvard in 1910 (and finished the next year in Munich; see Grover Smith, Jr., *T. S. Eliot's Poetry and Plays* [Chicago, 1955], p. 9). Indeed, Stevens' poems seem little more than fairly successful exercises in the poetic fashions of the nineties. A good example would be the sonnet, "Vita Mea," the second poem to appear in the *Advocate* (Dec. 12, 1898, p. 78):

> With fear I trembled in the House of Life,
> Hast'ning from door to door, from room to room,
> Seeking a way from that impenetrable gloom
> Against whose walls my strength lay weak from strife,
> All dark! All dark! And what sweet wind was rife
> With earth, or sun, or star, or new sun's bloom,
> Lay sick and dead within that place of doom,
> Where I went raving like the winter's wife.
>
> "In vain, in vain," with bitter lips I cried;
> "In vain, in vain," along the hallways died
> And sank in silences away. Oppressed
> I wept. Lo! through those tears the window-bars
> Shone bright, where Faith and Hope like long-sought stars
> First gleamed upon that prison of unrest.

The poem is melodramatic, strained and sentimental, but at the same time it displays a competent craftsmanship in the consistent development of the house-prison imagery, the regular fulfillment of the sonnet's rhyme-scheme, and the not ungraceful use of the basically iambic pattern—with such effects as "and sank in silences away."

The movement, imagery, and diction of the poem are distinctly Victorian and recall, for example, Tennyson's *Maud*, Part Three, which proceeds from Stanza 1: "My life has crept so long on a broken wing / Through cells of madness, haunts of horror and fear, . . ." to Stanza 5: "It is better to fight for the good than to rail at the ill; / . . . , / I embrace the purpose of God, and the doom assigned." A reminder of the central metaphor in "Vita Mea" is found in the title of Rossetti's sonnet sequence, *The House of Life*. These parallels are not meant to point out specific influences for Stevens' poem, but rather to indicate that such

imagery, diction, and tonal quality were part of the poetic atmosphere of the time.

Santayana, for example, in the nineties while teaching at Harvard, was writing more controlled sonnets, but in a style similar
to that of "Vita Mea," as the following passage from "Though
utter death should swallow up my hope" indicates:

> Yet have I light of love, nor need to grope
> Lost, wholly lost, without an inward fire;
> The flame that quickeneth the world entire
> Leaps in my breast, with cruel death to cope.[2]

And E. A. Robinson had included in *The Torrent and the Night
Before* (1896) not only many distinctive departures from conventional verse but also such poems as "Credo" (see *Selected
Early Poems and Letters*, ed. Charles T. Davis [New York, 1960],
p. 27), which is in the same manner as "Vita Mea":

> I cannot find my way: there is no star
> In all the shrouded heavens anywhere;
>
> . . . .
>
> No, there is not a glimmer, nor a call,
> For one that welcomes, welcomes when he fears,
> The black and awful chaos of the night;
> For through it all,—above beyond it all,—
> I know the far-sent message of the years,
> I feel the coming glory of the light!

"Vita Mea," along with several other student poems of its type,
was anthologized in *Harvard Lyrics* (published in Boston, 1899,
edited by alumnus C. L. Stebbins), probably for the very reason
which makes the poem so embarrassing from a later point of view:
its standard Victorian style and atmosphere (though there is
perhaps a faint glimmer of Stevens' later boldness of metaphor
in "raving like the winter's wife"). No wonder Stevens was to
say later in a letter, quoted by Samuel French Morse in Stevens'
Opus Posthumous, p. xvii, "Some of one's early things give one
the creeps."

That Stevens during this period had no particularly original

---

[2] Sonnet L, written 1895-1901, *Poems* (New York, 1935), p. 54. Any study of the
development of Stevens' theme would have to take Santayana's prose into account.
As Frank Kermode says, "*Interpretations of Poetry and Religion* (1900) is a key
book for the thought of Stevens" (*Wallace Stevens* [Edinburgh and London, 1960],
p. 81).

point of view which demanded original means of expression, and
that essentially these poems are juvenile exercises in the current
modes can be seen by examining another "Sonnet" which came
out in the *Harvard Monthly* a few months after "Vita Mea"
(March, 1899, p. 31):

> If we are leaves that fall upon the ground
> To lose our greenness in the quiet dust
> Of forest-depths; if we are flowers that must
> Lie torn and creased upon a bitter mound,
> No touch of sweetness in our ruins found;
> If we are weeds whom no one wise can trust
> To live our hour before we feel the gust
> Of death, and by our side its last, keen sound;
>
> Then let a tremor through our briefness run,
> Wrapping it with mad, sweet sorcery
> Of love; for in the fern I saw the sun
> Take fire against the dew; the lily white
> Was soft and deep at morn; the rosary
> Streamed forth a wild perfume into the light.

Here the apprentice poet seemed as ready to adopt the *carpe
diem* theme, with *fin de siècle* overtones, as that of faith and
hope, and the tonal quality is closer to Dowson's "Amor Pro-
fanus," for example, than to Tennyson. Again, as in "Vita Mea,"
the poem is excessively dramatic and figurative, with the ornate
diction and imagery that the moderns, including Stevens, were
to rebel against a decade or so later. But in spite of its overblown manner, the poem is partly redeemed by "For in the fern
I saw the sun / Take fire against the dew," an image that is specific
and vital, a sign of better things to come. Also, the rather skillful
use of enjambment shows that Stevens knew what he was doing
within the formal framework.

Another "Sonnet" (*Advocate*, April 10, 1899, p. 18), with its
insistent personification, its pretty but second-hand effects of
diction, and its echoes of Keats' "Bright Star!" is a formally
competent and conventional piece of work:

> There shines the morning star! Through the forlorn
>   And silent spaces of cold heaven's height
>   Pours the bright radiance of his kingly light,
> Swinging in revery before the morn.
> The flush and fall of many tides have worn
>   Upon coasts beneath him, in their flight

From sea to sea; yet ever on the night
His clear and splendid visage is upborn.

Like this he pondered on the world's first day,
Sweet Eden's flowers heavy with the dew;
And so he led bold Jason on his way
Sparkling forever in the galley's foam;
And still he shone most perfect in the blue,
All bright and lovely on the hosts of Rome.

In *Harvard Lyrics*, "Worth" (p. 97) is not the only student poem to use the imagery of Stevens' "Sonnet."

I saw the old white moon above the trees
That shone on Adam in his paradise,
That shines on the everlasting rise
And fall of realms and races, land and seas

Stevens also achieved a conventional facility in "Quatrain," with its rather tenderly coy personification (*Advocate*, Nov. 13, 1899, p. 63):

Go not, young cloud, too boldly through the sky,
To meet the morning light;
Go not too boldly through that dome on high—
For eastward lies the night.

In its prettiness and grace it is not unlike the quatrain in Tennyson's *Maud* (Part I, XVII):

Go not, happy day,
From the shining fields,
Go not, happy day,
Till the maiden yields.

Similarly graceful is Stevens' "Song" (*Advocate*, March 13, 1899, p. 150):

She loves me or loves me not,
What care I?—
The depth of the fields is just as sweet,
And sweet the sky.

She loves me or loves me not.
Is that to die?—
The green of the woods is just as fair,
And fair the sky.

This poem is an attractive version of a traditional theme.[3] It has lightness and restraint, qualities decidedly lacking in such poems as the following mawkish "Song," which appeared in the *Advocate* a year after the one above (March 10, 1900, p. 5) and well after Stevens had begun to explore new directions in his stories:

> Ah yes! beyond these barren walls
> > Two hearts shall in a garden meet,
> And while the latest robin calls,
> > Her lips to his shall be made sweet.
>
> And out above these gloomy tow'rs
> > The full moon tenderly shall rise
> To cast its light upon the flow'rs
> > And find him looking in her eyes.

This is one of the weakest of the Harvard poems; very possibly it was written earlier and then used as a space filler when Stevens became president of the *Advocate*. But it is just as possible that his performance was as uneven as this poem indicates.

Indeed, "Who Lies Dead?," the first of his poems to appear in the *Advocate* (Nov. 28, 1898, p. 57), shows more promise than any of the poems discussed so far.

> Who lies dead in the sea,
> > All water 'tween him and the stars,
> The keels of a myriad ships above,
> > The sheets on a myriad spars?
>
> Who lies dead in the world,
> > All heavy of heart and hand,
> The blaze of a myriad arms in sight,
> > The sweep of a myriad band?

The image in the first quatrain, dependent as it is on the unusual point of view of looking upward from the ocean floor, has a particularity and freshness that make it more effective than the lugubrious "impenetrable gloom / Against whose walls my strength lay weak from strife" ("Vita Mea"). The device of the unanswered questions, though obvious, is an attempt to

---

[3] See "Shall I Like an Hermit Dwell," *The Poems of Sir Walter Raleigh*, ed. Agnes M. C. Latham (London, 1929), p. 112: "If she undervalue me; / What care I how fair she be?" and "The Author's Resolution in a Sonnet," *The Poetry of George Wither*, ed. Frank Sidgwick, I (London, 1902), p. 138, "Shall I wasting in despair / Die because a woman's fair? / . . . . . / What care I how fair she be?"

leave the import of the martial images oblique rather than heavily explicit or merely figurative. What seems to be suggested is the paralysis of those unresponsive or dead to the beauty, wonder and purpose in life. By stretching the suggestion, one might find a slight hint here of one of Stevens' later thematic concerns: that beauty and meaning are to be found in this world if one's imagination is alive. But chiefly there is little more in the poem than a vague lament and a poetic impulse toward beauty and heroic spectacle, matched by the young poet's attempt to give the poem a lofty impressiveness. Still, "Who Lies Dead?" is a respectable effort within the limitations of its conventional style, which here includes the grand martial imagery, the phrase "heavy of heart," and the elegaic tone.

Lacking thematic certainty at this point, Stevens, like many of his contemporaries, tended to write poetry of religious or moral abstraction, self-conscious despair or fervor, tender love lyrics, and reverent nature poems. His attempts to provide vivid emotion were submerged in poetic language that was not only dated but also figurative, inflated, and sentimental.

It is in the stories and sketches, all published in the *Advocate* between January, 1899, and June, 1900, that Stevens' break from nineteenth-century poetic conventions becomes apparent. In prose, Stevens was free of the restrictions of popular poetic practice and could with greater flexibility work out what more and more became his central concern, the relationships between the actual world and that world as observed or transformed by the imagination. He could deal with a wider range of characters, situations, and points of view. But assuredly the stories are not accomplished works of art. They are too wooden and contrived for that, and are too full of such immaturities as the sentence, "The warm afternoon beat against the windows courageously." Samuel French Morse refers to the stories as "*fin de siècle* sketches" (*Opus Posthumous*, p. xvii), a characterization which is on the whole apt. Nevertheless, they are a noteworthy advance, containing in embryo many of Stevens' later qualities.

One of the ways in which the stories differ from the poems discussed so far is in the use of the kind of seamy detail that the naturalistic novelists were fond of. The most clear-cut example occurs in the third sketch of "Four Characters," Stevens' final piece in the *Advocate* (June 16, 1900, pp. 119-20) .[4] In this sketch the narrator accompanies a reporter (appropriately enough for the naturalistic situation) to investigate a death, and delivers a straightforward description of an old woman in a tenement, her newly-dead husband stretched out on an ironing board between two chairs and covered by the couple's only sheet. Even the bare mattress is described. Nothing but sordidness is evoked, though the sketch—one of a series of four on the contrasts between beauty and the banal—is placed in striking contrast between one which describes a beautiful summer day and one in which a lady describes the past splendor of her home ("painted in imitation of the ducal palace in Venice") before it became a boarding house. The dead body, the sheet and the milieu of the sketch perhaps contain the seed of the *Harmonium* poem " The Emperor of Ice-Cream," with its lines, " Take from the dresser of deal / ... that sheet / . . . and spread it so as to cover her face." [5]

But, paradoxically, at the same time that Stevens included more realistic and naturalistic detail he also felt free to introduce the fanciful, fantastic, or imaginatively beautiful — even precious—in counterpoint with the realistic. By means of such counterpoint he approached his theme indirectly. There is no explicit discussion of imagination and reality; rather Stevens narrates an incident in which the details symbolically dramatize the theme.

Even the first two of the stories to appear in the *Advocate* are rudimentary attempts in this direction. In a melodramatic piece called "Her First Escapade" (Jan. 16, 1899, pp. 104-6), beauty and romance are blunderingly obliterated by a man representing material success and heartless reality. Rothwald, a wealthy farmer, momentarily jealous when his young housekeeper tries to escape with a poor young farmer (Rothwald has been too obtuse to realize the girl's potential as a wife for himself), shoots in their direction, intending merely to frighten them, and unknowingly kills the girl. "A Day in February" (March 6, 1899, pp. 135-36), the next story to appear, has as its basis the dualism

---

[4] The magazine title *Harvard Advocate* will be omitted in the parenthetical documentation of the stories, since all of them were published in that periodical.

[5] "The Emperor of Ice-Cream," *The Collected Poems of Wallace Stevens* (New York, 1954), p. 64. Parenthetical documentation for other *Harmonium* poems will refer to page numbers in *Collected Poems*.

between winter, associated with barren college studies in philosophy, mathematics, and economics, and summer, which stimulates romance: a hint of warm air in February causes the narrator to feel like a knight, though he is in street clothes, and evokes pleasant memories of summer fields in Pennsylvania. Only hindsight, however, would lead the reader to see the possible origin here of the later symbolic role of winter and summer in Stevens' poetry. The sketch is hardly distinguishable from one any student might write on the subject of nature versus books.

But in the third story, "Part of His Education" (April 24, 1899, pp. 35-37), Stevens presented his theme with more clarity and force by developing it in terms of the antithetical motifs of crème de menthe and beer. Geoffrey, a prissy aesthete (everything about him creates the impression of art for art's sake), visits a barroom with Billy, a regular fellow, in order to "see the side of life he had never seen." In an atmosphere of coarse faces, smoke, and pictures of fighting cocks and pugilists (very naturalistic details), Geoffrey asserts his preciosity by ordering crème de menthe.[6] At this, he becomes a butt of ridicule and makes a fool of himself, calling the men pigs for desecrating a ballad; but finally he realizes his absurdity and atones by ordering beer all around. Geoffrey's precious elegance cannot exist in an ivory tower. He must accept reality, crude but vital, as the men, after laughing at him and being entertained at his expense, come to accept Geoffrey. As Billy had said earlier of the men, "They're like thirsty flowers longing for dew," the dew presumably suggesting beauty and meaning in their lives. The final reconciliation is contrived and sentimental, but the story stresses the need for such a reconciliation. And there is a basic grasp of symbolism in the use of crème de menthe and beer to show the conflict. Geoffrey must drink the beer of reality, but it is the crème de menthe which forms a beautiful rainbow, when Geoffrey, making a defiant gesture, inadvertently causes the liquor to fly out of his glass. This rainbow remains a point of poetic illumination; although it is a passing thing in the barroom, it is retained

[6] Just two months before "Part of His Education" appeared in the *Advocate*, Frank Norris had shocked the literary world with the publication of his naturalistic novel, *McTeague* (Feb., 1899). In it, perhaps by coincidence, McTeague ordered a glass of beer and Marcus "called for a 'Creme Yvette' in order to astonish the others." *McTeague* (New York, 1950), p. 167.

in the imaginative framework of the story. "Part of His Education" is an awkward *fin de siècle* piece, but with the difference
that it hardly endorses an escape from reality. In fact, it plunges
the aesthete into it. Stevens still had much to learn, but this story,
in its attempt at thematic complication and in its skeletal symbolic
construction, is a real turning point in Stevens' early writing.

Although the theme of conflict and interdependence of the
mundane and imaginative worlds runs through all of them, two
other stories clearly illustrate this theme and Stevens' search for
ways of dramatizing it. One is "Pursuit" (Oct. 18, 1899, p. 19),
in which a group of boys who "had eyes only for what was
bright and rare" chase an extraordinary butterfly, an obvious
symbol of aesthetic perfection. The boys are laughed at by the
boorish wife of a farmer, but when the butterfly "sailed down
in its luxury" at the feet of the farmer and his wife, clearly Philistines, "there was a piercing scream and in a wild panic the
farmer and his wife were gone." The wife, overwhelmed by a
sense of the power of pure beauty, is left "a breathless heap in
the dust . . . The vanquished clod [her husband] cut across the
country through a thicket of tall, pink-blooming milk-weeds."
After capturing the perfect butterfly, the boys, for a while for-
getful of ordinary things, remember the events the butterfly had
brought about and they return, as to reality and necessity, to
look for the farm woman in the dust, but she is gone.

The other story which illustrates Stevens' theme particularly
well is "The Nymph" (Dec. 6, 1899, pp. 86-87). Here, the
narrator is in the woods in Massachusetts in search of wildness,
but he finds instead a tall, slim girl of seventeen in a faded blue
skirt and white sweater, with a spray of eglantine in her hair
and a sketching pad in her hand, who responds to his curiosity
by declaring herself to be a nymph. "And in the winter—"
wonders the practical youth. "That's my secret," she replies.
She makes fun of his hard tack, dry beef, and canned beans,
offering in their stead—while playfully stepping on one of his
crackers—blackberries, mushrooms, wild cherries, and grapes.
Naming the woodland dainties in French, thus civilizing them
and intensifying the sense of their delicacy, she lists them on
her sketching pad (the distinction between this fare and the
gross food of the young man reminds us of that between crème
de menthe and beer in "Part of His Education"). The encoun-

ter of the boy and girl offers something considerably more striking than "Two hearts shall in a garden meet." The scene is
sophisticated and idyllic—nature heightened by the power of
the girl's imagination. The nymph's playful indoctrination of the
youth into the world of sophisticated experience definitely anticipates the plot of the girls in the *Harmonium* poem, "The Plot
against the Giant" (p. 6), to check, abash, and undo the giant
by providing the most delicate and beautiful stimulants to his
senses. But of the poems in *Harmonium* "The Plot" is not
alone. "Last Looks at the Lilacs" (pp. 48-49) and "Two Figures in Dense Violet Night" (pp. 85-86) both concern the humorous opposition of the gauche male and the suave female. Dora,
the nymph, is also a prototype of the more modest Ursula in
the witty, outwardly irreverent "Cy Est Pourtraicte, Madame
Ste Ursule, et Les Unze Mille Vierges" (pp. 21-22), as the comi-
cally presented narrator (in search of wildness) is a precursor
of the more experience-hungry Crispin—that "marvelous sophomore" in "The Comedian as the Letter C" (pp. 27-46).

In the stories Stevens not only discovered some of the possibilities of his theme, but also in working out variations of it
he first displayed some of the traits of style and technique that
later came to be characteristic of him. One of the chief innovations in the stories, for example, is their irony and wit. Inherent
in the very juxtapositions of the contrary worlds of imagination
and reality lay the basis for these qualities which implicitly repu-
diated the inflated softness of the early poems, many of which
were appearing in the *Advocate* at the same time that the bulk
of the stories came out. Stevens had learned that irony and the
comic point of view could exist side by side with the beautiful
and serious, and in fact both protect and enhance them. In
"Pursuit," for example, the triumph of the butterfly produces the
comic rout of the farm couple, and at the same time the rout
itself is not without its element of the beautiful; the farmer
flees through the "thicket of tall, pink-blooming milkweeds." In
"Part of His Education," the rainbow-like spray of crème de
menthe occurs as a result of the young aesthete's ridiculous
behavior. The boy and girl in "The Nymph" are interrupted
in their enumeration of pastoral delicacies in French by an insistent voice calling Dora to come: "The potatoes are cold, the flies
are in the jelly—oh, such a lunch as you'll have." The comic

deflation becomes complete when, arriving at a clearing, the narrator finds that his nymph works for a group of men who are playing cards outside their tents; a banner proclaims them the "Eureka Camping Club of Billville, Mass." The story ends on this triumph of banality, but not before the actual girl has created her imaginary mythological character and a few moments of rare beauty, which remain in our minds despite the comic deflation, or because of it.

Related to the ironic and comic are examples of Stevens' fondness for the eccentric, bizarre, and grotesque. The main character in " The Higher Life " (June 12, 1899, pp. 123-24) is an ex-variety-stage juggler turned college student in order to escape the rude world of vauderville and elevate himself to opera and tragedy. Nevertheless it is his nature to continue wearing a vest embroidered "with a multitude of little pink roses." "Hawkins of Cold Cape " (March 10, 1900, pp. 8-12) combines humor and weirdness. On the basis of a meteor's falling, a rumor develops that the end of the world is at hand. In the atmosphere of eeriness arising from the threat of imminent cataclysm, Hawkins, the unsuccessful editor of the local newspaper, uses the rumor and his imagination to create panic among the gullible townsfolk, and thus manages to acquire most of the town's livestock as well as a thriving butter and egg business. But " In the Dead of Night " (May 23, 1900, pp. 83-86) is the most flamboyantly bizarre; here Stevens' imagination was thoroughly liberated from the " impenetrable gloom " of "Vita Mea." In this farce, which can be characterized as something between a college humor sketch and some of Washington Irving's burlesques of the ghostly in *Tales of a Traveller*,[7] Cavanaugh, a servant disgruntled because he has been caught being too noisy, takes revenge by drugging the apple dumplings. The result is a wild midnight scene of mass hallucination in which the father of the house soberly discusses the Philippine question with Cavanaugh, who is trying to get away with the silverware. Meanwhile there is tobogganing on the main stairway to the accompaniment of shrieks and the singing of " Jingle

[7] New York and London, 1897. In these tales of ghosts, robbers, and the supernatural, one finds grotesquerie, a whimsical playing with fact and fancy, and strange antics in the middle of the night. See, for example, in Volume I, " The Adventures of My Aunt " (p. 41); " The Bold Dragoon " (p. 50); and " The Adventure of the Mysterious Picture " (p. 77).

Bells," while a Mrs. Fann keeps asking to be folded. There is a radically farcical quality in this nightmarish confusion, produced by the transposition of the outdoor, daylight activity to the indoors in the middle of the night, and by the release by Mrs. Fann of her suppressed obsession. The scene presents the opposite of ordinary daytime reality. It is an early caper by the poet who was to lament in " Disillusionment of Ten O'Clock " (p. 66),

> The houses are haunted
> By white night-gowns.
> None are green,
> Or purple with green rings,
>
> . . . .
>
> People are not going
> To dream of baboons and periwinkles.

It is in the relative freedom of the prose too that there occur a few specific effects of imagery and diction that would lead one to expect the manner of the mature poet. Compare, for example, the treatment of the wind in the poem " Vita Mea " with the more playful and striking use of it in " The Nymph." In the poem he says, ". . . And what sweet wind was rife / With earth, or sea, or star, or new sun's bloom, / Lay sick and dead within that place of doom." " Sweet wind was rife ": how trite. " Lay sick and dead ": how heavy and contradictory. But in the story the wind on that perfect day is likened to a giant. When the girl is summoned back to camp, she runs with the narrator in pursuit and cries over her shoulder "' Mures de ronce' . . . with a tantalizing laugh. ' De ronce, de ronce,' repeated the giant. ' De ronce,' I added instinctively." Here the obligato of the personified wind adds to the scene a quality that is at once slightly haunting and whimsical. It is also revealing of Stevens' progress to compare the personification used here with the excessively poetic personification in the " Sonnet," " There shines the morning star! . . . ," discussed above (pp. 95, 96). " The Nymph " is definitely a step toward greater originality and sophistication. Here also there is a foretaste of the grace and wit Stevens later derived from the use of French words and phrases, as in " The Plot against the Giant " (" Oh la . . . le pauvre! ") and in the titles of many of his poems.

In the stories there are a few other instances of relative fresh-

ness of expression. In "Pursuit," "the clouds strayed lazily into
the sky, like children into an open field . . ."; the movement of
the butterfly's wings is described as "such an opening of light,
such a closing of radiance, . . ." Then in the first sketch of
"Four Characters," an old man, whose gift of utterance ("My
tongue was like the Ba'am of Gilead") is a hindrance now that
he has been reduced, in the modern world, to peddling metal
polish, graphically describes the death of his horse, symbol of
his former glory: "But ol' Gold Dust lay there on her side,
her breath scattering the dust about her nostrils." It should be
stressed that expression indicative of the later poet is not often
evident in the prose, but two instances which point to the later
exuberance of word and sound might be cited. One is the use
of "gabble" and "bluster" in the sentence, "In another year
I shall be able to gabble your French and bluster your German,"
spoken by the ex-juggler in "The Higher Life." The other occurs
in "Part of His Education" at a point where Stevens was trying to convey the excitement and vitality of the music in the
barroom: "the banjo . . . thrilled and rattled with a volume
of clattering notes and chords." This is still far from the later
extravagant virtuosity—as seen in "Bantams in Pine Woods"
(p. 75), but "thrilled," "rattled," and "clattering" have in a
very elementary way some of the later almost tactile vibrato of
diction and sound, played "not on the psaltery, / But on the
banjo's categorical gut" ("The Comedian as the Letter C," p. 38).

One other element in the stories, an element in Stevens' work
that grew in importance, should be mentioned here—his interest
in color, both as a visual effect and as a symbolic device. The
third sketch in "Four Characters," essentially an amateurish
prose ode to the beauty of a natural setting complete with robin,
contains this specifically colorful but merely decorative description: "The horizon was blue, rimmed in the east with a pink
mistiness; in the west, with a warm yellowish red that gradually
died into thin whiteness." But in "The Revelation" (Nov. 13,
1899, pp. 54-56), Williams, a picture-frame maker, in helping a
college youth decide on an appropriate color for the frame of the
photograph of a pretty girl, provides half seriously a brief glossary
of color symbolism. Black is considered ominous, brown is thought
poetical, and white symbolic of clear weather (nothing is said of
blue). Finally gold, the color Williams uses for framing pictures

of Madonnas, is chosen for the picture of the girl, who, in her visits
to the shop to get her photograph of the youth framed, has become
Williams' idol. Thus Williams finds his Madonna in the actual
world.

In an editorial in the *Advocate* (March 24, 1900, p. 17) regard-
ing a proposed fence plan for Harvard Yard, Stevens said: "Putting a fence around the Yard strikes us as being the easiest way
of achieving order out of chaos . . . we have no point of concentration . . . bring back to the Yard some of the prestige
which it has lost . . . and thus the Yard would regain the hold
on our imagination which it is gradually losing." For Stevens
the imagination, order, and art were not simply literary matters;
they were relevant to experience, to the actual world. In a second
editorial on the subject (April 13, 1900, p. 49), he was against
those who wanted a wall-fence combination: "no more archi-
tectural *pot pourri*." In the final one (June 16, 1900, p. 114) he
wanted to avoid a fence that was pompous, dull, and useless:
"The fence must be utilitarian, not gorgeously commemorative;
it must be attractive, not depressive." It is such concentration
of interest that enabled Stevens, in the stories, to work out some
of the elements of his theme and make his first move toward his
later style. And the same interest had a corresponding effect on
some of his later undergraduate poetry.

By March, 1900, all but two of the stories ("In the Dead of
Night" and "Four Characters") had appeared in the *Advocate*,
and at that point (March 24, 1900, p. 18) Stevens published
"Outside the Hospital," a poem very different from the earlier
ones:

> See the blind and the lame at play,
>   There on the summer lawn—
> She with her graceless eyes of clay,
>   Quick as a frightened fawn,
> Running and tripping into his way
>   Whose legs are gone.
>
> How shall she 'scape him, where shall she fly,
>   She who never sees?
> Now he is near her, now she is by—
>   Into his arms she flees.
> Hear her gay laughter, hear her light cry
>   Among the trees.

> " Princess, my captive." " Master, my king."
>   " Here is a garland bright."
> " Red roses, I wonder, red with the spring,
>   Red with a reddish light? "
> " Red roses, my princess, I ran to bring,
>   And to be your knight."

Here is a pastoral scene with flowers, but it takes place on a hospital lawn, not " beyond these barren walls." [8] With its ironic juxtaposition of the grotesquely real and the gracefully imaginative which transcends the real, this is the first poem in which Stevens' central theme is unmistakably present. Also, the couple's lack of self-pity and their dialogue are in telling contrast with the overwrought qualities in the earlier poems. In fact, although the subject provides a greater risk of the sentimental than do the subjects of the first poems, it reveals instead a higher degree of emotional control. The very conception of the poem is more forceful; in the chiasmic reversal, the girl sees excellently in her mind's eye, and the legless boy runs in his imagination like a knight. The pair are like the nymph, Dora; although they do not speak French, they act and speak with regal elegance. The use of the word " garland " would be trite in the context of the earlier poems, but here it adds appropriately to the effect of light fantasy which is set off by the blunt statement of facts: a girl with " eyes of clay " plays with a boy " whose legs are gone." One recalls how frequently in his later poetry Stevens gave new life to archaic, poetic words, like " tinct " in " Cy Est Pourtraicte, Madam Ste Ursule, et Les Unze Mille Vierges " (p. 21).

Here, too, Stevens uses color more as he would in his later poetry. The girl, in her imagination, sees color very intensely, as if with a painter's eye; she sees " red with a reddish light." The basic red is heightened by a stroke of brighter red, as in the painter's technique, a device Stevens often used later in his *Harmonium* poems to give visual emphasis and a sense of texture: in " The Apostrophe to Vincentine " (p. 53), he says " Your dress was green, / Was whited green "; in " Six Significant Landscapes " (p. 74), " The white folds of its gown / Filled with yellow light ";

---

[8] A possible source of the hospital setting and the grimness in the poem is W. E. Henley's series of poems, " In Hospital " (*Works*, I [London, 1908], 3-46). Stevens might well have been struck by the way in which Henley introduced realistic details into his poetry.

or in " Nomad Exquisite " (p. 95) , " Beholding all these green sides / And gold sides of green sides."

Although the actual dates of composition cannot be proved, the general trend of publication in the *Advocate* makes it seem reasonable to conclude that the developments in the short stories had begun to be carried over to the poetry. Following " Outside the Hospital " there is a group of four poems collectively called " Street Songs " (April 3, 1900, pp. 42-43) . These have an unevenness that does not firmly consolidate the advance made by " Outside the Hospital," but they are much more ambitious than that poem and are definitely superior to the earlier poems as well as to three of those which followed.

I

THE PIGEONS

Over the houses and into the sky
    And into the dazzling light,
Long hosts of fluttering pigeons fly
    Out of the blackened night,
Over the houses and into the sky
    On glistening wings of white.

Over the city and into the blue
    From ledge and tower and dome,
They rise and turn and turn anew,
    And like fresh clouds they roam,
Over the city and into the blue
    And into their airy home.

II

THE BEGGAR

Yet in this morn there is a darkest night,
Where no feet dance or sweet birds ever rise,
Where fancy is a thing that soothes—and lies,
And leads on with mirages of light.
I speak of her who sits within plain sight
Upon the steps of yon cathedral. Skies
Are naught to her; and life a lord that buys
And sells life, whether sad, or dark, or bright.

The carvings and beauty of the throne
Where she is sitting, she doth meanly use
To win you and appeal. All rag and bone
She asks with her dry, withered hand a dreg
Of the world's riches. If she doth abuse
The place, pass on. It is a place to beg.

III

STATUARY

The windy morn has set their feet to dancing—
    Young Dian and Apollo on the curb,
The pavement with their slender forms is glancing,
    No clatter doth their gaiety disturb.

No eyes are ever blind enough to shun them,
    Men wonder what their jubilance can be,
No passer-by but turns to look upon them—
    Then goes his way with all his fancy free.

IV

THE MINSTREL

The streets lead out into a mist
    Of daisies and of daffodils—
A world of green and amethyst,
    Of seas and of uplifted hills.

These bird-songs are not lost in eaves,
    Nor beaten down by cart and car,
But drifting sweetly through the leaves,
    They die upon the fields afar.

Nor is the wind a broken thing
    That faints within hot prison cells,
But rises on a silver wing
    From out among the heather bells.

The title, "Street Songs," seems to have been chosen to give an air of casualness and detachment, though at our remove from the turn of the century it may seem closer to a pseudo-Neapolitanism. To read the poems, however, as a random collection of songs, as though they were merely descriptive vignettes, would be quite misleading, for "Street Songs" was an ambitious undertaking. Beneath the mask of casualness there runs a serious theme. This was Stevens' first attempt to write a suite of poems which amount, really, to one long poem in which the connections between the parts are oblique and the meaning is presented symbolically ("Four Characters," a couple of months later, was such an attempt in prose). The more one studies "Street Songs" the more one realizes that it is a very primitive version of what Stevens later did so magnificently in "Sunday Morning": in spite of great stylistic differences and some differences in emphasis, there are noteworthy similarities in what the two poems have to say about nature and religion. The trouble is that in the early poem the style and technique were not adequate for the elaborate aim. Some of the stylistic qualities remind one of those in the earliest poems, and the result is a clash between those qualities and the demands put upon them.

That Stevens was trying to work by indirection and to make order or pattern of his imagery becomes apparent upon examining the movement and theme of the poem. To begin with, the pigeons, coming out of the darkness into the light, are vaguely mystical ("hosts . . . On glistening wings of white"). Their ascent out of the blackness "Over the city and into the blue" suggests a transcendent renewal and, in the context of the whole poem, a stimulus to the imagination. If this is the case, it may be the first instance of the association, however unconscious, of blue and the imagination. In "The Beggar" there is a reversal: in the midst of light there is darkness. The imagination here cheats one ("fancy is a thing that . . . lies") and art ("The carvings and beauty of the throne") is perverted. The beggar woman, with an obliviousness to actual nature ("Skies are naught to her"), seems to suggests that the church and formal religion have turned lifeless and materialistic ("It is a place to beg"). The structure established to care for souls misleads them. In place of the excitement of the pigeon's ascent, there is stagnancy (the beggar is sitting) and ugliness. "Statuary" is an antidote to all this. The combination of nature ("The windy morn") and art (the statuary) removes the blindness and produces dancing, gaiety, and a free imagination. Significantly, Dian and Apollo are pagan, pre-Christian gods with attributes of nature—the woods, moon, and sun—but also they are associated with music, poetry, and prophecy. Whether one imagines in "Statuary" actual youths transfigured by the imagination and described by the metaphor of statuary, or the actual statuary described by the metaphorical "movement" of actual dancing, a motion within stillness ("No clatter doth their gaiety disturb"), a vitally imaginative scene is suggested. Finally, one's imagination having been set free by the atmosphere of pagan innocence and joy, "The Minstrel"—a minstrel rather than any other kind of evangelist—takes one with a now pristine vision to nature itself. But it is a nature from which one derives both poetic and mystical elevation. It is a world of green *and* amethyst, green and yet with the poetic suggestions of amethyst. It is a world "Of daisies and

of daffodils" but also "Of seas and of uplifted hills," a phrase
with biblical and spiritual connotations.[9] Suggestion of art are
found in the title itself and in the "bird-songs." Further suggestions of the spiritual quality in nature are found in "rises on a
silver wing"—one is reminded of the flight of pigeons, which in
retrospect can be seen as a kind of symbolic annunciation—and
"heather bells," rather than church bells. Thus in the four-part
poem there is a rejection of formal religion and an avowal of a
mixture of art and a kind of pantheistic religion.

On an elementary level, then, "Street Songs" is concerned with
essentially the same theme as the later "Sunday Morning" (pp.
66-70), even to the ambiguous cycle of death and renewal in
nature: in "The Minstrel," in a mist "Of daisies and of daffodils,"
the wind "rises on silver wing" following the death of the bird-
songs "upon the fields afar"; in "Sunday Morning," Part VIII,
"Sweet berries ripen in the wilderness," and

> At evening, casual flocks of pigeons make
> Ambiguous undulations as they sink,
> Downward to darkness, on extended wings.

But there are other parallels, not merely thematic, which indicate
that "Street Songs" was an embryonic version of the mature
poem. There are the symbolic, transcendent pigeons in both
poems; there are the pagan Dion and Apollo in "Statuary" and
Jove and the more "savage source" in "Sunday Morning," Parts
III and VII. There are "sweet birds" in "The Beggar"; "bird-
songs," the "world of green," and the mist and fields in "The
Minstrel," while in "Sunday Morning," Part IV, there are also
birds with "their sweet questionings," "April's green," and "misty
fields." Also, the question, "Why should she give her bounty to
the dead?" in Part II of "Sunday Morning" is a vivid reminder
of "The Beggar" in "Street Songs":

> . . . she doth meanly use
> To win you and appeal. All rag and bone
> She asks with her dry, withered hand a dreg
> Of the world's riches.

Finally, the movement from city to country in "Street Songs"

---

[9] See, for example, Isaiah, II, 14: "Upon all the hills that are lifted up," or Psalm
95, 4-5: "In His Hand are the deep places of the earth; the strength of the hills
is His also. The sea is His, and He made it; and His Hands formed the dry land."

is roughly parallel to the movement from the Matisse-like urban luxury to the fields and the deer on the mountains in the more sophisticated "Sunday Morning."

But to compare the two poems at all is to measure the growth in Stevens' poetry in the fifteen-year period between them, for "Street Songs" was an interesting failure in which the young poet overextended himself. There are too many elements which blunt the high purpose. In "The Beggar," for example, there is an ill-disguised spite that breaks through the carefully assumed air of detachment in the group as a whole. In contrast to this lack of control there is the more playful urbane satire of the later "A High-Toned Old Christian Woman" (p. 59), as well as the controlled ambivalence with which Christian myth is treated in "Sunday Morning" itself. Also, part of the purpose of the whole group is obscured by the over-emphasis on the theme of nature versus the city. "The Minstrel" becomes almost entirely a conventional poem on this theme; one must not stay long in city pent. Further, "Of daisies and of daffodils," "beaten down by cart and car," and "faints within hot prison cells" are remnants of the diction and imagery of his earlier poems. The subtlety of "heather bells" as a substitute in nature for church bells is ruined by the unfortunate triteness of the surface; it is clever as an image, but it falls flat taken unmetaphorically. Finally, no particular ends seem to be served by the use of the sonnet form in "The Beggar" and the quatrain form in "Statuary" and "The Minstrel." These forms are shells of Stevens' early exercises and are not very successfully filled by his new purpose.

But there are in "Street Songs" hints of the later poet— despite "yon cathedral" and the doth's. "The Pigeons" certainly has a tighter relationship between form, meaning and rhythm than do the earlier poems. The repetitions, especially in the line, "They rise and turn and turn anew" (which herald the similar technique in the *Harmonium* poem "Domination of Black," with its ominous turning of leaves, pp. 8-9), help to give a sense of the sweeping, circling upward movement of the pigeons, and of the excitement and awe over their radiant flight. Also, the emotion in each stanza is sustained beyond the length of the customary quatrain. In "The Beggar" there is the sudden simplicity of style in the sentence, "It is a place to beg." In its abrupt statement of what is, it faintly anticipates "The Emperor of

Ice-Cream": "If her horny feet protrude, they come / To show how cold she is, and dumb" (p. 64). In "Statuary" the word "jubilance" and the light play on "fancy free" have a touch of the later flair. And in the title, "The Minstrel" (not identified in the poem), there is an oblique relevance, an added implication, that we find in many of the later, usually more humorous and ironic, titles. As a whole, "Street Songs" is a *mélange* of new purpose and old style, but the new purpose was beginning to have its effect on his style.

This point is apparent in "Ballade of the Pink Parasol," of the undergraduate poems the one which in style seems most indicative of what was to appear in *Harmonium* (*Advocate*, LXIX, No. 6 [May 23, 1900], 82).

> I pray thee where is the old-time wig,
>   And where is the lofty hat?
> Where is the maid on the road in her gig,
>   And where is the fire-side cat?
>   Never was sight more fair than that,
> Outshining, outreaching them all,
>   There in the night where the lovers sat—
> But where is the pink parasol?
>
> Where in the pack is the dark spadille
>   With scent of lavender sweet,
> That never was held in the mad quadrille,
>   And where are the slippered feet?
> Ah! we'd have given a pound to meet
>   The card that wrought our fall,
> The card none other of all could beat—
>   But where is the pink parasol?
>
> Where is the roll of the old calash,
>   And the jog of the light sedan?
> Whence Chloe's diamond brooch would flash
>   And conquer poor peeping man.
> Answer me, where is the painted fan
>   And the candles bright on the wall;
> Where is the coat of yellow and tan—
>   But where is the pink parasol?
>
>   Prince, these baubles are far away,
>   In the ruin of palace and hall,
>   Made dark by the shadow of yesterday—
>   But where is the pink parasol?

This poem, like the two before it, is obviously a variation on Stevens' central theme. "Outside the Hospital" focused on the

ironic juxtaposition of imaginative beauty and painful reality—
reality is made bearable, and more than bearable, by the imagination. "Street Songs," in a more philosophic vein, concerns
the imaginative and, by extension, religious construct one makes
of nature. " Ballade " is a frivolous lament for the ordered elegance
a past age had created in the midst of, or out of, reality. Time,
a central element of reality, obliterates such creations. And what,
it is implied, has the present that will serve the function previously served by the pink parasol? In "Ballade" Stevens found
a subject and form which, at that point in his career, not only
expressed his theme but also were most conducive to liberating
his penchant for the exuberant and elegant. Though it is influenced by the ballade vogue of the late nineteenth century, the
poem is an important step toward Stevens' later style.

This is especially evident in the obsolete diction which was
deliberately chosen for its forceful evocation of a recherché and
sophisticated elegance: wig, spadille, quadrille, calash, sedan chair.
But these words also carry with them, in their outdatedness, an
effect of the absurd, which enabled Stevens to include a conception
of refinement and beauty without being sentimental. He could
afford to indulge in the thing he simultaneously ridiculed in a
gentle way. Notice particularly the gusto of "Where is the roll
of the old calash," wherein the wit and humor are reinforced by
the repetitions of sound in roll, old, and calash. The joy in language and sound here brings Stevens much closer to his extravagant displays in *Harmonium*.

Stevens also avoided sentimentality by finding in the ballade
form the means to objectify and dramatize his theme; as he did
in "Outside the Hospital," he avoided self-conscious personae.
One can simply compare "Lo, even as I passed beside the booth
/ Of roses . . ." from another "Sonnet," which appeared in the
same issue of the *Advocate* as did "Ballade," with "I pray thee
where is the old-time wig" in order to see how Stevens was
working toward wit and a lightness of touch.

The pink parasol is decidedly functional in this poem, unlike
the trite and ineffectual "booth of roses" just mentioned. The
parasol, the essence of feminity, is treated with gaiety and exag-
gerated by alliteration. More important, however, the phrase
seems to have been chosen with some precision as the central
symbol of the poem. What, after all, was the function of the

parasol but to enable the user to go out in the sun of reality
without losing her aristocratic pallor, so artfully maintained?
Without the parasol, itself a thing of elegant beauty, to protect
within its shadow the world of aristocratic artifice—the painted
fan, the scent of lavender, the coat of yellow and tan—the dark
"shadow of yesterday" asserts itself and reduces the baubles
of sophisticated beauty to a flat banality. And so, under the
mask of lightness and wit, there is a genuine, if at the same
time amusing, sense of lament which emerges in the concluding
quatrain.

For Stevens' use of the ballade form itself there were many
precedents, ranging from Villon's ballades to several by E. A.
Robinson, which appeared in *The Torrent and the Night Before*
in 1896 and *Children of the Night* in 1897. Theodore de Ban-
ville, with his *Trente-Six Ballades Joyeuses* (1873), did much
to rekindle interest in Villon and in the ballade form in France.
With the help of Swinburne and Rossetti, the vogue for Villon
and the ballade form passed over to England.[10] Rossetti translated Villon's "Ballade des Dames du Temps Jadis" in 1869, a
poem of nostalgic lament for past beauty, and Swinburne wrote
his double ballade of tribute to Villon, "A Ballade of François
Villon, Prince of all Ballad-makers," as well as "A Ballade of
Dreamland" (*Works* [London, 1925], III, pp. 125, 78), the latter
very Swinburnian in style: "I hid my heart in a nest of roses."
However, William Ernest Henley, Andrew Lang, and Austin Dobson made more extensive use of the form, and in ways which would
be more likely to inspire Stevens. There are, for example, Henley's
"Ballade of a Toyokuni Colorprint" (*Works* [London, 1908], I,
81-82), and Lang's "Ballade of Blue China" (*Works* [London,
1925], I, 197), with their exotic and rococo details.

Austin Dobson, however, is the most interesting of the possible
influences, for in his other work as well in the ballades we find
a thorough-going affection for the eighteenth-century world of
graceful and quaint artifice, both English and French. In "A
Gentleman of the Old School" (*Collected Poems* [New York,
1895], I, 10), he writes of a "canary vest / With buds brocaded,"

---

[10] For a pertinent discussion of the ballade form and its influence on English Parnassianism, see James K. Robinson, "Austin Dobson and the Rondeliers," *MLQ*, 14
(1953), 33, and the same author, "A Neglected Phase of the Aesthetic Movement:
English Parnassianism," *PMLA*, Sept., 1953, 733-54.

which is very like the juggler's vest "embroidered with a multi-tude of little pink roses" in Steven's sketch, "The Higher Life." In Dobson's "The Old Sedan Chair" (II, 7-8) there is a recol-lection of past elegance:

> And yet—can't you fancy a face in the frame
> Of the window,—some high-headed damsel or dame
> Be-patched and be-powdered, just set by the stair,
> While they raise up the lid of that old sedan chair?
>
> Can't you fancy Sir Plume, as beside her he stands,
> With his ruffles a-droop on his delicate hands,
> With his cinnamon coat with his laced solitaire,
> As he lifts her out light from the old sedan chair?

These examples would certainly have appealed to Stevens, but this is even more true of Dobson's ballade, "On a Fan That Belonged to the Marquise de Pompadour" (I, 249-50), which seems in many ways a possible model for "The Ballade of the Pink Parasol," though it cannot be said that Stevens necessarily knew of the poem:

> Chicken-skin, delicate, white,
>   Painted by Carlo Vanloo,
> Loves in a riot of light,
>   Roses and vaporous blue;
>   Hark to the dainty *frou-frou!*
> Picture above if you can,
>   Eyes that could melt as the dew—
> This was the Pompadour's fan!
>
> See how they rise at the sight,
>   Thronging the Œil de Boeuf through,
> Courtiers as butterflies bright,
>   Beauties that Fragonard drew,
>   *Talon-rouge*, falbala, queue,
> Cardinal, duke—to a man,
>   Eager to sigh or to sue—
> This was the Pompadour's fan!
>
> Ah, but things more than polite
>   Hung on this toy, *voyez-vous!*
> Matters of state and of might,
>   Things that great ministers do;
>   Things that, maybe, overthrew
> Those in whose brains they began;
>   Here was the sign and the cue—
> This was the Pompadour's fan!

Envoy

Where are the secrets it knew?
    Weavings of plot and of plan?
—But where is the Pompadour too?
This was the Pompadour's *fan!*

" Chicken-skin " is certainly repellent, but in " On a Fan " there
is the use of a dainty feminine accessory to evoke nostalgia and
sophisticated wit. There are also the savoring of recherché words
and an emphasis on elegance and beauty. There is even the reference to intrigue, with death implied, as there is in the Stevens
poem:

Ah, we'd have given a pound to meet
    The card that wrought our fall,
The card none other of all could beat—

But of course what really stands out in Stevens' poem, when
one notes the similarities of the two poems, is the line, " Answer
me, where is the painted fan / . . . ? " Surely Stevens was aware
of the ballade vogue and quite possibly of Dobson's " On a Fan "
in particular.

If Stevens was influenced by Dobson's poem, with all its rococo
details and the reference to Fragonard, and by other Dobson
poems, such as one called " After Watteau " (I, 234), it was
only a short step to the *fêtes galantes* elements in Verlaine's
poems and in the paintings by Fragonard and Watteau. But
whether Stevens had already in college discovered Verlaine and
the paintings is difficult to say. Nonetheless, Stevens' fondness
for the *fêtes galantes* atmosphere at this time can be seen in the
fourth sketch of " Four Characters " (see above, p. 99), in which
the lady who owns the boarding house describes her former garden
parties:

. . . the garden! How we used to dance there in summer evenings!
—with the trees bright with little lanterns, and the rose bushes tied
up with little ribbons, and the sweetest orchestra of guitars and
mandolins hidden somewhere in the foliage . . . .

Even though " Ballade of a Pink Parasol " is derivative, it is
derived from a vogue that was part of a general attempt to
bring new effects into English poetry. Stevens' ballade, like
Dobson's does not avoid quaintness, but resurrected with the
language and trappings of eighteenth-century culture there are

detachment and wit which prevent the staleness of some of the more prevalent nineteenth-century modes. The very literature overthrown by Romanticism had by the end of the nineteenth century become remote enough to be itself "Romantic." Here was one way of instilling new life into a stagnant tradition. Modern poets would try other ways generally overlooked by nineteenth-century English and American poets. Stevens, for one, had by "Ballade" come abreast of the movement that more and more brought French influences to bear on English poetry. In his undergraduate interest in things French—the French-speaking nymph, the ballade vogue, the *fêtes galantes* atmosphere—he found a means of introducing into his work details that were exotic, elegant, and at the same time more original. This was an interest that would lead more distinctly to Verlaine and then to the French Symbolists and Ironists—though that is not at all to say that he was to be exclusively devoted to French influences.

Certainly Victorian poets—and, indeed, Romantic poets—had been concerned with the fate of subjective, imaginative and artistic ideals in a world of science and materialistic values. But the pressures of the actual world were increasing, and art to survive at all in a meaningful way had to change, to become somehow more potent and not retreat into the quiet, safe territory reserved for it. Stevens seems to have surmised this, as he became absorbed with his theme and took steps to make his writing more vital. In the undergraduate work, there is a liberation of his matter and style from the confines of the standard poetic practices of the time. There is the emergence of irony, wit, and humor; there is more color, more boldness, more control. Of course the work is hardly distinguished, but it is a respectable—even promising—beginning, with tendencies that would be fulfilled in the mature work when it appeared. Stevens' first real triumphs, indeed his first published poems after he left Harvard, were still fourteen or fifteen years away, but the Harvard work points out the direction he was to follow in his later work.

IV

WALLACE STEVENS,
BERGSON, PATER

BY SAMUEL FRENCH MORSE

The fourteen poems which Wallace Stevens and Harriet Monroe finally came to agree on as suitable for publication under the collective title "Pecksniffiana" appeared in *Poetry* for October, 1919. A year later they won the Levinson Prize, the magazine's most distinguished award. This triumph meant more, perhaps, to Miss Monroe than to Stevens: he had been one of her proudest discoveries, and "Pecksniffiana" had dazzlingly confirmed her judgment that he was of the elect. He had not been completely satisfied with the group. He had wanted "to make the design as belle as possible,"[1] and had persuaded her to omit "Piano Practice at the Academy of the Holy Angels" because it was "cabbage instead of the crisp lettuce intended."[2] But although Stevens

---

[1] Letter to Harriet Monroe, Aug. 27, 1919. Thanks are due to the University of Chicago Library for permission to quote from the Stevens-Monroe correspondence; to Mr. Thomas McGreevy; and to Mrs. Holly Stephenson.

[2] Letter to Harriet Monroe, Aug. 16, 1919. Stevens' fondness for describing his failures in Candide's kitchen-garden idiom lasted at least until he had worked it into "The Comedian as the Letter C." He also took special delight in the name "Peter Parasol," that he had chosen as the pseudonym under which to submit his first poems to *Poetry* and as the title for one of the poems he tried to persuade Miss Monroe to omit from "Pecksniffiana." "The element of pastiche," he argued, would "not be apparent and the poem [would] go off on its substance and not its style." When he came to assemble the manuscript of *Harmonium*, he first included "Peter Parasol," and then decided to leave it out. He never reprinted it, although Marianne Moore referred to it as an illustration of his skill in getting "a special effect with those adjectives which often weaken . . ." ("Well Moused, Lion," *Dial*, LXXVI [1924], 87.) Many years later, when Wilfrid Mellers wrote him for permission to use the poem as a text for a choral work, he replied that he had forgotten everything about it except that it had been in some way unsatisfactory, and that he had never liked it. Stevens intended the poem to be an imitation of the ironic sentimentalities that Apollinaire handles with such skill in *Le Bestiaire* (some of which he knew by heart and recalled in "Lions in Sweden," with its reference to Dufy's illustrations for the original edition) and *Alcools*, but it does not quite come off. It overstates the finickiness of its protagonist without making its irony clear.

On the other hand, he played with the parasol as a symbol of the imagination for a long time. It first appears in the best of his undergraduate poems, "Ballade of

felt that "Pecksniffiana" was "under the curse of miscellany," he was pleased to have won the prize. "I am much more modest," he wrote Miss Monroe, "than you think, or than the overblown bloom I am suggests. Really, the bouquet in this month's poetry will drive me to back alleys and the suburbs." He added as a token of his gratitude, "I shall be sending you another patch of things bye and bye, but prefer to allow your panegyrics to fade a little out of mind before I reappear." [3] He knew that nothing could have delighted her more; for all his growing self-confidence in his poetic powers, he enjoyed taking advantage of the opportunities that she gave him to "let go" as a person and as a poet. The "patch" he finally sent her turned out to be the group published in October, 1921, under the title "Sur Ma Guzzla Gracile," twelve poems about which neither he nor Miss Monroe had any second thoughts. He had sent to *Poetry* what he considered his best work; moreover, "Sur Ma Guzzla Gracile" represented about half of all he had written in two years. Of the rest, "Invective against Swans," "Infanta Marina," and two inconsequential bits of grotesquerie called "Lulu Gay" and "Lulu Morose" were published in Robert McAlmon's *Contact*; "Cortege for Rosenbloom" appeared in *The Measure*, as a favor to Pitts Sanborn; and "The Man Whose Pharynx Was Bad," in *The New Republic*. The others remained unpublished.

Bergson's theory of comedy, which had contributed much to the design of "Carlos among the Candles" and "Bowl, Cat and Broomstick," was equally important in shaping the poems written between 1915 and 1921. The belief that "just as objects in nature affect us . . . so, on the other hand, we affect objects in nature, by projecting our moods, emotions, etc.," which Stevens had attempted to demonstrate in his plays, squared neatly with his own interpretation of Pater and Bergson's theories of comedy and art. *Laughter* contributed more than Pater, however, to the

the Pink Parasol." It crops up again in "The Comedian as the Letter C" at the moment when Crispin is about to renounce the imagination for his peculiar kind of realism, and still later in "Of Hartford in a Purple Light" and "Certain Phenomena of Sound," in which imagination is restored to what for Stevens was its proper status as "the will of things." In his "Adagia" he notes that "All of our ideas come from the natural world: trees=umbrellas." But a parasol inevitably suggests artifice and fiction; it makes the imagination an ambiguous power. Like Pascal, whom Stevens greatly admired, he was sometimes of two minds about the imagination.

[3] Letter to Harriet Monroe, Dec. 2, 1920.

creation of most of the oddly disaffected types whose meditations are dramatized in the poems of "Pecksniffiana" and "Sur Ma Guzzla Gracile"; for a time, at least, it provided the stylistic scaffolding for Stevens's developing manner. Bergson raises the social implications of comedy to a level of greater significance than Stevens ever does: for him, truth, vice, and virtue are conventionally moral terms which Stevens regards as irrelevant to "the morality of the right sensation." But his recognition of the fact that "the comic does not exist outside the pale of what is strictly human," like his understanding that "a landscape may be beautiful, charming and sublime, or insignificant and ugly" but "never laughable," must have seemed to Stevens a reflection of his own ideas. The "Six Significant Landscapes" are exercises that illustrate and support the proposition on which the plays are founded; but in one instance at least, Bergson seems to have supplied the essential metaphor. "You may laugh," Bergson observes, "at a hat, but what you are making fun of . . . is not the piece of felt or straw, but the shape that men have given it,—the human caprice whose mould it has assumed." In the sixth of his "Landscapes," Stevens observes:

> Rationalists, wearing square hats,
> Think, in square rooms,
> Looking at the floor,
> Looking at the ceiling.
> They confine themselves
> To right-angled triangles.
> If they tried rhomboids,
> Cones, waving lines, ellipses—
> As, for example, the ellipse of the half-moon—
> Rationalists would wear sombreros.

The most elaborate development of this theory of comic resemblances is "The Comedian as the Letter C," in which Crispin, "Like Candide, / Yeoman and grub," appropriately enough sees the world at the end of his adventures in the same way that he has always seen it, as a turnip. Between the quasi-imagistic notations of "Six Significant Landscapes" and the most ambitious of his "preliminary minutiae" lie all but one or two of Stevens's most remarkable early poems.

Stevens once noted that the vice of imagism was its failure to recognize that all objects are not "equal." Bergson, early in his essay, says, ". . . give your sympathy its widest expansion: as though at the touch of a fairy wand you will see the flimsiest of objects assume importance, and a gloomy hue spread over everything. Now step aside, look upon life as a disinterested spectator: many a drama will turn into a comedy." Here, perhaps, Stevens found a suggestion as to how he could satisfy his passionate desire to be a poet, maintain his natural detachment, and indulge his fondness for " the flimsiest of objects," without having to make all objects "equal." It gave him, as he discovered, a method of objectifying his own eccentricities without becoming their victim. Bergson goes on to say:

. . . the vice capable of making us comic . . . is that which is brought from without, like a ready-made frame into which we are to step. It leads us to its own rigidity instead of borrowing from us our flexibility. We do not render it more complicated; on the contrary, it simplifies us. . . . A drama, even when portraying passions or vices that bear a name, so completely incorporates them in the person that their names are forgotten, their general characteristics effaced, and we no longer think of them at all, but rather of the person in whom they are assimilated; hence, the title of a drama can seldom be anything else than a proper noun. On the other hand, many comedies have a common noun as their title: *l'Avare, le Joueur,* etc. . . . The reason is that, however intimately vice, when comic, is associated with persons, it none the less retains its simple, independent existence, it remains the central character, present though invisible, to which the characters in flesh and blood on the stage are attached. . . . Look closely: you will find that the art of the comic consists in making us so well acquainted with the particular vice, in introducing us, the spectators, to such a degree of intimacy with it, that in the end we get hold of some of the strings of the marionette with which [the comic poet] is playing, and actually work them ourselves; that it is that explains part of the pleasure we feel.

The meditating mind of " The Weeping Burgher," for example, although eccentric rather than vicious, is self-indulgent and, as Bergson notes, " unconscious of its self-indulgence ":

> It is with a strange malice
> That I distort the world.
>
> Ah! that ill humors
> Should mask as white girls.
> And ah! that Scaramouche
> Should have a black barouche.

The sorry verities!
Yet in excess, continual,
There is cure of sorrow.

Permit that if as ghost I come
Among the people burning in me still,
I come as belle design
Of foppish line.

And I, then, tortured for old speech,
A white of wildly woven rings;
I, weeping in a calcined heart,
My hands such sharp, imagined things.

The burgher has no name; he is identified only as a city dweller by a term both surprising and faintly ironic in the context of twentieth-century usage. His words reveal him as a displaced figure of classical comedy, a *précieux ridicule* isolated from the ordinary world by his longing for past elegance. He is, however, sensitive to his difference from his fellow-citizens; his "malice" lies in his refusal to accept the vulgarity of the world in which he lives, the vulgarity of "things as they are." He is the epitome of those who, when Stevens was an undergraduate at Harvard, argued that "all the poetry had been written and all the paintings painted." He is also the man whom Stevens satirized in his acceptance speech when he received the National Book Award in 1951: the man who asks, "Do you really think that any of these [modern poets] are as good, say, as Sir Walter Scott?" But although his heart is "calcined," he is no Ethan Brand, and he has committed no unpardonable sin. As Bergson observes of certain characters in Molière, he is unsociable; he "inverts" common sense and spends his time "following up his one idea." His eccentricity is that of the dreamer who "feels he has not ceased to be what he is; yet he has become someone else. He is himself and not himself. He hears himself speak and sees himself act, but he feels that some other 'he' has borrowed his body and stolen his voice." Finally, his language creates a comic effect by "transposing the natural expression of an idea into another key." The burgher exploits words as much for their sound as for their meaning; his syntax is deliberately, rather than spontaneously, wayward.

Bergson deals at length with such points: *Laughter* is a kind of encyclopedia of comic strategies. Stevens did not, of course, write

"Pecksniffiana," "Sur Ma Guzzla Gracile," or "Le Monocle de
Mon Oncle" simply as illustrations of Bergsonian doctrine, or to
disguise his own impulse to burn with a hard gem-like flame. He
discovered very quickly how little he had in common with his
fellow-contributors to *Others*, *The Rogue*, and *Poetry*. He knew
himself better than the critics who casually lumped him together
with Kreymborg, Williams, Bodenheim, Skipwith Cannèll, and
John Gould Fletcher. As a person he fitted somewhat uneasily
into the literary atmosphere of the New York "gang." He did not
thrive on the literary life, nor did he have much time for it. He
kept in touch. He read a good deal. He saw Harriet Monroe
whenever he was in Chicago. He picked up a certain amount of
literary gossip. He corresponded with friends who could tell him
things and, if they were abroad, could satisfy his pleasure in books
by sending him what he wanted, as McAlmon sent him from
Montreux "a box of what the natives call glazed fruit." He was
able to take advantage of his position as business man and poet;
he could be off-hand, when he chose, about literary causes that
for some of his contemporaries were almost matters of life and
death, and he cultivated his natural detachment effectively. He
had time to write to Miss Monroe from Indianapolis:

A further postponement will defer my seeing you for about a month.
From to-day's train:

I

The cows are down in the meadows, now, for the first time.
The sheep are grazing, under the thin trees.
My fortune is high.
All this makes me happy.

II

Fickle Concept
Another season of illusion and belief and ease.

III

First Poem For the Meditation on Infants
Gather together the stones around the tree and let the
  tree gather its leaves and fruit.

IV

Earth-creatures, two-legged years, suns, winters . . .

V

Poupée de Poupées
She was not the child of religion or science
Created by a god or by earth.
She was the creature of her own minds.

VI

Certainties cutting the centuries
Je vous assure, madame, q'une promenade à travers the soot-
deposit qu'est Indianapolis est une chose veritablement étrange.
Je viens de finir une telle promenade. Le jour après demain je
serai a Pittsburg d'ou je partirai pour Hartford. Au revoir,

Recevez, madame, etc.[4]

Or, again:

Apparently Bodenheim, our poetic Junius, is back in this vulgar
region. It was very decent of him to say a good word for Rodker.
Rodker's publications last winter were by all odds the most
sympathetic of the year. There is, of course, a cliché of the
moment as well as a cliché of the past; and I rather think that
Rodker merely represents the cliché of the moment, without really
being, in the sense in which the Little Review uses the word
"being." My friend Ferdinand Reyher is spending the winter in
London, and I expect shortly to receive various odds and ends
from him, so that when you come to Hartford again we may be
able to make you more content than you imagine.[5]

In his role as comedian he could employ the devices of exaggeration and caricature he enjoyed without becoming personally
involved in literary causes and movements. His independence
gave him the self-protection he liked and needed, and saved him
from having to make explanations. He parodied the dilettante,
including the dilettante in himself, rather than the dandy; good
literary manners were important to him. On the rare occasions
when something he had published aroused the indignation of a
reader for whom literature was the utterance of high moral truths
or a harmless pastime, his detachment proved useful. When, for
example, William Stanley Braithwaite passed on to him the
comment of a reader who had been outraged by the inclusion of
"Cortège for Rosenbloom" in the *Anthology of Magazine Verse*
for 1921, he replied in a note that combined lofty forbearance,

[4] Letter to Harriet Monroe, Apr. 25, 1920.
[5] Letter to Harriet Monroe, Dec. 2, 1920.

asperity, and candor with the clear implication that the confidence between two men of letters was not to be violated:

> I have your letter of November 25 enclosing a copy of Miss Fowler's letter of November 9 in regard to the Cortège for Rosenbloom. I don't know whether Miss Fowler is looking for exegesis of the poem itself or apology for your choice of it. Is she entitled to either? I shall be much interested to see a copy of your notice in the Transcript.
>
> From time immemorial the philosophers and other scene painters have daubed the sky with dazzle paint. But it all comes down to the proverbial six feet of earth in the end. This is as true of Rosenbloom as of Alcibiades. It cannot be possible that they have never munched this chestnut at Tufts. The ceremonies are amusing. Why not fill the sky with scaffolds and stairs, and go about like genuine realists?
>
> I hope that this will throw a little light on the subject, although it may still leave your own choice of the poem unexplained. Please do not involve me in any correspondence with the damsel.[6]

For the most part, however, his poems aroused not even this kind of response. "The Weeping Burgher," "Peter Parasol," and the speakers in "Anecdote of the Jar," "Banal Sojourn," and "Colloquy with a Polish Aunt" could hardly be considered Pecksniffs in any serious moral sense. Their hypocrisy or cant involves only "the flimsiest of objects," although it is expressed in the most precisely elegant language. Bergson had noted Dickens's special fondness for exaggeration as a device to "express in reputable language some disreputable idea," adding that such a technique is "far more artificial" than the conventional mockheroic. But the ideas expressed by the characters of "Pecksniffiana" are contrary and perverse rather than disreputable, despite Marianne Moore's "resentment" of "the temper of certain of these poems":

Mr. Stevens is never inadvertently crude; one is conscious, however, of a deliberate bearishness—a shadow of acrimonious, unprovoked contumely. Despite the sweet-Clementine-will-you-be-mine nonchalance of the "Apostrophe to Vincentine," one feels oneself to be in danger of unearthing the ogre and in "Last Looks at the Lilacs," a pride in unserviceableness is suggested which makes it a microcosm of cannibalism.[7]

Like Bergson, Miss Moore takes a more moral view of comedy

---

[6] Letter to William Stanley Braithwaite, Dec. 5, 1921.
[7] "Well Moused, Lion," *Dial*, LXXVI (1924), 86.

than Stevens; even so, it seems quite likely that Bergson's reference to Dickens suggested "Pecksniffiana" as a title.

The only thing "disreputable" about "Ploughing on Sunday" is its superb high spirits, its festive defiance of the biblical dictum that Sunday should be the Lord's Day and a day of rest: the poem is a hymn to celebrate the "truth" of a proposition re-stated in a later poem, "The Sense of the Sleight-of-Hand Man":

> One's grand flights, one's Sunday baths,
> One's tootings at the weddings of the soul
> Occur as they occur.

The only hypocrisy of "Ploughing on Sunday" is an irrelevantly private one: its contradiction of the fact that the Stevenses did maintain the old custom of performing no physical labor, not even cooking, on Sundays. "Anecdote of the Jar" pricks the balloon of local pride by suggesting that God's country of Tennessee is "slovenly," but it implies that man's contribution to the landscape is equally unattractive. That Stevens was of two minds about Tennessee the poem makes clear. That he said so explicitly in letters contemporary with the poem is certainly of interest, if not of tremendous importance. He said in a letter from Chattanooga, "I have always been of two minds about Tennessee. Sometimes I like it . . . I know well that I like the far South, along the Gulf; but this midway South is uncertainty." [8] The next day he wrote, "I feel quite sure that I rather like Knoxville. The Tennessee River makes a great bend through the woods and cliffs and hills, and on the horizon run the blue ranges of the Appalachian Mountains." [9] But from Nashville, the view was different, and he had "noticed that in a letter O. Henry asked, 'Is it possible for anything to happen in Nashville?' Certainly not without outside help. This applies to the state as a whole." [10] The famous jar, which is the "outside help," is not only "round . . . and tall . . ." but also "gray and bare." As between jar and wilderness, then, the poem makes no choice. The one hypocrisy of the "Anecdote" is its seeming contradiction of Steven's great pleasure in "fabricated things" and in "atmospheres" and "the principle of order." The tone of the poem, despite the zest for order which it reveals, is undeniably sardonic. "Pecksniffiana" remains an ambiguously

[8] Letter to Elsie Stevens, Apr. 18, 1918.
[9] Letter to Elsie Stevens, Apr. 19, 1918.
[10] Letter to Elsie Stevens, Apr. 20, 1918.

rhetorical title, a pointed joke that complicates as much as it clarifies.

"Sur Ma Guzzla Gracile" is equally ambiguous. The songs created on this instrument are all in some way gracefully and gently disaffected; their tone is comic rather than pathetic. The bitter meditations of "The Cuban Doctor" and Don Joost ("From the Misery of Don Joost") make up in sophistication what they lack in intensity of feeling. The moodiness of the "disbeliever" in "Palace of the Babies," or the snow man's "Mind of winter" has the quality of a serious and elaborate hoax. In "Hibiscus on the Sleeping Shores," the mind that "roamed as a moth roams, / Among the blooms beyond the open sand," indulges itself with a guilty awareness that "the flaming red / Dabbled with yellow pollen" disturbs the "stupid afternoon." The poem presents the meditation of a mind unable to cope with boredom except by aesthetic shock: the red of the hibiscus is a "red as red / As the flag above the old café." The commonplace café and the dullness of the afternoon are heightened by the contrast with the context in which they appear. The mind that speaks in "Hibiscus on the Sleeping Shores" is as guilty in its self-consciousness as Max Beerbohm's young man whose secret vice was drinking Bovril in his attic room at midnight.

The tempering influence of Bergson's reflections on the comic spirit protected Stevens from his fondness for the exotic, the "strange dyes, strange flowers, and curious odours," that he shared with Pater. On the one hand, the "Conclusion" of *The Renaissance* spoke directly to him; the whole drift of his thought agreed with Pater's final words:

... we have an interval, and then our place knows us no more. Some spend this interval in listlessness, some in high passions, the wisest in art and song. For our one chance is in expanding that interval, in getting as many pulsations as possible into the given time. High passions give one this quickened sense of life, ecstasy and sorrow of love, political or religious enthusiasm, or the 'enthusiasm of humanity.' Only, be sure it is passion, that it does yield you this fruit of a quickened, multiplied consciousness. Of this wisdom, the poetic passion, the desire for beauty, the love of art for art's sake has most; for art comes to you professing frankly to give nothing but the highest quality to your moments as they pass, and simply for those moments' sake.

Yet he was practical enough to accept the world as it happened to be; like a sophisticated Candide, he took Hartford as an adequate, even admirable compromise, for it was ultimately his imagination, "the power of the mind over the possibilities of things," that made him a poet. He could go his own way with greater freedom in Hartford than in an atmosphere which would have violated his sense of privacy by identifying the figure of the poet with the eccentric. Not that Hartford escaped his eye unscathed; but he reserved his most acid comments for those who found in art an excuse to show off, whether as art-lovers, critics, or artists. His comment on the opening performance of *Four Saints in Three Acts*, like his characterization of "salesmen disguised as catalogues or chairs in New York galleries," defines his feeling about such matters perfectly:

While this is an elaborate bit of perversity in every respect: text, settings, choreography, it is most agreeable musically, so that, if one excludes aesthetic self-consciousness from one's attitude, the opera immediately becomes a delicate and joyous work all around.

There were, however, numerous asses of the first water in the audience. New York sent a train load of people of this sort to Hartford: people who walked round with cigarette holders a foot long, and so on. After all, if there is any place under the sun that needs debunking, it is the place where people of this sort come to and go to.[11]

"Aesthetic self-consciousness" was an aspect of "the merely personal" that he struggled to suppress in himself, not only because it was synonymous with pretense but also because it threatened the freedom of the mind that he valued so greatly. More often than not he defended his business associates from the charge that they were philistines, although he was shy for a long time about talking of poetry with them. His image of "The Whole Man: Perspectives, Horizons," as projected in the address with that title, bore a striking resemblance to himself as he hoped to be. There he speaks of Whitehead as a man with a "rapacious and benign mind," and in his own way describes the qualities that his detachment had helped him to achieve. Between 1914 and 1922, he was learning how to keep a balance between life and literature; and what in the letters of most other poets would have remained merely personal became, in the last years of his life, part of his unfinished theory of poetry. He knew the dangers of his position; to the critics who complained that his work lacked a sense of the

---

[11] Letter to Harriet Monroe, Feb. 12, 1934.

tragedy of life, he replied that the dark night of the soul was a fiction, too; and in commenting on the work of a younger poet, he wrote:

. . . to say that only the peasant desires happiness and that the evil man does evil as a dog barks overlooks the idea that the Drang nach den Gut is really not much different from the Drang nach the opposite. You are fascinated by evil. I cannot see that this fascination has anything on the fascination by good. A bird singing in the sun is the same thing as a dog barking in the dark. Again, your antithesis between evil on the one hand and thought and art on the other involves quite other ideas.[12]

He went even farther, when he said of another writer's work:

. . . the pages of this book . . . contain not literary exercises but the text of a life: the life of a young woman constantly thoughtful of injustice and afraid and frightened of the present and of the years to come. I should suppose that she had read and searched a great deal of poetry, particularly English poetry, and that she had been moulded by the poetry that she had read. In the conflict that came of all this she was unhappy enough not to have had the strength to prevail. She had not mastered life and I am very much afraid that, for that reason, she had not mastered her own poetry. There are many striking things in the book. . . . It seems to me, in the face of so much that moves one, so much that excites sympathy and pity, that it would be wrong to speak of any aspects of the book other than these personal and human ones. After I closed the book I said to myself *la malheureuse*.[13]

Although criticism for him had to take into account " the presence of the determining personality " in addition to " subject and manner," poetry was not personal. When a work failed to convey a sense of all three qualities as an integrated whole, it had to be judged on other than valid artistic grounds. The distinction between " Art, broadly," as " the form of life or the sound or color of life," which he believed to be " often indistinguishable from life itself," and works of art remained clear in his own mind, but he sometimes shuffled the terms about in his writings with as much pleasure as he took in other kinds of improvisation. Paradox and irony were as natural to him as the ambiguity for which he became famous, but they were matters of sensibility rather than of intellect. The fastidiousness with which he chose the poems to be

[12] Letter, Oct. 9, 1950. (I am obliged to omit the name of the recipient of this and the following letter.)
[13] Letter, Mar. 14, 1955.

included in *Harmonium* ironically pointed up the fastidiousness
of the poems themselves, which even among the few readers he
trusted, might be mistaken for preciosity. He protected himself
from swallowing Pater whole by noting that "It is life that we
are trying to get at in poetry," and by asserting that "Art involves vastly more than the sense of beauty."

No aesthetic doctrine had suffered more by World War I than
Pater's. To "burn with a hard gem-like flame" was as absurd
as any other Victorian ideal in the eyes of those committed to
self-conscious modernisms. Yet it remained an ideal for many
artists, including Stevens. The fundamental irony of "The Comedian as the Letter C" is that it is the "anecdote" of a man
who is unable to achieve the wisdom of spending his "internal"
in art and song; but its purple, which is also its wit, was so different
from Pater's that it looked like a satire of Pater's substance as
well as of his style. Indeed, the mere notion of a comic character
as the protagonist of views as solemn as Pater's would have
seemed at the time an insupportable whimsy. Nevertheless, the
poem is concerned "with the movement, the passage and dissolution of impressions" at which "analysis leaves off," and records
"that continual vanishing away, that strange perpetual weaving
and unweaving" of the self to which, Pater says, "what is *real* in
our life fines itself down." As a "realist," Crispin chose the purple
of the "good, fat, guzzly fruit," at the expense of the plum "Harle-
quined and mazily dewed and mauved / In bloom"; but Stevens
did not have to choose—or if he did, he knew that the choice
"was not a choice / Between excluding things." He sought "the
whole, / The complicate, the amassing harmony," and as his ideas
of order took shape, the influence of Pater became more shadowy.
He came almost as close to Pater as he would ever come before
writing "The Comedian," in "Tea at the Palaz of Hoon," where
the comic manner all but disappears:

> Not less because in purple I descended
> The western day through what you called
> The loneliest air, not less was I myself.
> What was the ointment sprinkled on my beard?
> What were the hymns that buzzed beside my ears?
> What was the sea whose tide swept through me there?
> Out of my mind the golden ointment rained,
> And my ears made the blowing hymns they heard.
> I was myself the compass of that sea:

I was the world in which I walked, and what I saw
Or heard or felt came not but from myself;
And there I found myself more truly and more strange.

The poem begins at the moment when "reflection begins to act
upon [external] objects" and "they are dissipated under its influence; the cohesive force is suspended like a trick of magic; each
object is loosed upon a group of impressions—colour, odour, texture,—in the mind of the observer." And it continues "to dwell
on this world . . . of impressions unstable, flickering, inconsistent,
which burn and are extinguished with [the] consciousness of them"
until "the whole scope of observation is dwarfed to the narrow
chamber of the individual mind." Paradoxically, as Pater says,
this moment of withdrawal, if it communicates a "sense of the
splendour of our experience and of its awful brevity" becomes
more significant than "some interest into which we cannot enter,
some abstract morality we have not identified with ourselves. . . ."
Stevens, it is true, touched the sacerdotal purple and gold with his
own irony, in the "buzz" and "blowing" of the hymns and the
apparently absurd enigma of the title, to give the opulence of the
moment an unexpected dimension. To those who asked what
"Hoon" meant, incidentally, Stevens always gave the same
answer: that he could not remember its origin, and that as well
as he could judge, it meant "everybody, or rather, anybody."
But Hoon appeared again in a later poem, "Sad Strains of a Gay
Waltz," where he is also identified with "the individual in his
isolation":

> There's that mountain-minded Hoon,
> For whom desire was never that of the waltz,
>
> Who found all form and order in solitude,
> For whom the shapes were never the figures of men.
> Now, for him, his forms have vanished.

It is unlikely that Hoon was in any literal sense a disguise for
Pater or for the self Stevens described in his *Adagia* when he
noted that "Life is an affair of people not of places. But for me
life is an affair of places and that is the trouble." If Hoon meant
"everybody, or . . . anybody," it meant everybody who shared the
same sense of splendor that Stevens shared with Pater at those
moments when the balance between order and disorder was
threatened. It is not surprising, in retrospect, that Stevens did

not often achieve the balance in the poems that were to comprise the body of his first book. Nevertheless, the ambiguities Stevens had stated so plainly in " Thirteen Ways of Looking at a Black-bird "—

> I was of three minds,
> Like a tree
> In which there are three blackbirds.—

had, by 1921, been all but disciplined into a way of looking and composing.

Success on the scale of " Pecksniffiana " and " Sur Ma Guzzla Gracile," or even in the more complicated comic mode of " Le Monocle de Mon Oncle," did not long provide all the satisfactions Stevens sought in poetry. He wrote Miss Monroe just after " Sur Ma Guzzla Gracile " appeared in *Poetry*:

The early part of October found me dreadful drove; I seemed to be dealing with fanatics on all hands and scarcely had time to read my own poems. One evening G. Taggard came to dinner with us and told me that there was an impression abroad that the poems were hideous ghosts of myself. It may be.[14]

Even allowing for his exaggeration, Stevens was hardly revealing any secrets. He had not, as a matter of fact, quite mastered his impulse to " fidget with points of view." When Matthew Joseph-son and Gorham B. Munson asked him for a contribution to the magazine that ultimately appeared as *Secession*, all he had to send them was " This Vast Inelegance," which Josephson refused with a comment that sums up the defects of the false starts Stevens usually kept to himself:

. . . this poem is rather bad—an unfortunate moment in the life of the author of " Pecksniffiana " and the " Worms at Heaven's Gate." Thinking of the solid, martial, organ-like verses of " The Worms " and other poems of yours, this poem fails to get going into any rhythms of its own. Its first line is frankly bad. Most of the others are merely neutral—and labored. The alliterations employed are quite obvious. Here and there are glimpses of your most personal method. The whole poem, then, offers the mechanics of your art and not the fruition thereof.[15]

He had reached a point at which he felt " an inclination to look back as well as forward," as he told Thomas McGreevy many

[14] Letter to Harriet Monroe, Oct. 29, 1921.
[15] Letter from Matthew Josephson, Feb. 22, 1922.

years later in commenting on the completion of *The Auroras of Autumn*. " One grows tired of being oneself and feels the need of renewing all one's thoughts and ways of thinking. Poetry is like the imagination itself. It is not likely to be satisfied with the same thing twice." At the moment, however, he contented himself with transcribing some of the " Schemata " and " Memorias Antiguas " he had collected on bits of paper. Some of these contained the germs of poems which would in time get themselves written down. One group of " Schemata " ranged from " Twenty quail flying in moonlight," and " A vivid fruit in a vivid atmosphere," to " The grand simplifications " and " Poetry supreme fiction " by way of such wisps of matter as " Holly, kingfishers, grapes and cosmos," " Mrs. Bonfanti's cakes," " Mr. Goldsmith's desire to live it out in Guatemala " and " Experiments on Adam." Others included " A Nice Shady Home," " On Being One's Own Native," " The Man Who Wanted to Think of One Thing Only," " The Error of Crispin Approaching the Carolinas," " The Idea of a Colony," " The World without Imagination," and " Book of Moonlight," all of which eventually contributed their share to " The Comedian as the Letter C." About half these notations grew into poems; some never amounted to anything: " The Dame Who Carried Her Cane in Her Coffin," " Bandits in Plum Thickets," " The Man Who Could Not Sell Even Nectarines." He did not write an " Anecdote of the Commonplace," but he did make a draft of an " Anecdote of the Abnormal ":

> He called hydrangeas purple. And they were.
> Not fixed and deadly (like a curving line
> That merely makes a ring).
> It was a purple changeable to see.
> And so hydrangeas came to be.
>
> The common grass is green.
> But there are regions where the grass
> Assumes a pale, Italianate sheen—
> Is almost Byzantine.
> And there the common grass is never seen.
>
> And in those regions one still feels the rose
> And feels the grass
> Because new colors make new things
> And new things make old things again . . .
> And so with men.

Crispin-valet, Crispin-saint!
The exhausted realist beholds
His tattered manikin arise,
Tuck in the straw,
And stalk the skies.

It was from this unpromising bit of self-imitation that "The Comedian as the Letter C" seems to have derived. The Crispin of the "Anecdote" is no more than a witty antithesis, and the poem establishes no correlation between "Crispin-valet, Crispin-saint" and the "exhausted realist" who evokes them. The Crispin of "The Comedian" is both "realist" and "manikin"—in Bergson's sense, Stevens and his marionette—whose adventures bring him full circle, and for whom "new things" and "old things" do blur into one. If the saintly aspect of Crispin survives at all in "The Comedian," it is only as a shadow, as the idealist and ascetic who "denied himself" many poems before composing his "first central hymns," and who "projected a colony" of believers like himself. The Crispin-valet of classical comedy, however, contributes a great deal to the personality of Stevens' hero. But he is no longer the type-character who is a ready assistant in the love-affairs of an aristocratic master, except as a device Stevens employs to satisfy his own natural flair for rhetoric. As a character, he is his own master, and it is significant that the reader first meets him on the high seas as an emigrant from Europe on his way to Carolina. He is a poet—a truer poet than Jonson's Crispinus, who is a poetaster with a fondness for odd words he is forced to spew up at his arraignment by Horace and Virgil—much given to high-flown language. Whatever he may have owed to his ancestors, this emancipated descendant of the tribe of Harlequin is the manipulator and victim of his own fate.[16]

[16] How much the poem owes to *Poetaster* can only be surmised. Jonson presents Ovid as a young law student, who tells his father that he will "prove the unfashion'd body of the *law* / Pure elegance, and make her ruggedst straines / Runne smoothly as Propertius *elegies*," if only his father will be more tolerant of his ambitions as a poet. When Lupus tells Ovid *senior*, "Come, do not misprize him," the latter replies "*Misprize?* I, mary, I would have him use some such words now: They have some touch, some taste of the *law*. He should make himselfe a stile out of these, and let his Propertius *elegies* goe by." Another character, Albius, observes to his wife, "Gaine savours sweetly from any thing; He that respects to get must relish all commodities alike; and admit to no difference betwixt oade, and frankincense; or the most precious balsamum, and a tar-barrell," which is suggestive of the way Crispin "savored rankness like a sensualist." The banquet at which the young poets assume the roles of gods and goddesses Cytheris calls "a fiction . . . fit for the fit of a poet"; and in the

The gap between "Anecdote of the Abnormal" and "The Comedian as the Letter C" is too wide, in any case, to be closed by even the most staggering leap of imagination or speculation. By the time Crispin emerged as a character in his own right, he had come to resemble his creator in several important respects. By profession he is a poet—well acquainted, incidentally, with the Latin of law; and he is at least as eccentric as the character that Kreymborg had made of Stevens in his play "At the Sign of the Thumb and Nose," and as different from the New York "gang" as they believed Stevens to be. He is not only "the Socrates / Of snails, musician of pears, principium / And lex," a "wig / Of things," a "nincompated pedagogue," but also

> The lutanist of fleas, the knave, the thane,
> The ribboned stick, the bellowing breeches, cloak
> Of China, cap of Spain, imperative haw
> Of hum, inquisitorial botanist,
> And general lexicographer of mute
> And maidenly greenhorns . . .

in short, the poet of "Hibiscus on the Sleeping Shores" ("in-

---

discussion of the appropriateness of the term "fiction" which follows, Gallus asks, "Who knows not, Cytheris, that the sacred breath of a true *poet*, can blow any vertuous humanitie, up to *deitie?*" But the most amusing of all these (possibly) chance resemblances occurs after Crispinus has been purged of his vocabulary—retrograde, incubus, glibbery, defunct, magnificate, childblain'd, clutcht, quaking custard, obstrupefact, among others. Virgil passes sentence on Crispinus and his associate Demetrius Fannius, with the following warnings:

> You must not hunt for wild, out-landish termes,
> To stuffe out a peculiar *dialect*;
> But let your *matter* runne before your *words*:
> And if, at any time, you chaunce to meet
> Some Gallo-belgick phrase, you shall not straight
> Racke your poore verse to give it entertainment . . .
> Demetrius Fannius, thou shalt here put on
> That coate, and cap; and henceforth, thinke thy selfe
> No other, then they make thee . . .

Finally, the "Apology" that follows *Poetaster* gives Jonson's answer to the charge that all his writing "is mere rayling":

> Ha! If all the salt in the old comedy
> Should be so censur'd, or the sharper wit
> Of the bold *satyre*, termed scolding rage,
> What age could then compare with those, for buffons?

—a reminder that even Crispin knew "One eats one paté, even of salt, quotha." When, at last, the Author says to his friends, "Leave me. There's something come into my thought, / That must, and shall be sung, high and aloofe, / Safe from the wolves black jaw, and the dull asses hoofe," one can only recall Steven's remark to Harriet Monroe that since he had "elected to regard poetry as a form of retreat," the opinion of other people was "neither here nor there."

quisitorial botanist "), and " The Paltry Nude Starts on a Spring
Voyage" ("lexicographer"), among other pieces. Although his
absurdities relate him to the comic madman that Bergson cites
as the ideal comic character, the unsociable observer obsessed
by a single idea, his self-knowledge ultimately saves him from
insanity. He is also Bergson's " robber robbed," but he has enough
wit to be amused at the end of his adventure by his own decline
and fall.

If Stevens momentarily thought of himself as an "exhausted
realist" in the fall of 1921, all he really needed to stimulate him
was a project ambitious enough to challenge him. The announcement in *Poetry* of a contest sponsored by the Poetry Society of
South Carolina, for a poem of some length, was what he wanted.
Just before Christmas he wrote to Harriet Monroe:

> I return your greetings, most sincerely, and in these Mrs. Stevens
> joins, although possibly in her case, rather gingerly, for I have made
> life a bore for all and several since the announcement of the Blindman
> prize in your last issue. To wit: I have been churning and churning,
> producing, however, a very rancid butter, which I intend to submit
> in that competition, for what it may be worth, which, at the moment,
> isn't much. But what's the use of offering prizes if people don't make
> an effort to capture them. My poem is still very incomplete and im-
> perfect and I have very little time to give it. But I am determined to
> have a fling at least and possibly to go through the damnedest dol-
> drums of regret later on. But Merry Xmas and a happy New-Year to
> you and to your house.[17]

No copy of "From the Journal of Crispin" survives. Apparently, if the evidence of the "Schemata" can be trusted, it con-
sisted of four sections: "Concerning the Thunderstorms of Yucatan," "The Idea of a Colony," "Approaching the Carolinas," and
"The World without Imagination." If this plan represented the
order of the sections, the poem must have been quite different
from "The Comedian" as we have it. At any rate, "From the
Journal of Crispin" did not win the prize. Amy Lowell, who acted
as sole judge of "some three hundred and fifty manuscripts"
submitted, gave first place to "Variations on a Theme," by Grace
Hazard Conkling. Stevens received the first of eleven honorable
mentions, although, according to Hervey Allen, she "hesitated a
long time" between Mrs. Conkling's poem and the "Journal."
Allen tactfully observed to Stevens that it would probably be

---

[17] Letter to Harriet Monroe, Dec., 1921.

"cold comfort" to say that he had "almost got the prize," and added: "Thank you so much for handing this lovely thing in for the competition. There are very few of the poets writing now who glimpse the whole earth as the background for their hero's 'soul.' I like your planetary attitude." [18]

Stevens did not begin to revise his poem until after the announcement that the award had gone to Mrs. Conkling. Business kept him at home; "There has been so much to do that I have stayed here like a turtle under a bush," he told Miss Monroe in a letter written early in April; "Carl Sandburg came to Hartford a month or so ago and V. Lindsay comes next week with other early songsters. Autograph copies of his poems are to be sold in the lobby of the High-School. My word!" [19] He made another trip to the Middle West in May, but he and Miss Monroe talked about making arrangements for her sister, Mrs. Calhoun, to send him lapis lazuli and jasmine tea from Peking. Toward the end of August, he wrote again:

It is a pleasant surprise to have your card from North Carolina with its *news* from Peking. One of these days, when the different things on their way to Hartford from Peking, Paris, Geneva, London & Mexico (cigars), actually arrive I shall have exhausted the possibilities of life within my scope. I suppose, however, that the simple cure for that will be to leave Hartford. I have been here all summer and do not expect to go away unless for a day or two. I prefer very much to go to Florida in the winter time. A few weeks ago I came to the substance of an agreement with Mr. Knopf for the publication of a book in the fall of 1923. This, by the way, is confidential for the present; but I don't know of anyone more entitled to first news of it than yourself. The book will naturally be a collection of things that have already appeared, for since the manuscript is to be ready by November 1 this year it will not be possible for me to do anything new in the interim. The long summer spells of quiet are very good for me and at times I have been in a most excellent state of spontaneity, but nothing has survived the subsequent Katzenjammer. One's desires keep a good way ahead. And then too I have done a great deal of reading this summer, so that in the long run I have accomplished little or nothing. Williams drove through town a few weeks ago on his way to Vermont with one of his children and a dog. It was a blessing to see him

[18] Letter from Hervey Allen, Apr. 20, 1922. The other honorable mentions, "in the order named," went to Babette Deutsch, Hildegarde Flanner, Janet Lewis, Harold Monro, Robert J. Roe, Thomas W. Dean, Mary Bowman, Herbert Read, N. S. Bushnell, and Beatrice Ravenal. Miss Lowell was at least catholic in her taste as well as generous in her award of praise.

[19] Letter to Harriet Monroe, Apr. 6, 1922.

although we were both as nervous as two belles in new dresses. I hope to see him again on his return trip. I also saw Marcel Duchamp in New-York recently. He seemed like a cat that had been left behind. Everybody else seems to be out of sight. Your post-card gives me the most exciting ideas. The land of the sky has always struck me as one of the hollowest of phrases; but it is evident that I can know nothing of the matter until I have stood on the shores of Lake Toxaway. In my case, mountain lakes are among the rare things of life. If the Japanese make miniature gardens . . . there's a good idea. Moreover, there is something integrally American (or the robust thing that goes by that name) in all these southern places and among the people there. I was in Charleston in July and while it is true that like any antiquated seaport it contains Armenian priests, Scotch Presbyterians and so on, nevertheless the place is beautifully and sedately the early and undefiled American thing. I love the south for this quality. Your mountains are a compendium of it in land-scape.[20]

Interesting as the letter is on several counts, it is important at the moment for what it reveals about Stevens' attitude toward his accomplishments during a summer that had not given him sufficient time for poetry—whether it was cigars from Mexico, postcards from Lake Toxaway, seeing Marcel Duchamp in New York, or letting his imagination go in "a most excellent state of spontaneity." He had, as a matter of fact, revised "From the Journal of Crispin" and had found time during the first half of the year to write a dozen short poems. When Miss Monroe wrote him in September to ask about the possibility of publishing "The Comedian as the Letter C" in *Poetry* before it appeared in his book, he said:

About the Crispin poem. Pitts Sanborn, one of my oldest friends, expects that he *may* be called upon to edit the Measure one of these days for a period and, as I am under many obligations to him, I have promised to let him have this poem if he wants it. During the summer I re-wrote it and in its present form it would run to, possibly, the greater part of twenty pages of print. A long poem is what he wants, for of the three numbers that he would have to edit, this would account for one. And this promise I made to him long ago, when he went on that miserable sheet. So there you are. During the coming week, he sails from Havre bringing for me my autumnal bon-bons from the Place de l'Opera not to speak of a number of books etc which he has picked up for me. How, then, could I have the face to disappoint him?[21]

[20] Letter to Harriet Monroe, Aug. 24, 1922.
[21] Letter to Harriet Monroe, Sept. 23, 1922.

The end of summer and the arrival of friends from Europe bearing gifts provided the excitement that saved him from "the malady of the quotidian" and the "Katzenjammer" that was synonymous with whatever interfered with poetry "as a form of retreat." But he did not want to disappoint Miss Monroe, and by way of apology, he added:

When I get back from the South I expect to do some short poems and then to start again on a rather longish one, so that sooner or later I shall have something for Poetry, to which I send what I like most. But it takes time and, besides, I have no desire to write a great deal. I know that people judge one by volume. . . . The desire to write a long poem or two is not obsequiousness to the judgment of people. On the contrary, I find that this prolonged attention to a single subject has the same result that prolonged attention to a senora has, according to the authorities. All manner of favors drop from it. Only it requires a skill in the varying of the serenade that occasionally makes one feel like a Guatemalan when one particularly wants to feel like an Italian. I expect that after a while Crispin . . . will become rudimentary and abhorrent.[22]

His next "longish" poem was "Academic Discourse in Havana," which went to *Broom*. Then came "Sea Surface Full of Clouds," published in *Dial* for July, 1924. But he had nothing in *Poetry* until 1932, when he found a "scrap" ("Good Man, Bad Woman") to send Miss Monroe for the twenty-fifth anniversary issue of the magazine. Having committed himself to a book, and having to put together a manuscript, he took stock of what he had done; and although he still considered Miss Monroe the person in whom he could confide most, he had nothing to offer her except a characteristic apology, like the one in a letter written just before the manuscript of his book went off to New York:

All my earlier things seem like horrid cocoons from which later abortive insides have sprung. The book will amount to nothing, except that it may teach me something. I wish that I could put everything else aside and amuse myself on a large scale for a while. One never gets anywhere in writing or thinking or observing unless one can do long stretches at a time. Often I have to let go in the most insignificant poem, which scarcely serves to remind me of it, the most skyey of skyey sheets. And often, when I have a real fury for indulgence I must stint myself. Of course, we must all do the same thing. Ariosto probably felt the same thing about the solid years he spent on Orlando. If farmers had summers ten years long what tomatoes they would

[22] *Ibid.*

grow and if sailors had universal seas what voyages they could take. Only, the reading of these debilitated and outmoded poems does make me wish rather desperately to keep on dabbling and to be as obscure as possible until I have perfected an authentic and fluent speech for myself. By that time I should be like Casanova at Waldheim with nothing to do except to look out of the window. So that I shall have to swallow the rotten pill.[23]

He had to be satisfied with his own version of "things as they were" at the moment, with a copy of *Ulysses* "and other things including some liqueur from Santa Maria Novella" which Pitts Sanborn had brought him from Europe.

The favors dropped from "The Comedian" included "Bantams in Pine-Woods," "A High-Toned Old Christian Woman," "O Florida, Venereal Soil," "The Emperor of Ice-Cream," and "To the One of Fictive Music." But to a poet committed to the suppression of the merely personal, the writing of a long poem must have been primarily a problem in strategy. The only story "The Comedian" has to tell is that of a poet in search of his subject, a way of looking at himself and the world around him which will satisfy his need for aggrandizement and allow him to keep his sense of humor. His discovery that the world is just what he had thought it was, from whatever point of view he looked at it, is almost as unsurprising to Crispin as it is to the reader because, although Crispin is no more than a marionette, he has the power to pull his own strings. He is, after all, a poet, a maker; but his progress is really a progress from metaphor to metaphor. He begins with the proposition that "man is the intelligence of his soil," but comes to the conclusion that "his soil is man's intelligence" is "better," and "worth crossing seas to find." Yet the world, which was a turnip to begin with, remains a turnip. The reader knows that for Crispin the resemblances between things are what matter: they are the basic reality. Crispin is a "profitless philosopher" because his basic propositions are nothing but metaphors, too. Stevens' joke on Crispin consists in letting Crispin confuse fancy and imagination, so that, although Crispin comes to terms with his own nature, accepting his lot as yeoman and grub, he never quite vanquishes his egotism. Stevens' joke on the reader is his refusal to judge Crispin's failure with the harshness of a stern moralist; he leaves it to the reader to judge

[23] Letter to Harriet Monroe, Oct. 28, 1922.

for himself whether Crispin is a "hideous ghost" of his creator. The apology with which the poem concludes is ambiguous enough to satisfy the reader for whom all art is autobiography, however ingeniously disguised, or the reader for whom "design" is the "pith" of art.

Many years later, when Stevens had partly satisfied his desire to "write a long poem or two"—including "Owl's Clover," "The Man with the Blue Guitar," "Notes toward a Supreme Fiction," "Esthétique du Mal," and "An Ordinary Evening in New Haven" —he looked back at "The Comedian" with considerable pride, and with an affection that makes it quite clear how little he had meant it when he told Harriet Monroe that he expected Crispin to become "rudimentary and abhorrent." He told Renato Poggioli, his Italian translator, in 1953:

> It may be a little difficult to translate *The Comedian as the Letter C.* The sounds of the letter C, both hard and soft, include other letters like X, K, etc. How would it be possible to translate a line like
> Exchequering from piebald fiscs unkeyed,
>   and
> preserve anything except the sense of the words? However, it is true that the poem has made its way without reference to the sounds of the letter C. There is another point about the poem to which I should like to call attention and that is that it is what may be called an anti-mythological poem. The central figure is an every-day man who lives a life without the slightest adventure except that he lives it in a poetic atmosphere as we all do. This point makes it necessary for a translator to reproduce the every-day plainness of the central figure and the plush, so to speak, of his stage.[24]

The significance of "the sounds of the letter C" can be taken with a grain of salt; but the "anti-mythological" character of the poem and the "every-dayness" of Crispin are somewhat more complicated. Some critical analyses of "The Comedian" reduce it to a metaphysical exercise, although it has never given critics a great number of allusions to chew on in order to prove their mettle as source-hunters. The poem clearly reduces Crispin's pretensions as a poet to absurdity, but it does not thereby make him a symbol of the modern artist's alienation from society. It pierces the "mythology of self" which, as an "insatiable egotist," he has cultivated, but it does not destroy his ego altogether because to do so would be tantamount to the destruction of his identity.

[24] Quoted in *Mattino Domenicale ed Altre Poesie*, trans. Renato Poggioli (Torino, 1954), p. 169.

Stevens' assertion that Crispin " lives a life without the slightest adventure " implies that the voyage from Bordeaux to Carolina, his marriage, and family really make no difference to his way of looking at things: the " realist's " self he comes to accept is as limited in the end by his fancifulness as the " romantic " one which had been dissolved by the sea and frightened by the thunder-storms of Yucatan. To put it another way, Crispin is a poet who thinks of his poetry and of the world as a means to an end—as a source of awards and honors—not as ends in themselves. He never learns that " The poet must put the same degree of intent-ness into his poetry as, for example, the traveler into his adven-ture, the painter into his painting "; nor does he believe that " The most beautiful thing in the world is, of course, the world itself," except as the world can provide satisfactions for his ego. By separating poetry and the world, he fails to understand them as they are, although he thinks he sees through them both. He recog-nizes them as fictions, but he cannot believe in them. Life passes him by, leaving him with " the sounds of the letter C," with nothing but rhetoric. Congenial as the rhetoric is to his tempera-ment, it never quite becomes a statement of his " unaffected per-ception of the thing."

Stevens shared some of Crispin's failings and predilections. He complained occasionally that he " shrivelled up living in the same spot, following the same routine "; and since most of his traveling had to be undertaken purely on business, he did not have time for the meditation which would have made travel worth the effort. For a long time Florida satisfied him: at least as long as it remained like the land of Oz; and even after it had ceased to excite his imagination, he enjoyed his vacations at Key West and at Pirates' Cove (where he began " Farewell to Florida "), where he went with his friends Judge Powell and Philip May. When an admirer of his work expressed surprise that he had never been to Europe, Stevens explained that Mrs. Stevens was " not a good traveler," or that Hartford had more advantages than disadvan-tages for him because he had learned to " feel like a native " there. Furthermore, he preferred the Europe of his imagination to an actual Europe which would not resemble the one he had had much pleasure in inventing. Such a Europe was a fiction in which he could believe, knowing it was a fiction. And although his ex-planations may not wholly account for his never having been to

Europe, they square with his belief that "It is the explanations of things that we make to ourselves that disclose our character: The subjects of one's poems are the symbols of one's self or of one of one's selves." That Stevens had already formulated the proposition of poetry as the supreme fiction in 1922 is, in retrospect at least, very clear.

Stevens resembled his poetic hero in other ways, too, as, for example, in his fondness for "breakfast ribands, fruits laid in their leaves, / The tomtit and the cassia and the rose," "cream for [his] fig and silver for the cream, / A blonde to tip the silver and to taste / The rapey gouts." The autobiographical elements of "The Comedian as the Letter C," although they do not bear on its value as a poem, are of considerable importance in relation to its structure and its place in the total body of his work. Simply as a long poem it poses certain questions of design. As the ideological culmination of his early work and the cornerstone of all his later poetry and prose, it recognizes and accepts the flux as its governing principle. The poem is "anti-mythological" not only in its attack upon Crispin's carefully cultivated "mythology of self" but also in its attempt to disperse all other *a priori* assumptions about man and the world of extended reality except to acknowledge the existence of the self and that world, the hero and his "poetic atmosphere," as given. Ultimately, the success of the poem depends upon the willingness of the reader to go along with its style. Not every reader, of course, can accept the constantly shifting point of view and the deliberate gaudiness of the language; but the fable is one that is as applicable to our own age of disbelief as it was to the Twenties, and the high spirits are as engaging as they ever were. Only a prig would inveigh against them.

"Nota: man is the intelligence of his soil, / The sovereign ghost." So the poem begins, but whether this utterance represents a pronunciamento made by Crispin, by an anonymous observing intelligence, or by Stevens speaking in his own private person, would be difficult to say. As a poetic device, however, it is familiar: it is both prologue and argument in a parody of the sententious style, and echoes the "polished moralizing," the gilded aphorism, that is a commonplace in Dryden and Pope and classical comedy. What it lacks in substance it makes up in wit. Yet its humanistic substance is also a commonplace, lending itself to ironic uses as effectively as Dryden's "All human things are subject to decay." Any reader sensitive to inflections is unlikely to miss the satirical overtones; but even the reader with no special equipment can miss the absurdity of what follows almost as an afterthought by way of explanation:

> . . . As such, the Socrates
> Of snails, musician of pears, principium
> And lex.

The tone defines itself as one of witty self-ridicule; what is said is mocked in the saying. Not only the idea but the language becomes suspect. The Latin is a bit of fancy dress, appropriately inappropriate.

> . . . Sed quaeritur: is this same wig
> Of things, this nincompated pedagogue,
> Preceptor to the sea?

The rhetorical ornamentation masking this characterization of man as "The glory, jest, and riddle of the world" has already recoiled upon itself. It has descended from the universal to an irrelevant particular, distorting the grandiose and metaphorical "soil" by juxtaposing it to the literal "sea." The technique is one Bergson formulates in "The Comic in Words" as a law: "A comic effect is obtained," he says, "whenever we pretend to take literally an expression which was used figuratively; or, once our attention is fixed on the material aspect of a metaphor the idea expressed becomes comic."

The stage has now been set for the appearance of Crispin. He is introduced, in the words of a later poem, as "A most inappropriate man / In a most unpropitious place":

> . . . Crispin at sea
> Created, in his day, a touch of doubt.
> An eye most apt in gelatines and jupes,
> Berries of villages, a barber's eye,
> An eye of land, of simple salad-beds,
> Of honest quilts, the eye of Crispin, hung
> On porpoises, instead of apricots,
> And on silentious porpoises, whose snouts
> Dibbled in waves that were mustachios,
> Inscrutable hair in an inscrutable world.

This barber of Bordeaux, this Candide uprooted from his kitchen garden, gives the poem's original proposition still another turn. As a barber, apparently, Crispin can see the ocean only in the lingo of his trade. As a farmer, he is wholly unprepared to explain porpoises. His fixed point of view has become so rigid that, as Bergson says, he looks at things absentmindedly. Exposed to a reality too big for his ego to grasp, Crispin sees himself reduced to the "merest minuscule." His romantic assumption that a man may be what he chooses has amounted to nothing. But the ego is not so easily destroyed. The landscape of Yucatan provides him with birds and flowers gorgeous enough to satisfy his hankering for the decorative, although fresh from his sobering experience with the sea, he indulges his fondness for the exotic as a tourist, a "connoisseur of chaos" who overestimates his ability to absorb "the dreadful sundry of the world." When a real tropical storm breaks around him, he retreats to the cathedral like the natives, and he suffers the ignominy of discovering that he is no braver or better than anyone else. He sets sail again, this time for Carolina, which he has always identified with the North, and not merely the North, but the Arctic.[25]

What he is looking for is an environment in which he can truly be the man he wants to be: "an abundant zone, / Prickly and obdurate, dense, harmonious, / Yet with a harmony not rarefied / Nor fined for the inhibited instruments / Of over-civil stops." In short, he is looking for the Carolina that Stevens described to Miss Monroe as "beautifully and sedately the early and undefiled American thing" which he had found Charleston to be, in spite of its "Armenian priests, Scotch Presbyterians and so on." For Armenian priests, Scotch Presbyterians and so on are realities Crispin's imagination can cope with:

> . . . Tilting up his nose,
> He inhaled the rancid rosin, burly smells
> Of dampened lumber, emanations blown
> From warehouse doors, the gustiness of ropes
> Decays of sacks, and all the arrant stinks
> That helped him round his rude aesthetic out.
> He savored rankness like a sensualist.
> He marked the marshy ground around the dock,
> The crawling railroad spur, the rotten fence, . . .

[25] Crispin's imaginary America has no ground in actuality. It is no more than "a metaphor of a metaphor." In the *Adagia* Stevens later recorded his conviction that "One does not progress through metaphors. Thus reality is the indispensable element of each metaphor. When I say that man is a god it is very easy to see that if I also say that a god is something else, god has become reality." Crispin's failure

Such things—whether Crispin knows it or not—are merely " Curriculum for the marvelous sophomore ": in other words, the facts of life with which a fundamentally temperate man can feel at home. They are the facts of life in Bordeaux, from which he had emigrated, but which in his vanity and pursuit of an impossible romanticism, he "never saw at all." Unwilling to give up living his life on the basis of a thesis, he formulates a new proposition: "Nota: his soil is man's intelligence." But the poems he writes to illustrate its truth turn out to be as trivial as those he had written before, for they concern " The florist asking aid from cabbages, / The rich man going bare, the paladin / Afraid, the blind man as astronomer, / The appointed power unwielded from disdain," which hardly differentiates them from the work of the Crispin who was "lutanist of fleas, . . . inquisitorial botanist, / And general lexicographer of mute / And maidenly greenhorns . . . ."[26]

He discovers, in other words, that he cannot escape the limits of his sensibility. Unwittingly he has tried to search life for "unprecedented experiences." A man of fancy, he has mistaken fancy for imagination. It is no wonder, then, that he has failed to "master life." He settles for the plum as " good, fat, guzzly fruit," rather than the fiction of the plum which hangs

> In the sunshine placidly, colored by ground
> Obliquities of those who pass beneath,
> Harlequined and mazily dewed and mauved
> In bloom. . . .

without realizing that both views are "fictions," and that either may be a "man's unaffected perception of the thing." But he has come to terms with his own nature. He has recognized his need for something in which to believe and has accepted the satisfactions of his poverty without losing his self-respect. If he has learned everything and understood nothing, he at least knows the right question to ask:

> Was he to company vastest things defunct
> With a blubber of tom-toms harrowing the sky?

to understand that " the imagination must not detach itself from reality " accounts in part for his inability to distinguish fancy from imagination.

[26] Crispin cannot see that a fair exchange, in his case, is still a robbery. The inquisitorial botanist is no more absurd than the florist asking aid from cabbages. He has not really solved his problem; he has simply inverted his egotism.

Scrawl a tragedian's testament? Prolong
His active force in an inactive dirge,
Which, let the tall musicians call and call,
Should merely call him dead? Pronounce amen
Through choirs infolded to the outmost clouds?
Because he built a cabin who once planned
Loquacious columns by the ructive sea?
Because he turned to salad-beds again?
Jovial Crispin, in calamitous crape?
Should he lay by the personal and make
Of his own fate an instance of all fate?
What is one man among so many men?
What are so many men in such a world?
Can one man think one thing and think it long?
Can one man be one thing and be it long?

He has only his ego—his wit and his senses—to rely on. He
ends where he began, knowing what he knew to begin with but
attempted to deny, that a man cannot violate his own nature.
The apology with which the poem concludes echoes the final
paragraphs of *The Renaissance* with an irony that Pater could
hardly have foreseen, with the awareness of an irony that Bergson
seems to have overlooked by asking the question, "What is the object of art?" in an essay on comedy. Bergson denies the comedian
the status of the true poet. But the sense of self—the individual
way of looking at things which distinguishes the poet from other
men—and the self-forgetfulness that Bergson demands as the
necessary prerequisite for poetic creation present a paradox.
"However interested a dramatist (i.e., a true poet) may be in the
comic features of human nature, he will hardly go, I imagine,
to the extent of trying to discover his own," Bergson says. But
for Stevens, "plumbing the depths of his own nature in so powerful an effort of inner observation, that he lays hold of the potential in the real, and takes up what nature has left as a mere outline or sketch in his soul in order to make of it a finished work of
art" led directly to a discovery of his own "comic features."
Simply to accept Bergson's opinion that the discovery was *prima
facie* evidence that he was no poet would have been for him un-
thinkable. The "disguised pronunciamento" of "The Comedian"
is a categorical denial of Bergson's conclusion. The poem turns
the comic strategies set forth in *Laughter* against their author in
an attempt to disprove their validity. Stevens knew how much he
had in common with the characters he had created in his work

long before Genevieve Taggard told him of the rumor that the
characters in the poems of " Sur Ma Guzzla Gracile " were " hideous ghosts " of himself; but he was not thereby persuaded that
the comic view of life was necessarily superficial. "The Comedian " may not have proved that his point of view was true, but
it gave him an opportunity to try on a large scale how far the
strategies that Bergson believed appropriate to comedy would
take him.

For the poem does explore those strategies in almost bewildering profusion. Bergson observes of comic sayings, for example,
that " if we laugh at them, we are equally entitled to laugh at their
author "; and as the victim of his own fondness for rhetoric,
Crispin is certainly laughable. But, Bergson goes on to say, " This
latter condition . . . is not indispensable, since the saying or expression has a comic virtue of its own. This is proved by the fact
that we find it very difficult, in the majority of these cases, to
say whom we are laughing at, although at times we have a dim,
vague feeling that there is someone in the background." This
" someone " may be the Crispin who is clever enough to take
advantage of his own pretensions, who has enough detachment
at times to see his own absurdity. It may be the author, whom
the reader must admire for the skill with which he pulls the strings
of his marionette. It may be the reader himself, whenever he
recognizes his own absurdities in those of Crispin. It may be
Bergson, who, in answer to the question " With whom has the wit
to deal? " says:

First of all, with his interlocutors themselves, when his witticism is a
direct retort to one of them. Often with an absent person whom he
supposes to have spoken and to whom he is replying. Still oftener,
with the whole world,—in the ordinary meaning of the term,—which
he takes to task, twisting a current idea into a paradox, or making use
of a hackneyed phrase, or parodying some quotation or proverb. If
we compare these scenes in miniature with one another, we find they
are almost always variations of a comic theme with which we are
well acquainted, that of the " robber robbed." You take up a metaphor, a phrase, an argument, and turn it against the man who is, or
might be, its author, so that he is made to say what he did not mean
to say and lets himself be caught, to some extent, in the toils of
language.

Bergson characterizes wit itself as a " gift for dashing off comic
scenes in a few strokes—dashing them off, however, so subtly,

delicately and rapidly, that all is over as soon as we begin to notice them," and he adds that "in every poet there is something of the wit." If this definition of wit is correct, "The Comedian" must be reckoned a failure. Its wit, though often subtle, is expansive and self-indulgent. Bergson, like Dr. Johnson, emphasizes brevity. But as a *tour de force*, as the demonstration of comic strategies and of an argument turned "against the man who is, or might be, its author, so that he is made to say what he did not mean to say and lets himself be caught . . . in the toils of language," "The Comedian" merits a good deal of praise. Ultimately, the poem turns the tables not only on Bergson but on Stevens and Crispin, who comes to the conclusion that "The words of things tangle and confuse."

It is a final irony that Crispin's ambition has been to achieve that state of clairvoyance and "immediate communion with things" and with himself which Bergson—like Pater—calls the object of art. Crispin's ego, rather than the need to live with "the acceptance only of the *utilitarian* side of things in order to respond to them by appropriate reactions," defeats him. He is so self-conscious of his own point of view that he never succeeds in loving "colour for colour and form for form," perceiving them "for their sake and not for his own," and therefore it is never "the inner life of things that he sees appearing through their forms and colours." Crispin's "good, fat, guzzly fruit" which "survives its poems" lacks the particularity of "the thing itself" far more than its romantic counterpart does; but in both cases the plum becomes entangled and confused in the words used to describe it. It becomes a symbol or an emblem. Unlike the pears in a later poem, "Study of Two Pears," the plum is seen too much "as the observer wills." Crispin uses his experience as a means of self-aggrandizement. He has not learned that the poem, not the plum, has to be the symbol. His natural detachment is not quite sufficient to be characterized as "innate in the structure of sense or consciousness, which at once reveals itself by a virginal manner, so to speak, of seeing, hearing, or thinking." "Were this detachment complete," Bergson goes on to say, "did the soul no longer cleave to action by any of its perceptions, . . . it would perceive all things in their native purity: the forms, colours, sounds of the physical world as well as the subtlest movements of the inner life."

Stevens remained sceptical of the soul all his life. But in Berg-

son and Pater he nevertheless found the confirmation of his own
desire "to live in the world but outside of existing conceptions
of it." He was too ambitious and too practical to be satisfied with
waiting for the world "to arrange itself in a poem." "The Comedian" gave him an opportunity to take stock of himself, and of
two theories of poetry which had helped him discover his own.
Although he would modify and interpret their doctrines in many
ways, he accepted almost unchanged the beliefs that the wisest
men spend their "interval" in art and song, and that "the loftiest
ambition of art . . . consists in revealing to us nature." The artist
who "for a few moments at least . . . diverts us from the prejudices
of form and colour that come between ourselves and reality" is
the artist he hoped to become. "Poetry," he said, "has to be
something more than a conception of the mind. It has to be a
revelation of nature. Conceptions are artificial. Perceptions are
essential." The examples of "Carlos among the Candles," "Le
Monocle de Mon Oncle," and "The Comedian as the Letter C"
had already made him aware that "The poet is the intermediary
between people and the world in which they live and also, between people as between themselves; but not between people and
some other world."

He may have been more self-defensive than he knew when he
wrote Miss Monroe that *Harmonium* would "amount to nothing,
except that it [would] teach [him] something," but he had already
learned enough from the "outmoded and debilitated poems" he
sent to Knopf to give his own theory of poetry a solid foundation.
Nothing he was to write later would achieve the particular comic
quality of these early exercises, but as the tone of the poetry
deepened, he could look back at *Harmonium* without embarrassment. Perhaps the judgment made years afterward on the accomplishments of Leon-Paul Fargue came close to the truth about
his own accomplishment as he saw it in 1922:

All during the autumn [1950] I have been reading Fargue . . . I suppose
that everyone in Paris knew him. Claudine Chonez has written a little
book about him which I finished yesterday. In substance, she dismisses him as of no value although she concedes that he had many
gifts. She thinks that he was of no value because he did not let himself go. This means that he remained superficial. He never went to
the extremes of Rimbaud or Michaux. For my own part, I came to
about the same result, but for a different reason. Chonez makes a
great point of this: that the imagination is always made active by

some contact with reality. Rimbaud followed the imagination in its own right. The trouble with Fargue is that he follows it in the right of reality; that is to say, he substituted Paris for the imagination. Chonez, who has carefully analyzed his work, says that something like 60% of his poems are about Paris. Within the range of that 60% he very often said extremely perceptive and enchanting things. But, after all, Paris is not the same thing as the imagination and it is because Fargue failed to see the difference, that he is not first rate.[27]

" The Comedian " had spelled out the consequences of confusing fancy with imagination and the error of assuming that imagination or reality by itself was sufficient to live by. The poet was, after all, a man with a monocle: one eye naked to reality, one eye looking at the world imaginatively. The double view, he believed, would compose to a single inclusive vision, once he had come to terms with himself.

[27] Letter to Thomas McGreevy, Nov. 5, 1950.

V

WALLACE STEVENS AND THE SYMBOLIST IMAGINATION

BY MICHEL BENAMOU

The starting point of this inquiry is a stanza of " Extracts from Addresses to the Academy of Fine Ideas ":

> Where is that summer warm enough to walk
> Among the lascivious poisons, clean of them,
> And in what covert may we, naked, be
> Beyond the knowledge of nakedness, as part
> Of reality, beyond the knowledge of what
> Is real, part of a land beyond the mind?

While the first half of this quotation superabounds with echoes and fragrances from Baudelaire, the second half has in intent, if not in style, the ascetic character of Mallarmé's quest. With the first we associate the nostalgic tone of:

> J'aime le souvenir de ces époques nues . . .[1]

and:

> Au milieu de l'azur, des vagues, des splendeurs
> Et des esclaves nus, tout imprégnés d'odeur . . . .[2]

With Mallarmé's search for an absolute poetry, we associate Stevens' use of words which he may have learned from the French master: *knowledge, nakedness, beyond*. But we soon become dissatisfied with our associations. Whatever sameness struck us at first pales in the glare of essential differences. Baudelaire remembers nature before the fall; Stevens projects his Adamic hopefulness.[3] Mallarmé seeks a land of the mind beyond reality; Stevens a land beyond the mind, as part of reality. Because of

---

[1] Charles Baudelaire, *Oeuvres Complètes* (Paris, 1931), p. 87.

[2] *Ibid.*, " La Vie antérieure," p. 93.

[3] This essay was written in part to answer a question asked by Roy Harvey Pearce in *The Continuity of American Poetry* (Princeton, 1961), p. 7. I took cognizance of his brilliant history of the Adamic tradition after publishing an article in *Critique*, " Sur le Prétendu Symbolisme de Wallace Stevens," dissociating Stevens from the French tradition.

92

such exchanges among words and symbols shared by Baudelaire, Stevens, and Mallarmé, parallelisms must be checked out beneath their words, at the boundaries of their imaginary worlds.

One motive for metaphor has to do with clothing, concealment, protection, placation. It metamorphoses the world into pleasurable likenesses, multiplies its colors, its perfumes, and its sounds, yet stresses their profound unity. In poetry of this kind, the images enhance bodily well-being, the value of nutrition, the feminine presences of Night, Moon, and Earth, in their maternal role of dispelling fear. The imagination successfully creates a world whose vitality does not deny, but veils or beautifies death's finality. The lyric dictionary of such an imagination enters phrases like "éternelle chaleur" and "eternal bloom" (Baudelaire's in "La Chevelure"; Stevens' in "Le Monocle de Mon Oncle"). It is romantic by its arrest of time. Its rhetoric makes of metaphor the chief vehicle of its discoveries especially by use of the synecdoche which creates a world within a world, as though language had the same innate fecundity as Nature. Its poetics welcome lexical opulence. Its aesthetics have, since Baudelaire found their name, Correspondances. Its religion is a mystic humanism, hedonistic rather than heroic. The poetry of the beautiful surface with the dark terror beneath does not, however, escape the facts of death and suffering. It is a means of overcoming terror. Hence the invention of the gods and the worship of the imagination. *Harmonium*, and some poems of *Les Fleurs du Mal*, will admit the reader through a passage going down [4] into the secure interiors

[4] For Stevens, the Moon is *down*, and the sun is *up*. No poet seems more conscious than he of the Jungian archetype of the Moon as a feminine, descentional movement of the imagination, as the "Mother of pathos and pity," as the truly maternal and protective symbol of the imagination in its role of euphemizing the vital fears. Howard Baker was first in connecting Stevens with the collective unconscious and Jungian archetypes. The self-awareness of Stevens in moving from one constellation of his images to the other was remarkable, and one should give full meaning to the substantivation of adverbs in Crispin's lines:

> Thus he conceived his voyaging to be
> An *up* and *down* between two elements,
> A fluctuating between sun and moon,
> A *sally* into gold and crimson forms,
> As on this voyage, out of goblinry,
> And then *retirement* like a turning *back*
> And *sinking down* to the indulgences
> That in the moon have their habitude.

The moon is reached by a movement inward, or backward, to the maternal origins. Ernst Robert Curtius has shown that the myth of the Great Mother entered Middle Age

of a world of "indulgences." But we must qualify the oversim-
plified view of Stevens as a hedonist. In fact, as Richard Ellman
has suggested it,[5] death is the constant obsession of the poet from
the first [6] to the last. In *Harmonium*, almost no poem dodges the
theme, almost none refuses to minister the solace of poetry, only a
few face the fact of death with derision or dirge.

During the late twenties a change occurred in Stevens' imagery.
He summarized this change in "Farewell to Florida," consciously
placing this poem, written in 1936, at the threshold of his new
Ideas of Order. True, all its themes were already in *Harmonium*;
yet too much cannot be made of the poet's self-realization. Quite
lucidly, he stated that for him the imagination of Night, with its
constellating images of the South, the Moon-Woman, vegetation,
summer, nature, music, must give way to the masculine constellation of Day, North, men, mud, winter, society, and violence.
Thus, he was making his adjustment to reality, which now included misery for millions, the Depression, the impending world
catastrophe. The change of symbols entailed a change of style.
The very structure of the poem tells us that the protected world
of the synecdoche has been abandoned for the fight of mind
against chaos. Antithesis, both in composition and syntax, produces a poetry of "ghostlier demarcations," "contrary theses,"
sharp light effects. A new motive for the poet's craft appears,
the pursuit of a knowledge of reality. The aesthetics of "order"
makes a cleavage between "reality" and "imagination" in spite
of "their incessant conjunctionings." [7] The theme of nakedness
takes hold of Stevens' imagination during this period, perhaps
under the influence of Mallarmé's ascetic example. As the opposition of word and world grows in his mind, Stevens yearns for
transparence. Metaphor cloaks reality. The image of green leaves

---

literature with Bernard Sylvestris' *De Universitate Mundi* (*European Literature
and the Latin Middle Ages* [New York, 1953], pp. 108-13). I am struck by the moon's
convergence with the archetype, which Bernard called Natura; the moon is "the mid-
point of the Golden chain, navel of the upper and lower worlds." It is in the sky and
within us. But this is so only within the context of Bernard's theory of correspondances, another striking emanation of the Archetype: the Macrocosm is *in* the
Microcosm. Cf. also: John Senior, *The Way Down and Out* (Ithica, N. Y., 1959).

[5] Richard Ellman, "Wallace Stevens' Ice-cream," *Kenyon Review*, Winter, 1957.

[6] Samuel French Morse relates from letters that in 1918, Stevens had a conversation
about death with Miss Harriet Monroe, and allowed that "the subject absorbed
him." See "Lettres d'un Soldat," *Dartmouth College Bulletin*, Dec., 1961, p. 50.

[7] Statement on the dust-jacket of *Ideas of Order* (New York, 1936).

covering the "basic slate" of death changes into the image of veils that must be stripped. Hence a tendency toward the abstract, a refining of poetic vocabulary. But Stevens, even at his wintriest, never followed Mallarmé's rarities, and kept something of his original gaiety and bigness of diction. The symbols of the sun, light, air, mountain-tops, and hero now constellate in a poetry of pure sight, of sight purified by poetry. The dreams of heroic humanism soar up, and their verticality lends to them a moral meaning somewhat absent in *Harmonium*. The poetry of divestment and naked sight even takes on a collective significance when both Stevens and Mallarmé envisage a "supreme fiction." These are the common directions; many are the divergences.

The imagination's sex, always androgynous in all poets, follows the dialectics of animus and anima. Primitive androgyneity, Stevens' later poetry seems to say, is the absolute poetic state, the mystic equilibrium.[8] The final result of the "up and down between" sun and moon, is a happy marriage between the giant projection of the masculine self and the earth-spouse; it is a cyclic gesture unifying season with season and world with word, a marriage and a cycle whose stylistic icon is often Stevens' repetitive pattern of three-line stanzas, as opposed to Mallarmé's hieratic tombstones.

This is of course an abstract schema—but voluntarily so, because our endeavor is to trace the polarity veiling-nakedness through the inner space, symbolism, and poetics of Stevens and his French confreres.

STEVENS AND BAUDELAIRE

This old, black dress,
I have been embroidering
French flowers on it.[9]

Recent phenomenological criticism[10] has disengaged at least

---

[8] Jung's terminology, "anima" and "animus," was known and used by Stevens, e. g., "His anima liked its animal" in a passage about the maternal archetype, *The Collected Poems of Wallace Stevens* (New York, 1954), p. 322.

[9] "Explanation," *Collected Poems*, p. 72. Imagination "embroiders" on the *black* dress: death is old, permanent. The flowers are fragile, but they add color, in the way a French word does to a sentence. They are artificial, not natural flowers. William York Tindall quotes this poem in his *Wallace Stevens* (Minneapolis, Minn., 1961), p. 15, and we should follow his advice to read alongside it Baudelaire's "Eloge du Maquillage."

[10] Chiefly J.-P. Richard, *Poésie et Profondeur* (Paris, 1955), and G. Poulet, *Les*

three Baudelaires from the complex formula: " De la concentration et de la vaporisation du Moi, tout est là " (Mon Coeur mis à
nu). To which was Stevens attentive? To the poet of nature's
infinite dilation (symbolized by the sea, perfumes, far horizons),
whose very dissemination in space brought about the anguish of
emptiness and dissolution? Or to the poet who fought the vertigo
of expansion and natural fecundity (symbolized by the teeming
carrion), and fought it by a thickening, almost a solidification of
the self, to the point of immobility: art giving this counter-natural
fixity? Or, again, was Stevens attentive to the Baudelaire who
conjugated the two movements into one, and whose imagined
paradise combined the memory of limitless space within the protective shell of the temple, the ship, the island, the sky felt as
a cup?

It is difficult to answer on behalf of Wallace Stevens, because he
limited his allusions to and borrowings from Baudelaire to a few
excerpts (e. g. " my semblables " transferred from " Au lecteur "
to " Dutch Graves in Bucks County "), one or two parodies (e. g.
the five French lines in " Sea Surface Full of Clouds ") a pro-
nouncement on the aesthetics of decreation at the end of *The
Necessary Angel*, and the beautiful analysis of the opening lines of
" La Vie Antérieure," which is perhaps the most revealing published document of his way of reading French poetry.[11] Stevens'
comments show him a keen and sympathetic judge of Baudelaire's
imaginary experience. The kind of sympathy which Stevens
evinces is akin to an affinity. It is a sympathy which enabled
Stevens to feel the importance to Baudelaire of the phrase " au
milieu de l'azur," rendered by " at the *centre* of azure " and of the
" vast porticoes," endowed by Stevens with more than casual or
romantic value:

We stand looking at a remembered habitation. All old dwelling-
places are subject to these transmogrifications and the experience of
all of us includes a succession of old dwelling-places: abodes of the
imagination, ancestral or memories of places that never existed.[12]

Métamorphoses du Cercle (Paris, 1961). I disagree with their attempt to turn
Baudelaire into a poet of infinite space. No " solar tropism " verticalizes Baudelaire's
dreams. In fact, as Gaston Bachelard pointed out, he was a terrestrial, not an aerial
poet (*L'Air et les Songes* [Paris, 1950], p. 158). Stevens, on the contrary, partook
in the " Nietzschean imagination " of pure air, and did not need to translate space
in terms of depth and swimming, as Baudelaire always did.

[11] *Opus Posthumous* (New York, 1957), pp. 202-16.   [12] *Ibid.*, p. 204.

Quite rightly, Stevens was tuning his ear to a theme which it is rather easy to miss in Baudelaire's more expansive moods. Critics miss it, who pick up only the Wagnerian melody of "expansion infinie." But even that most hackneyed of all romantic images, "la nature est un temple," possesses the charm of "a remembered habitation." It is a pity that critics do not mention that the sonnet "Correspondances" is the recounting of a hashish dream. The "temple" of the first line, with its "living pillars" speaking "garbled words" and casting "familiar glances" to man, is the "transmogrification" of a remembered habitation, an artificial paradise, as a matter of fact probably a room in an inn.[13] No wonder, then, that there should be so few instances of "correspondances" (apart from the rather trite device of synesthesia) in Baudelaire's poetry as a whole. These mystic moments required a "temple" and the intoxication caused by a drug, or their substitutes: an alcove and a woman's perfume. In no case did the vistas of outdoor nature—suggested by a casual reading of "Correspondances"—produce the conditions of the experience. Baudelaire's paradise was the transfiguration of trivial details printed on wall-paper; his sky, a ceiling deepened by imagination; his synesthesia, a real sound or sight fragranced by hallucination. To him, paradise had the ambiguous shape of a cage: a temple, pillars, vast porticoes, that retain the poet's self while it expands. Nature

[13] My proof for this unorthodox view comes from two prose poems by Baudelaire: "Du Vin et du Haschisch," 1851, and "Le Poème du Haschisch," 1858. In the first, he wrote: "Les hallucinations commencent . . . Les sons ont une couleur, les couleurs ont une musique . . . Les peintures du plafond . . . prennent une vie effrayante . . . Toute contradiction est devenue unité. L'homme est *passé* dieu." In the second, the ceiling becomes a vault, then a cage: ". . . Je me considérais comme enfermée pour longtemps, pour des milliers d'années peut-être, dans cette cage somptueuse, au milieu de ces paysages féeriques, entre ces horizons merveilleux . . ." then the "living pillars" and "familiar books" appear: "Mais toutes les divinités mythologiques [allegorical figures painted on the walls of the room] me regardaient avec un charmant sourire. . . ." The same pattern appears in the next dream: a ceiling deepens, painted figures look understandingly, symbols and synesthesias develop: "les peintures du *plafond* revêtiront une vie effrayante; les plus grossiers papiers peints qui tapissent les *murs* des auberges se creuseront comme de splendide dioramas. Les nymphes aux chairs éclatantes vous *regardent* avec de grands yeux plus profonds et plus limpides que le ciel et l'eau; les personnages de l'antiquité . . . échangent avec vous par le simple *regard* de solennelles confidences . . . Cependant se développe cet état mystérieux et temporaire de de l'esprit, où la *profondeur* de la vie . . . se révèle *tout entière* dans le spectacle . . . qu'on a sous les yeux,—où le premier objet venu devient *symbole parlant*. Fourier et Swedenborg, l'un avec ses *analogies*, l'autre avec ses *correspondances,* se sont incarnés dans le végétal et l'animal qui tombent sous votre regard, et au lieu d'enseigner par la voix, ils vous endoctrinent par la forme et par le couleur . . . ."

was dreamed from a room, the walls of which receded to the controlled depths of dioramas. "Expansion infinie" yes, but within
a "temple."

In "La Chevelure," a perfume signals the inward movement by
which Baudelaire discovers a larger world within the happy vessel
of his paradise:

> Je plongerai ma tête amoureuse d'ivresse
> Dans ce noir océan où l'autre est enfermé
> Et mon esprit subtil que le roulis caresse
> Saura vous retrouver, ô féconde paresse,
> Infinis bercements du loisir embaumé!

By deepening a sea and a sky inside his mistress's black hair,
then peopling it with bright sails, lazy cradling motions, eternal
warmth, the poet turned into pleasure his habitual sense of the
inner void. His desire for a *plenum* was fulfilled by an imaginative paradox well-known to the mystics. The large in the small
is discovered through metaphors of containment. A hemisphere
is contained by a woman's hair, a macrocosm by a microcosm, a
world of images by a draft of wine, the wine by the woman-bottle.
At the core of the imagination of correspondances, the vessel
archetype manages the successive sensual discoveries of "La
Chevelure."

The same imagination of prenatal comfort and aesthetic pleasure links Stevens with the spirit of Baudelaire's correspondances.
The image "The high interiors of the sea" recurs in contexts
reminiscent of the exotic settings of "La Chevelure" or "La Vie
Antérieure." Exoticism in Stevens and Baudelaire followed an
inward movement. For instance, "ce noir océan où l'autre est
enfermé" corresponds with "Jasmine's Beautiful Thoughts under-
neath the Willow," a dream

> Of bliss submerged beneath appearance,
> In an interior ocean's rocking
> Of long, capricious fugues and chorals.[14]

Although Stevens warns us that his "titillations have no footnotes," the image seems incomplete without the pedantic gloss
that the willow is the symbolic tree of Hecate, the goddess of
death. It is she who, in "Sunday Morning," "makes the willow
shiver in the sun." She is the secret which Baudelaire and Stevens

---

[14] *Collected Poems*, p. 79.

share, the common denominator of their paradisial poetry. For at the end of " La Vie Antérieure," Baudelaire hints at " the grievous secret that made [me] pine." Hashish, drunkenness, art, were the best *veils* (his word) to fill the inner void, the giddy tomb hollowed within him, or at least to hide it. The imagination, at its most expansive in " Correspondances," seemed to Baudelaire man's best protection against the vast spaces ready to engulf him. But mothered by Madame Aupick and a Jansenist tradition, his vivid imagery of death often overpowered the maternal archetype.

There are very few " fecundity " images in Baudelaire, in contrast to Stevens. If I have pleasure in imagining that my body corresponds, limb for limb with the World's Body, it is because nature is both beautiful and good. But Baudelaire could imagine nature as a bountiful mother only in a remote past, before the Fall:

> Du temps que le Nature en sa verve puissante
> Concevait chaque jour des enfants monstrueux,
> J'eusse aimé vivre auprès d'une jeune géante,
> Comme au pied d'une reine un chat voluptueux.[15]

Fecundity and poetry, creation and speech: close companions. Baudelaire nostalgically fuses them in a pun.[16] Verve and Verb both created, in some " anterior " world which was, we know, also an " interior " world. But those times were ended by some corruption of Nature, probably the appearance of death. The giant queen whose speech could create, the feminine archetype as Nature, no longer allows the poet to nestle in her lap. The only communication he has with her bounty is through the hallucinations of hashish and the vessel-type imagery of " Correspondances."

Stevens' poetry, on the contrary, has its generating center in the archetype. All but six poems of *Harmonium* exemplify the maternal role of the imagination. The six exceptions are: " The Snow Man," " The Emperor of Ice-Cream," " The Bird with the Keen, Coppery Claws," " Tea at the Palaz of Hoon," " New England Verses," and possibly " Anatomy of Monotony ": they announce the sun-style to come. (See the Appendix.) Critics of Stevens' hedonism have generally failed to see the tragic darkness which underlies the gorgeous colors and funny little sounds of *Harmonium*. " The quirks of imagery," as we read in Stevens'

[15] Baudelaire, " La Géante," *Oeuvres Complètes*, p. 97.
[16] Pointed out by Judd D. Hubert in *L'Esthétique du Mal* (Geneva, 1953).

exemplary poem of "swallowing," "Frogs Eat Butterflies. Snakes
Eat Frogs. Hogs Eat Snakes. Men Eat Hogs," are there because
"the night is not the cradle that they cry." The night is hostile,
and imagination safeguards us. The moon is one of its inventions.
She is "mother of pathos and pity"[17] and her counterpart the
candle will even outlast her as a symbol of the imagination: the
"valley candle" of *Harmonium* still shines in *The Rock*, when
the moon has long ago failed because too ambiguous (or too clear!
"The moon is a tricorn / Waved in pale adieu"[18]). The lamp in
a child's room remained associated with the tales which Stevens
loved, and with images of protection:

> Within its vital boundary, in the mind.
> We say God and the imagination are one . . .
> How high that highest candle lights the dark.
>
> Out of this same light, out of the central mind,
> We make a dwelling in the evening air,
> In which being there together is enough.[19]

The insistence on the role of the imagination, even the symbolism
of the light in the dark,[20] and the impulse toward the vessel are
of the same imaginary type as Baudelaire's. The difference is in

---

[17] *Collected Poems*, p. 107.

[18] *Ibid.*, p. 495.

[19] *Ibid.*, p. 524.

[20] Cf. "Les Phares," in which painters are compared to beacons in the abysmal
night. Also, "Le Voyage":

> Ah! que le monde est grand à la clarté des lampes!

This latter poem may have influenced Stevens, who may have noted Baudelaire's ambiguous attitude to the imagination, as a safeguard against *ennui*, as a means to
renew our world. By "Au fond de l'inconnu pour trouver du nouveau," does Baudelaire
mean the same things as Stevens: "We accept the unknown even when we are most
skeptical" (*Opus Posthumous*, p. 288)? Stevens' worship of imagination, in "Disillusionment of Ten O'Clock" for instance, is less mitigated than Baudelaire's:

> O le pauvre amoureux des pays chimériques!
> Faut-il le mettre aux fers, le jeter à la mer,
> Ce matelot ivrogne, inventeur d'Amériques
> Dont le mirage rend le gouffre plus amer?   (Le Voyage)

as compared with:

> Only, here and there, an old sailor,
> Drunk and asleep in his boots,
> Catches tigers
> In red weather.   (Disillusionment of Ten O'Clock)

Of this image, Howard Baker wrote it was "interesting in itself but nonsignificant"
("Wallace Stevens," *The Achievement of Wallace Stevens*, [New York, 1963], p. 88).
If it has its genesis in Baudelaire, it expresses a much more positive attitude toward
imagination in general.

the metaphysics of the " central mind." For Stevens the imagination has no extra-human source, and " the world imagined " (by man) "is the ultimate good." It is a world shored up by the miracle of imagery against the vital fears of night. Thus the birds of black which haunted the " walker in the moonlight " [21] became in another poem " euphemized " into thirteen blackbirds, all except one concealing the terror they evoked.[22] The abysmal night of chaos still gapes in the gloom of " Heaven considered as a Tomb," and it recalls another side of Baudelaire, the poet of gnawing worms and icy hells.

But it would be a mistake to compare " The Worms at Heaven's Gate " to " Une Charogne." In Stevens' poem, the imagination conquers the horror of death by a sea-change. No foul smell or teeming infection; the irony comes from the subtle tension between separation and wholeness: death as itemization versus life as organism. The wit of Stevens carries the theme of swallowing even into the name, Ba-droul-ba-dour, even into the syntax: " we her chariot." [23]

Much more successfully than Baudelaire, Stevens can conjure up the Lady of Darkness. The imagination can master night:

> Donna, donna, dark,
> Stooping in indigo gown
> And cloudy constellations,
> Conceal yourself or disclose
> Fewest things to the lover—
> A hand that bears a thick-leaved fruit,
> A pungent bloom against your shade.[24]

Ceres, the archetype as Mother-Nature, protects the lovers against Hecate. Here the symbols of fecundity (fruit) and concealment (thick-leaved) converge with the feminine:

> The night is the color
> Of a woman's arm:
> Night, the female,
> Obscure,
> Fragrant and supple,
> Conceals herself.[25]

Stevens' night hides the original dark with colors which are euphemizations of black, mostly green and purple. Elsewhere

[21] *Collected Poems*, p. 77.
[22] Directly opposed to Ellman's interpretation of the blackbird as the force of life.
[23] *Collected Poems*, p. 49.   [24] *Ibid.*, p. 48.   [25] *Ibid.*, p. 73.

(*Collected Poems*, pp. 223, 267), he repeats that "Green is the night" . . . "the archaic queen." Thus among the symbols of vestment and concealment used by Stevens, foliage plays a major role. Be it Pennsylvania's green or Florida's green, the color is dreamed in depth as well as perceived. It is an emanation of the archetype, the product of natural fecundity, as well as the "fictive covering" which man's imagination disposes over the "basic slate," the bare rock of fact and death. In *Harmonium*, the darkness remains precariously kept under control. "Domination of Black" presents a notable exception to the color symbolism of the book, in which statistically *green* is first (*43*), *blue* second (*28*), *white* third (*21*), then *gold* (*20*), *black*, *dark*, and *purple* (*14* each), *red* (*12*) and *yellow* (*7*). "Green is the night" . . . and green the "fusky alphabet" taught "Phosphor" by "that elemental parent." [26]

A Sears and Roebuck list of Stevens' symbols would just catalogue his favorite garments; he loved sombreros. But basic movements of the mind reveal more than its inventory. In *Harmonium* the reflex to cloak expresses a relationship between clothes and language, between language and the clothes which language weaves, almost like leaves and almost like fabric, at once manmade and natural. The gowns of grammarians are like "the speech of clouds," [27] the theme of embroidery parallels the efforts of the imagination,[28] cloak-moon-singer is a recurrent cluster [29] and in spite of Crispin's decision, taken late in the development of *Harmonium*, to "lay bare" his "cloudy drift," to tear the veils of Spring "irised in dew and early fragrancies" and to seek "a sinewy nakedness," [30] we shall see this dual symbolism of fecundity and language persist throughout Stevens' poetry. In fact this relationship may have been what he grasped of the rapport between poetry and reality, when at the end of "Notes toward a Supreme Fiction" he called by name his muse, the archetype, "Fat girl, terrestrial . . . my green, my fluent mundo." [31] The earth is green, round, maternal, fecund—an image seldom found in Baudelaire's poems, but present in Stevens'. To the end, the imagination of covering will resist the intelligence of divestment:

[26] *Ibid.*, p. 267.   [28] *Ibid.*, pp. 72, 84, 64.   [30] *Ibid.*, p. 36.
[27] *Ibid.*, p. 55.   [29] *Ibid.*, pp. 57, 74.   [31] *Ibid.*, pp. 406-7.

> Then Ozymandias said the spouse, the bride
> Is never naked. A fictive covering
> Weaves always glistening from the heart and mind.[32]

The happy color, green, the reticular web secreted by the imagination, joins man with nature, the fecund woman.

Dandyism, our second parallel, attaches a good deal of importance to sartorial symbols. It interests us as a signal of aesthetic
feeling rather than as an aspect of politics. Gorham Munson, its
inventor, brilliantly forestalled Jean-Paul Sartre's analysis [33] when
he noted the difference between " the metallic shell secreted by
a restless man against a despised social order " and Stevens' " well-
fed, well-booted dandyism of contentment," which, he added, reminded him of " the America of baronial estates." [34] It was a
remarkable judgment, especially in view of its date, 1925. Hindsight makes us more cautious, however. As early as 1920, Stevens'
poetic hero cut a much less impeccable figure than we were led
to believe. We read in " Anecdote of the Abnormal ":

> Crispin-valet, Crispin-saint!
> The exhausted realist beholds
> His tattered manikin arise,
> Tuck in the straw,
> And stalk the skies.[35]

This announced the rejection of " regalia " by the Comedian, and a
succession of ragged figures, who, in self-irony, projected Stevens'
image of the ideal poet! At mid-point down the line of heroes,
the virile young poet, poorly dressed and intent on the sun, won
in an aesthetic see-saw over an elegant lady, whose dress and
moonlight were one (" Mrs. Alfred Uruguay "). It was clear that
an essential redefinition of elegance was in process, and Stevens'
by now familiar cosmic symbols (repeated in " The Well Dressed
Man with a Beard ": " No was the night. Yes is this present sun ")
lent general meaning to the reversal. All these imaginary functions
converged: the sun, light, the eye, the masculine hero, and nakedness as a mode of knowing. The " final elegance " was to be reserved for the Chaplinesque figure at the end of " It Must Be

[32] *Ibid.*, p. 396.
[33] Jean-Paul Sartre, *Baudelaire* (Paris, 1947), p. 161: " Le dandysme baudelairien
est une réaction personnelle au problème de la situation sociale de l'écrivain."
[34] Gorham Munson, " The Dandyism of Wallace Stevens " in *The Achievement of
Wallace Stevens*, p. 43.
[35] *Opus Posthumous*, p. 24.

Abstract," in "Notes toward a Supreme Fiction," proof that a
clown, not a dandy, was the destination of Stevens' masks; now
metaphysics gone, man stands alone:

> Cloudless the morning. It is he. The man
> In that old coat, those sagging pantaloons,
>
> It is of him, ephebe, to make, to confect
> The final elegance . . .[36]

What do the dandy's clothes mean? To Baudelaire, the meaning is spiritual. The Symbolistic *askesis* stems from his series of
articles in *Curiosités Esthétiques* as directly as from any other
single source. "Dandyism is akin to spiritualism and stoicism." [37]
The latter word justifies Munson's analysis; the former suggests
something else, perhaps a purification. The next article says in
effect: the natural female is abominable, but a fashionable woman
is a dandy's love ". . . fusing both woman and the dress into an
indivisible totality." [38] In the next article, Baudelaire progresses
to the praise of make-up, which brings the human body closer
to the immobility of a statue: "idole, elle doit se *dorer* pour être
adorée . . . pour consolider et diviniser (sa) fragile beauté." [39]
Art receives the task of hardening the shell of human appearance,
in order to create a supernatural and magic being, indivisible
from its dress, whose flesh becomes, so to speak, materialized by
the artifice. A refusal of change, of time? Perhaps something
more: a need to fill the inner space with substance, or to contain
its expansion? The "gouffre" of death, let us remember, is to
Baudelaire both space and time: statues seem to him *divine*.

In *Les Fleurs du Mal*, Baudelaire's dandyism has its feminine
counterpart. He does not extol his langorous tropical natives
nearly as much as the stylized deities who torment and charm
him: "statue with jet eyes, bronze-browed angel," he says to one
of them, showing the link between spirituality and pure matter.
His metaphors mine inorganic nature for symbols of sterility and
frigidity: metals and minerals that are hard and cold. It would
be wrong to interpret these images as Parnassian conventions.
They are the active agents of the denaturalization of woman.
They effect a metamorphosis. Sonnet 27 lets us see, line by line,
this progressive, Ovidian, incantatory petrification of a woman's

---

[36] *Collected Poems*, p. 389.
[37] Baudelaire, *Oeuvres Complètes*, p. 907.
[38] *Ibid.*, p. 910.
[39] *Ibid.*, p. 913.

lithe body, until in the last alexandrine shines, like a star, "the cold majesty of the sterile woman." In a large group of poems dealing with natural woman in "ascetic terms," the sonnet to Beauty occupies a central position. Rather than a neo-classic ideal, it enacts the intellectual *askesis* of Baudelaire's life:

> Je suis belle, ô mortels! comme un rêve de pierre,
> Et mon sein, où chacun s'est meurtri tour à tour,
> Est fait pour inspirer au poète un amour
> Eternel et muet ainsi que la matière.[40]

Here, the metallic shell of dandyism becomes shaped into the artist's dream, a *plenum*, no longer a protection against nature, but a new, completely *artistic* state of being. Rather than a neo-classicist, this love of petrified life makes Baudelaire a precursor of the Surrealists, those innocence-seekers for whom "the way to purity is through mineralization."

Michel Carrouges, in *La Mystique du Surhomme*, quotes this revealing dream of Baudelaire:

". . . j'étais un morceau de glace pensant, je me considérais comme une statue taillée dans un seul bloc de glace; et cette folle hallucination me causait une fierté, excitait en moi un bien-être moral que je ne saurais définir." [41]

This mystique of cold and insensitivity comes directly out of Baudelaire's wish to purify nature, for the Dandy's beauty "consiste surtout dans l'air *froid* qui vient de l'inébranlable résolution de ne pas être ému." [42] But his "cold" and his "freezing" is not the result of naturally cold mountain air, as it is in Nietzsche or Stevens. It is a petrification and a congealing of life wrought by a desire for a contracted, homogeneous, absolute purity. It is the reverse of the Nietzschean or the Stevensian expansion from an imaginary mountain-top. In Baudelaire's statue of ice we cannot recognize the prototype of Stevens' familiar "man of glass, / Who in a million diamonds sums us up." [43] The genesis of Baudelaire's purity is a progressive decreation: clothes to hide animality, make-up to hide time, jewels to replace flesh, and the final petrification and divinization. Baudelaire's man of ice is the result of a centripetal movement, toward nothingness, but this new creation he reaches is the product of art: clothes-in-depth. Whereas Stevens' man of ice lives in change, and is nudity-in-depth.

[40] *Ibid.*, "La Beauté," p. 96.
[41] *Ibid.*, pp. 93-97.
[42] *Ibid.*, p. 909.
[43] *Collected Poems*, p. 250.

If, indeed, Stevens took up dandyism as a profession, this must be understood as a gesture of self-protection, not self-purification and *askesis*. It would be wrong to call it " a dandyism of contentment " any longer. Yet the clothing metaphors in *Harmonium* belong to a universe of colors and shapes as imaginative safeguards. Its aesthetics are the Baudelairian " correspondances " between nature and man, not the opposite Baudelairian exclusion of nature. And when eventually, after a silence of six years, the *askesis* of *Ideas of Order* appears, it will seek purity in an Adamic innocence, not an artistic petrification.

STEVENS AND MALLARMÉ

> He wanted to see. He wanted the eye to
> see
> And not be touched by blue. He wanted
> to know,
> A naked man who regarded himself in
> the glass
> Of air, who looked for the world beneath
> the blue,
> Without blue, without any turquoise tint
> or phase,
> Any azure under-side or after-color. . . .[44]

Among the poetic notions linking Stevens to Mallarmé, that of " purity " fosters the most satisfying impression of a resemblance between the two poets. Did not Stevens admonish himself to " seek those purposes that are purely the purposes of the pure poet . . ." ? The same entry in *Adagia* defines " purity " almost in the terms of Poe's *The Poetic Principle*, thus seeming to close the loop of tradition spiraling from Poe to Mallarmé, Valéry, and Abbé Brémond:

> To give a sense of the freshness or vividness of life is a valid purpose for poetry. A didactic purpose justifies itself in the mind of the teacher; a philosophical purpose justifies itself in the mind of the philosopher. It is not that one purpose is as justifiable as another but that some purposes are pure, others impure.[45]

Wallace Stevens' " sense of the freshness or vividness of life " is a snug fit to Poe's " Poetic Sentiment ": " He recognizes [it] . . . in

[44] *Ibid.*, p. 241.   [45] *Opus Posthumous*, p. 157.

the volutes of the flower—in the clustering of low shrubberies—in the waving of the grain-fields—in the slanting of tall, Eastern trees —in the blue distance of mountains—in the grouping of clouds. . . ."[46] Had Mallarmé read *The Poetic Principle*, he might have based Poe's angelism on earth. Somehow, Stevens repatriated the angel to the American soil, and restored the original meaning of "pure poetry":

> In spite of M. Brémond, pure poetry is a term that has grown to be descriptive of poetry in which not the true subject but the poetry of the subject is paramount.[47]

The difference between Stevens and the French tradition hinges on the metaphysical meaning of the word *pure*. It is a contrast between feeling purity in the world, and reaching purity out of this world by an angel's flight.

Mallarmé's distortion of Poe ("giving a purer meaning to his nation's words") takes the form of an angel wielding a naked sword: he is the angel of death, whose symbol of purification and severance typifies Mallarmé's imagination rather than Poe's. It is an imagination of dualistic structures, of earth and sky as enemies, "du sol et de la nue hostiles," of light and darkness, of antithesis, of the monster and the hero fighting.[48] Stevens insists, on the contrary, that *his* angel has "neither ashen wing nor wear of ore" and is one of the countrymen:

> I am one of you and being one of you
> Is being and knowing what I am and know.
>
> Yet I am the necessary angel of earth,
> Since, in my sight, you see the earth again,
>
> Cleared of its stiff and stubborn, man-locked set . . .[49]

The genesis of this image (a picture by Tal Coat representing a Venetian glass and earthenware round it) associates "Angel Surrounded by Paysans" with all the other poems by Stevens in which the poetic act is symbolized by a metamorphosis into glass, and in which purity is the result of cleared sight.

---

[46] Edgar A. Poe, *The Poetic Principle*.

[47] *Opus Posthumous*, p. 222.

[48] Stéphane Mallarmé, "Le Tombeau d'Edgar Poe," *Oeuvres Complètes* (Paris, 1945), p. 70.

[49] *Collected Poems*, pp. 496-97.

Mallarmé, whose influence on Stevens was exercised mostly from 1931 on, may have originated the meaning of " pure " as ideally transparent and visible. It is a key-word, occurring no fewer than seventeen times in a small body of poetry. However, several other notions are mixed with that of sheer visibility, for instance in

Le pur vase d'aucun breuvage.[50]

It is absence made visible. Purity will have to shed its Mallarméan connotations of inaccessibility and non-being before finding its way into Stevens' imaginary world. Yet the relationship of *pure* poetry unites the two poets, at least in dissimilitude.

They shared a revealing enthusiasm for the Impressionists. Mallarmé called their art " clairvoyance," " abstract purification into the beautiful," and " the modern enchantment." [51] Of Manet's eye, he said that it was " virgin and abstract." [52] Purity, then, has its origin deep in the artist's sight, not in the world. Its brilliance is an emanation of the artist's eye:

Le Maître, par un oeil profond, a sur ses pas,
Apaisé de l'éden l'inquiète merveille
. . . pluie ou diamant, le regard diaphane
Resté là sur ces fleurs dont nulle ne se fane.[53]

The Master is not a painter but a poet, Théophile Gautier, whose ever-freshening gaze stops the decay of flowers. Poetry and painting reach purity. But the metamorphosis is a swift passage from sheer visibility (" regard diaphane ") to essential notion. The slow, Ovidian metamorphosis belongs to the imagination of the vessel: the metaphor as shell. Mallarmé's is the metaphor as fold. An earthly flower becomes a " pure " flower, " absente de tous bouquets " by an ontological jump into abstraction. No doubt that Mallarmé's definition of poetry as the " Orphic explication of the earth " calls upon the poet to *unfold* flatly a world distanced from the visible one by negative analogy. The transaction between the eye and reality is a " transposition ":

A quoi bon la merveille de transposer un fait de nature en sa presque disparition vibratoire selon le jeu de la parole, cependant, si ce n'est qu'en émane, sans la gêne d'un proche ou concret rappel, la notion pure.[54]

---

[50] Mallarmé, *Oeuvres Complètes*, p. 74.
[51] *Ibid.*, p. 536.
[52] *Ibid.*, p. 532.
[53] *Ibid.*, p. 55.
[54] *Ibid.*, p. 857.

A symbol duplicates a "fact" in the mind; abstract, it is "pure."
An imagination such as Mallarmé's will not create a paradise of
calm sensual presences, beautiful shapes and colors; it will de-
create appearances, bring death to forestall death, thus master
death, and save from decay a "pure" world in the mind:

> Oui, dans une île que l'air charge
> De vue et non de visions
> Toute fleur s'étalait plus large
> Sans que nous en devisions.
>
> Telles, immenses, que chacune
> Ordinairement se para
> D'un lucide contour, lacune,
> Qui des jardins la sépara.
>
> Gloire du long désir, Idées . . . .[55]

Stevens, who quoted the last line while prefacing a Valéryan
dialogue, could not have recognized this paradise as native ground.
For Mallarmé's paradise of perception is a mental island outside
nature. A clear outline separates it from earthly gardens. Purity
means schism. Divorce, not marriage, is the law of the poet's
hygienic vision.

To Stevens, on the contrary, transparence brought participation. His comments on the Impressionists bespoke his delight that
their art removed a barrier between him and nature.[56] The main
notion conveyed, sixteen times out of nineteen occurrences, by his
use of the word "pure," is a cleansing of the verbal medium.
Reality is pure. The Adamic tradition does not accept the sense
of a Fall. Then purity results from clearing sight of its "man-
locked set" of religious ideas and mythological metaphors. The
object is not made pure by the artist's eye, it is cleansed by it,
until "The poem refreshes life so that we share, / For a moment,
the first idea . . . ."[57] The terms in which Stevens speaks of pure
reality are unequivocally the language of romantic participation.
His "first idea" is not at all Mallarmé's Platonic *Idée*. He explained it in terms of pictorial visibility:

---

[55] *Ibid.*, p. 56.

[56] " I share your pleasure in the Impressionistic school. In the pictures of this school:
so light in tone, so bright in color, one is not conscious of the medium. The pictures
are like nature. . . ." Letter to Mlle. Paule Vidal, Jan. 30, 1948. I am grateful
to Mrs. Holly Stevens Stephenson for permission to quote from the letters of Wallace
Stevens.

[57] *Collected Poems*, p. 382.

Someone here wrote me the other day and wanted to know what I meant by a thinker of the first idea. If you take the varnish and dirt of generations off a picture, you see it in its first idea. If you think about the world without its varnish and dirt, you are a thinker of the first idea.[58]

The linguistic equivalent of such a cleaning-up (which, incidentally, makes man a god [59]) takes place in many poems in which Stevens, instead of Poe, gives a "purer" meaning to his nation's words; most clearly in "A Primitive like an Orb," where the words for tree and cloud and sky "lose the old uses" that men made of them. Would not the poet luxuriate in the joy of a pure language: a language whose words might readily take the place of things, like the painter's brush strokes? He would then become as "clairvoyant" as an Impressionist, since his medium would lose its opacity, and he could release "Free knowledges, secreted until then." [60]

Both Stevens and Mallarmé wanted a necessary relation between words and things. But they differed in their way of coming to terms with the inescapable arbitrariness of language. In accord with his aesthetics of separation, Mallarmé sought to purify by cutting. He broke each word away from its wonted associations. Hence the fragmented sentence, in which each word, gemlike and pure, reflects the next unearthed jewel. Almost nothing of this divisive technique in Stevens' style: metaphors seem to generate one another instead of being juxtaposed forcibly by *folding* one word on top of another. Another contrast is vocabulary: while Mallarmé purified by sterilizing (two thousand different words in all), Stevens freshened by renewing (most words are used only once or twice in any collection of his poems into books). Note how exact Stevens' terminology was when he said "the poem refreshes life"—not the world, "so that we share the first idea"—not pure "azur." Since all we want is a new *sense* of things, renewing the words will do. The Impressionist impulse goes toward the transparence of the medium, and eschews the issue of absolutes. Stevens takes "pure poetry" to mean poetry written "because one grows tired . . . of one's imagination." [61] Or in another wording: "Poetry constantly requires a new relation." [62]

Even more than Mallarmé, Stevens is the poet of nakedness.

[58] Letter to Henry Church, Oct. 28, 1942.
[59] See Pearce, *The Continuity of American Poetry*, p. 419.
[60] *Collected Poems*, p. 441.   [61] *Opus Posthumous*, p. 221.   [62] *Ibid.*, p. 178.

By "more" is meant both quality and quantity. Relatively to the prose of his time, Mallarmé's high proportion (*nu* and *nudité* used twenty times) defines "nu" as a key-word.[63] Terms like "bare," "bareness," "nude," "nudity," "naked," "nakedness" recur in all ninety times in Stevens' *Collected Poems* alone. More significant are the imaginary structures that actually make these words "key-words" and that differentiate Stevens' poetic world from Mallarmé's.

Mallarmé's imaginary space, that is the space generated by his imagery in the reader's mind, is characterized by partitions, dividing surfaces, which are at the same time transparent and forbidding. One of these images recurs with connotations of beauty and death: it is the mirror. It reveals nakedness but also locks it out of reach:

> Elle, défunte nue en le miroir, encor
> Que, dans l'oubli fermé par le cadre, se fixe
> De scintillations sitôt le septuor.[64]

Charles Mauron psychonanalyzed this image of the poet's dead sister or mother, as a source of guilt and desire. Not only the mirror, but the cenotaph slab is imagined as translucid and as a means of keeping a distance between the self and the naked body. But whether or not the Freudians are right, whether or not they can add a third dead woman to Mallarmé's private morgue,[65] does not matter to us, as readers, although Stevens was aware of Mauron's theory. What matters is the impossibility of crossing the dividing surface, or the punishment which attends its crossing. Mallarmé conceived this act as his aesthetic and metaphysical achievement: "It is now two years since I committed the sin of seeing the Dream in its ideal nakedness, whilst I ought to have heaped between it and me a mystery of music and forgetting," [66] he writes to a friend while at work on *Hérodiade*. Direct sight of nakedness is to Mallarmé both a goal and a taboo.

Mallarmé cogently placed nakedness on the other side of a partition which the poetic act must penetrate. Nakedness is akin to a metaphysical rebirth. The terms "naïf" or "natif"

---

[63] P. Guiraud, *Index du Vocabulaire du Symbolisme*, III (Paris, 1953).

[64] Mallarmé, *Oeuvres Complètes*, p. 69.

[65] Cf. L. Cellier, *Mallarmé et la Morte Qui Parle* (Paris, 1959).

[66] Cited by R. Champigny, "Mallarmé's Relation to Platonism and Romanticism," *Modern Language Review*, July, 1956, p. 356.

associate with nudity. But it is an impossible rebirth. The most misunderstood instance of this theme is perhaps " Le Pitre Châtié." We must ignore the early version produced by Dr. Bonniot, and which may indeed address Marie Gerhard's eyes. The new poem introduces the theme of " Les Fenêtres," the break-through:

> J'ai troué dans le mur de toile une fenêtre.
>
> *   *   *
>
> Tout à coup le soleil frappe la nudité
> Qui pure s'exhala de ma fraîcheur de nacre.[67]

Once through the wall, the clown falls, finds both purification and a " thousand tombs," innocence and the dead sister (Ophelia, objectifying the good Hamlet),[68] but the forbidden water of the lake-mirror dissolves the film of make-up which was his " whole art." His skin has lost the purity of youthful innocence, and its nudity is left exposed to the sun's punishment. The 1884 version of " Le Pitre Châtié " tells almost the reverse of the first version: not that the love of a woman distracts the artist from his art, but that the quest for an ideal nakedness has failed. The attempt to replace the relationship with words (which are, like soot, a grimy make-up of ideality) by a relationship of naked, undistanced, unmediated vision, was an ontological impossibility. With this poem, the polarity of the veiled and the naked completes a striking image of the Symbolist poet. *Qua littérateur*, he praises make-up.[69] But *qua* poetic hero, he yearns for a virginal nudity, with its imagery of frozen lakes and immobilized swans bringing him death and sterility. Indeed, we can see how the nakedness of the poet, symbolizing linguistic *askesis*, is a strange and terrible metaphor. It makes aesthetics similar to a glacier both transparent and denying transparence to the poet it will eventually paralyze.

There is a third image: the poet as *voyeur*. J.-P. Richard shows

[67] Mallarmé, *Oeuvres Complètes*, p. 31.

[68] " Reniant le Mauvais Hamlet " should be construed with reference to Mallarmé's notion that Hamlet was in fact divided into a bad Hamlet and a good one impersonated by Ophelia " the virgin objectified youth of the lamentable royal heir." (Mallarmé, " Hamlet," *Oeuvres Complètes*, p. 302.)

[69] He even sells it in his fashion magazine, *La Dernière Mode*. As the promoter of cold-cream, Mallarmé is the subject of a brilliant analysis by J.-P. Richard, *L'Univers Imaginaire de Mallarmé* (Paris, 1961), pp. 91-93. Also cf. this telling passage, " Je lisais donc un de ces chers poèmes (dont les plaques de fard ont plus de charme pour moi que l'incarnat de la jeunesse)." Mallarmé, *Divagations*, p. 24.

its relevance. For beside cold nudity, Mallarmé knows summer desire. Beside the Virgin Muse live the nymphs of "L'Après-midi d'un Faune" and the heroines of *Contes Indiens*. Stevens (whose Harvard friend Walter Arensberg translated "L'Après-midi d'un Faune" in his book *Idols*) was at first more attentive to nudity as such than as aesthetic symbol. Indeed the Voyant-Voyeur relationship links Stevens with Mallarmé. One cannot read "Apostrophe to Vincentine" without recalling the beautiful vowel and color contrasts of Hérodiade's "native unveiling" ("De mes robes, arôme aux farouches délices / Sortirait le frisson blanc de ma nudité"),[70] and W. Y. Tindall rightly affiliates "The Virgin Carrying a Lantern" to "Une Négresse par le Démon Secouée."[71] Other poems in the voyeuristic manner of Mallarmé are "Cy Est Pourtraicte, Madame Ste Ursule, et Les Unze Mille Vierges" and of course "Peter Quince at the Clavier."

If *Harmonium* is largely a book of nudes and beautiful barenesses, *Ideas of Order* the book of a bare, unpoetic reality, *Parts of a World* can be called the book of heroic nakedness. The distribution of the terms "nude," "bare," and "naked"—a distinction unavailable in French—grows with the use of the words "abstraction," "purity," and "nothingness."[72] The statistics of this development show that the influence of Mallarmé came late; that without doubt the habit of using the words "naked" and "nakedness" with their crucial aesthetic or epistemological mean-

[70] Mallarmé, *Oeuvres Complètes*, p. 47.
[71] *Wallace Stevens*, p. 18.

[72]
	Nude	Bare	Naked	Pure	Nothingness	Abstraction
Harmonium	5	10	8	3	2	0
Ideas of Order	2	7	3	0	4	0
Blue Guitar	0	1	1	0	0	2
Owl's Clover	0	1	0	0	0	0
Parts of a World	1	2	16	5	1	6
Transport to Summer	2	5	9	7	6	8
Auroras of Autumn	0	7	8	4	6	4
The Rock	0	0	2	0	2	1

Nude and nudity, bare, bareness, and barenesses, naked and nakedness, pure and purity, abstract and abstraction were lumped together.

Grateful acknowledgments are hereby given to Professor Thomas Kurtz and Mr. Thomas Martin, of the Dartmouth Computing Center, and to the Research Committee of Dartmouth College for making this word-count possible.

The high proportion of words denoting nakedness (90 in all out of a total of about 83,000 words) is to be noticed relatively to the absence of these words in Dewey's 1923 count of 100,000 words. This differential is what makes them key-words according to Guiraud's definition (in *Index du Vocabulaire du Symbolisme*, III).

ings parallels the Mallarméan practice. What statistics do not show is that Stevens' definition of nakedness contradicts the French "nudité." Stevens' bare jar, "like nothing else in Tennessee," bore even less resemblance (except as poetic artifact) to Mallarmé's "pur vase d'aucun breuvage."

The fourth section of "Peter Quince at the Clavier" already implies that the peeping-Tom's perception of beauty was incomplete:

> Beauty is momentary in the mind—
> The fitful tracing of a portal;
> But in the flesh it is immortal.

This is impressionism triumphant. Appearance is all. The elders' *red* eyes see through their desire, in the mind. This kind of music will escape, fitful, momentary, because it is a subjective feeling ("music is feeling . . . not sound").[73] Permanent beauty is not a Mallarméan or neo-platonic Idea, but the revelation of an actual presence among us, on earth. In the teeth of Platonism and docetism, Stevens affirms what Robert Pack and Amos Wilder call the mystery of incarnation. The essence of things depends on their perishable existence. Such appears to be the difficult, modern, meaning of Susanna's legend. Stevens insists on nudity as essence revealed by existence:

NUDITY AT THE CAPITAL

> But nakedness, woolen massa, concerns an innermost atom.
> If that remains concealed, what does the bottom matter?

This defines nakedness as a quality at the center (the capital) of being, and not as something on the other side of a glass wall, like Mallarmé's "nudité idéale."

Nakedness at the center: the image links Stevens' private geometry with his mode of perception. It is a recurrent image, a key-image, important for the understanding of *Ideas of Order*, "The Man with the Blue Guitar," and *Parts of a World*. The search for centrality and for nakedness is a single movement, the ascensional movement of a human hero. Stevens' symbols have extraordinary power because of their very ordinariness: blue air, the mountain top, the giant, the circle, and the center. Majesty, clairvoyance, and nakedness coalesce. What we might call " Hoon's

[73] *Collected Poems*, p. 90.

complex" unifies the "high imagination" in which Stevens now sings triumphantly.

It is an old atomistic imagining that looking is actually like breathing, one that Lucretius accredited by calling things thus seen "spirantia." The transaction between the eye and the center of nakedness, by an odd parallel, often strikes Stevens as an exchange like breath:

> And *naked* of any illusion, in poverty,
> In the exactest poverty, if then
> One *breathed* the cold evening, the deepest inhalation
> Would come from that return to the subtle centre.[74]

This synesthesia makes the reader more conscious of the Romantic "communion" of the eye, Stevens' phrase in the same poem. It is, as an image, worth ten pages of aesthetic theory. For instance, it rejects Mallarmé's asceticism, much as Rémy de Gourmont did.[75] Purity is not something reaching out of the artist's eye at will. It is breathed in. Perception is participation, an organic relationship between the circle of appearances and the center of the self:

> . . . Breathe, breathe upon the centre of
> The breath life's latest, thousand senses.
> But let this one sense be the single main.[76]

Stevens' poetry is central in the sense that Nietzsche's poetry is central, that is, centered on the self. Its climate differs from the Symbolist descent into a dark room. It is real air, breathed on an imaginary or real mountain: a Mount Penn, or a Mount Chocorua, or a Mountain in Vermont,[77] or even Nietzsche's Alps.[78] The air breathed at the top gives all its values to the hero. It

---

[74] *Ibid.*, p. 258.

[75] See Glenn S. Burne's excellent summary of post-Mallarméan aesthetics, *Rémy de Gourmont* (Carbondale, Ill., 1963); "Indeed, Gourmont reversed the order of causality established by other Symbolists and asserted that it is not the will which places the artist in the center of a network of stimuli . . . sensation is the principal condition of creation," p. 49.

[76] *Collected Poems*, p. 264.

[77] See "Late Hymn from the Myrrh-Mountain," *ibid.*, p. 349.

"Chocorua to its Neighbor," p. 296.

"The Man with the Blue Guitar," p. 176.

"Three Travelers Watch a Sunrise," *Opus Posthumous*, p. 127.

"July Mountain," *ibid.*, p. 114.

[78] "The pensive man . . . He sees that eagle float
For which the intricate Alps are a single nest."
Collected Poems, p. 216.

makes him purer, larger, more central. In fact the *air makes* the hero, thus dilated to the limits of the universe, and at the same time concentrated:

> He was a shell of dark blue glass, or ice,
> Or air collected in a deep essay,
>
> *   *   *
>
> Upon my top he breathed the pointed dark.
>
> *   *   *
>
> The air changes, creates, and re-creates, like strength,
> And to breathe is a fulfilling of desire,
> A clearing, a detecting, a completing,
> A largeness lived and not conceived, a space
> That is an instant nature, brilliantly.[79]

As poet of air, Stevens differs from Baudelaire and Mallarmé. Their dream of metamorphosis into a "glorious body" seeks an escape from cosmic law. Baudelaire stops at petrification; Mallarmé conquers the freedom of nothingness beyond "L'insensibilité de l'azur et des pierres."[80] Because of a basic coalition of sight, breath, and touch in his perception, Stevens imagines his metamorphosis into a non-body as an increase of body-senses:

> To change nature, not merely to change ideas,
> To escape from the body, so to feel
> Those feelings that the body balks,
> The feelings of the natures round us here:
> As a boat feels when it cuts blue water.[81]

The joy of the hero is that sensual nakedness of the keel, that contact with elements, that immediate feel of reality touched, seen, breathed in like air or like water, "instant nature," brilliant, cleared, "lived and not conceived." It is the joy of being both on the horizon of the multiplied aspects of reality and at the naked center. Or rather nakedness is that quality of the object and of man which abolishes the irradiating distance between the circle and the center.

"The natures round us here": this alone establishes Stevens' originality. His movement from plural to singular goes from circle to center. And this figure is not the critic's device, but a structure of Stevens' imagination as well as a constant tenet of his aesthetics. From Crispin's idea that his soil is man's intelligence,

---

[79] *Ibid.*, pp. 297-301.   [80] "Tristesse d'Été."   [81] *Collected Poems*, p. 234.

to the notion that the "central man," the man of glass, "is the transparence of the place in which / He is," [82] it is evident that the centripetal structure develops. In contrast, the centrifugal moments are few: perhaps the concentric domination of man spreading a perimeter of order in the chaos of forms ("Anecdote of the Jar") or the mastery of song fixing zones and poles of light ("Idea of Order at Key West"), or the mad captain's take-over of the world by an ever-widening circle of the will ("Life on a Battleship"). Stevens' preferred figure of transcendance, on the contrary, is in the wording of the last poem, "to be / Merely the center of a circle." The restrictive adverb means, in its con-text, that man must return to the earth stripped of its myths, to the earth of "Sunday Morning." The centripetal imagination of Stevens moves toward a pure center where it will find peace.

What is that center: a man of glass, an essential poem, a giant of nothingness, a supreme fiction? The multiplicity of names might suggest divinity! And an unpublished letter from the poet to the keen critic of his metamorphoses might strengthen that impression:

... I do not want to turn to stone under your very eyes by saying "This is the centre that I seek and this alm." Your mind is too much like my own for it to seem an evasion on my part to say merely that I do seek a centre and expect to go on seeking it. I don't say that I shall not find it as that I do not expect to find it. It is the great necessity even without specific identification.[83]

This program for poetry differs from a mysticism. It is the quest not for a god, but for a man; not for an ideal perfection, but for reality. It also differs from Baudelaire's attempted identification with the infinite sphere and the infinite center of the Divinity, from his "vaporisation et concentration du moi." It differs again from Mallarmé's immobilization at the center of a circle of noth-ingness.[84] The metaphors of concealment and divestment help us to understand Stevens' difficuty: that center which he seeks is both reality and a self. It tends to naked reality through a cen-tripetal movement. For things reveal their essence as a sum of profiles. Stevens' ascetic look resembles the phenomenologist's *epoché* much more than it does the Symbolist's *askesis*:

---

[82] *Ibid.*, p. 250.
[83] Letter to Sister Bernetta, Apr. 7, 1949.
[84] Cf. Poulet, *Les Métamorphoses du Cercle* (Paris, 1961), p. 449.

>   . . . We seek
> The poem of pure reality, untouched
> By trope or deviation, straight to the word,
> Straight to the transfixing object, to the object
>
> At the exactest point at which it is itself,
> Transfixing by being purely what it is,
> A view of New Haven, say, through a certain eye,
>
> The eye made clear of uncertainty, with the sight
> Of simple seeing, without reflection. We seek
> Nothing beyond reality. Within it,
>
> Everything . . . .[85]

The "transfixing object" is a residue, at a "center of resemblance," like the pineapple "reduced" from the "sum of its complications": it is an image of convergence to a center.[86] Our imperfections, as Stevens calls our successive views of reality (Husserl's *Abschattungen*) form a circle of shapes, colors, metaphors. Keeping this world on the move will guarantee the fixity of its center: "It Must Change," so that the perceptive self may be evolved. The pure object reveals the pure self, or should; the naked thing mirrors a naked man, or should. Such are the abstract terms of the exchange. Stevens' poetry produces poems like "An Ordinary Evening in New Haven" out of a faith: the faith that the imagination can or should try to apprehend reality, and in so doing, apprehends itself. This view, offered as conclusion, can serve to distinguish on one side the dualistic imagination of Mallarmé and Valéry, issuing the same hyperbolic doubt of reality as Descartes' Cogito, and on the other side the Romantic imagination culminating in Husserl's Cogito:

The flux of living, my flux, as thinking subject, can be largely unapprehended, unknown to any extent of its past or future, it is enough to look at life in flux and actually present, for me to say, without any restriction and of necessity: *I am*, this life is, I live: *cogito*.[87]

---

[85] *Collected Poems*, p. 471.

[86] *The Necessary Angel* (New York, 1951), pp. 83-89.

[87] Edmund Husserl, *Ideen zu einer reinen Phänomenologie und phänomenologischen Philosophie*, I (The Hague, 1950), p. 85. That Stevens was attracted to phenomenology is quite certain. In a "Collect of Philosophy" *Opus Posthumous*, p. 194, he mentions a letter from Jean Wahl about Husserl's *Meditations Cartésiennes*, about Pascal's image of the infinite sphere and finally about Traherne's poetry. Incidentally, Traherne's circular imagery was recently treated in an article of *Etudes Anglaises*, Vol. 14-2, Apr.-June, 1961, by Jean Wahl.

But Stevens' final yes, born of a transparence turned to philosophic glass, was already present in the imaginative matrix of *Harmonium*.[88]

APPENDIX

An unexpected relationship exists between the distribution of words most repeated in *Harmonium* and the structures of the imaginary world based solely on the effect of symbolism on the reader. The sheer weight of words (their frequency) is after all responsible in part for the impression created by their association. A symbolistic-lexical table of the words of *Harmonium* is attempted below. The figures denote frequency. Feminine ♀ and masculine ♂ are clearly in a balance wholly favorable to the feminine archetype.

[88] There is no room left in this essay for the third large structure of Stevens' imagination, the cycle pattern. An approach to the subject will be found in my tentative study of Stevens' rehabilitation of the fecund woman, in *Dartmouth College Library Bulletin*, Dec., 1961, pp. 60-66.

	♀ (col 1)	♀ (col 2)	♀ (col 3)	Heaven 29	♂ (col 1)	♂ (col 2)
METAPHYSICS					Man 54	
					human 11	
				♀		♂
UP					Sun 30	Day 15
						think 36
						know 18
THOUGHT					Mind 12	clear 17
	Body 15					
SENSES	Color 11	green 43			eye 22	blue 28
		black 14				white 21
		dark 14				gold 20
		purple 14				
		ear 7				
	Music 20	wind 41				
		sound 17				
		voice 7	hymn 9			
		poem 7				
		speech 7				
		speak 7	bloom 23			
		grow 13	leaves 21			
			fruit 17	make 48		
ARCHETYPE	Earth 16		palm 10		air 14	
	nature 8		tree 9			
						frost 8
		Summer 18			Winter 5	snow 12
						north 7
	Sea 44					
	water 18	dew 5				
	mother 14	woman 10				
DOWN	Moon 44					
		darkness 25	light 18			
	Night 40		shadow 13			
	Dream 24					
		fall 24	Death 12			
	Sleep 17		dead 10			

VI

WALLACE STEVENS:

THE LAST LESSON OF THE MASTER

BY ROY HARVEY PEARCE

1

Accepting the National Book Award in 1955 (for his *Collected Poems*), Wallace Stevens said:

> Now, at seventy-five, as I look back on the little that I have done and as I turn the pages of my own poems gathered together in a single volume, I have no choice except to paraphrase the old verse that says that it is not what I am, but what I aspired to be that comforts me. It is not what I have written but what I should like to have written that constitutes my true poems, the uncollected poems which I have not had the strength to realize.

These words proclaim not only Stevens' imperious modesty, but the central being and import of his works: that, as in its totality it forever projected an "ultimate poem," the ground of all poetry, the assured existence of the *possibility* of poetry, it was the work "of the mind in the act of finding / What will suffice." The lines I quote are from "Of Modern Poetry," which is followed almost immediately in the *Collected Poems* by "The Well Dressed Man with a Beard," whose last line is "It can never be satisfied, the mind, never." Both poems were first collected in *Parts of a World* (1942), which is in Stevens' work a kind of resting-place and occasion for self-assessment. In the collections which came after, beginning the *Transport to Summer* (1947), Stevens moved into regions whose rarified ambiance was yet vigorous enough to sustain the spirit of the man who to his dying days appears to have insisted (the words are from his *Adagia*) that "God is a postulate of the ego."

His later work in the main records the quest of one whose reality principle was so capacious that, through the labors of the mind, it could be made to yield the very means by which it might be transcended, then enlarged—its fullest capacity at long last revealed. (The end of the process was that which Stevens came to

121

call "abstraction "; the method, that which he came to call " decreation.") It had to be not the product of instinct but the cause,
indeed not a principle but a kind of sublime therapeutic agent
(Stevens would come to say " cure ") whereby the limitations
that it marked out might be broken through. Again and again
in his later poetry Stevens sought to fix once and for all the
instant of the breaking-through. In " The Novel " (collected in
The Auroras of Autumn) a man sits before a fire and reads. The
novel he is reading takes hold of him and his little world and
transforms them from the merely real to the vitally unreal, the
sheer life, in which they have their source. " The fire burns as the
novel taught it how." Note: not " *as if* the novel taught it how ";
for in its art the novel directly renders appearance into reality and
so forces upon the reader the knowledge that the unreal is in the
end the real:

> The arrangement of the chairs is so and so,
>
> Not as one would have arranged them for oneself,
> But in the style of the novel, its tracing
> Of an unfamiliar in the familiar room,
>
> A *retrato* that is strong because it is like,
> A second that grows first, a black unreal
> In which a real lies hidden and alive.

The reader is an Argentine; he is reading Camus, but might as
well be reading Cervantes. Still, as the poem does its work, the
little anecdote proves to be not about the Argentine but about
the poet and his reader:

> It is odd, too, how that Argentine is oneself,
> Feeling the fear that creeps beneath the wool,
> Lies on the breast and pierces into the heart,
>
> Straight from the Arcadian imagination,
> Its being beating heavily in the veins,
> Its knowledge cold within one as one's own;
>
> And one trembles to be so understood and, at last,
> To understand, as if to know became
> The fatality of seeing things to well.

Understanding oneself in poetry of this order, then, is to be
understood. In the working of the poem the dissatisfactions of

the poet's mind become the dissatisfactions of the reader's. Time
at best has not a stop but a pause. In its very form and function,
the poem is an instance of the reality principle working to achieve
its necessary ends as it is empowered by the imagination.

So far as I know, Stevens never uses Freud's term "reality principle." But surely in the poems before *Transport to Summer* and
The Auroras of Autumn that is what it is—a terribly bounded
assurance of what, in the nature of things, our limitations in
this world of rocks and stones and trees "really" are. Yet by
the time of "The Rock," the most powerful of the poems first
collected in his seventy-fifth year, the assurance had become un-
bounded, was felt to exist only as it might lead to a certitude
in unboundedness. Of the "rock" of reality Stevens could write
that man must no longer rest satisfied with knowing it mediately,
in poems:

> We must be cured of it by a cure of the ground
> Or a cure of ourselves, that is equal to a cure
>
> Of the ground, a cure beyond forgetfulness.

Wanting to know so much, wanting in one's knowledge to be so
much—this is a kind of disease, the only cure for which is more of
the same. It is wanting to have God's mind. It is being willing,
thereby, to be responsible for God's thoughts—which are "reality." In this Stevens, the propositions which emerge from "Notes
toward a Supreme Fiction" (1942) and "Esthétique du Mal"
(1945), both collected in *Transport to Summer*, are developed
in extremis. Man suffers as God suffers: so that he may, with God,
suffer the world to suffer.

If the "cure" is successful, if man can will its success, "reality"
—the sad, gay, infinitely fragmented world of which man is a
part—will surely turn out to be a kind of mind, the kind which
Stevens most often called "imagination." Then the world, the
"real" world, which the act of the mind has rendered into poems
and so fragmented, would, if the process were pushed far enough,
finally be made whole once more. But it would be the mind's
world. God would be of His earth, the earth would be of its God,
and all would be right with the world. Because it would be the
mind's world. Of this ultimately "real" world, Stevens wrote at
the end of "The Rock":

> It is the rock where tranquil must adduce
> Its tranquil self, the main of things, the mind
>
> The starting point of the human and the end,
> That in which space itself is contained, the gate
> To the enclosure, day, the things illumined
>
> By day, night and that which night illumines,
> Night and its midnight-minting fragrances,
> Night's hymn of the rock, as in a vivid sleep.

The mind, then, would be satisfied—but only in a world like the one in this poem, where the thing contained has become the container; only in a sleep vivid enough to be the sleep of revelation; only, in the title of another late poem, when man can know himself as "A Child Asleep in Its Own Life." God is a revelation of the ego, because reality is.

There remained, however, life day-to-day—with the never-to-be-satisfied mind seeing and knowing reality so sharply as to know itself absolutely cut off from what it sees and knows. Day-to-day, indeed, one might have his proper doubts about the vivid sleep and its night hymn to the power of the mind. Thus Stevens put at the end of his *Collected Poems,* six pages after the ultimate affirmation of "The Rock," this poem, called "Not Ideas about the Thing but the Thing Itself." Note: Not even "thing-*in*-itself," but "thing itself."

> At the earliest ending of winter,
> In March, a scrawny cry from outside
> Seemed like a sound in his mind.
>
> He knew that he heard it,
> A bird's cry, at daylight or before,
> In the early March wind.
>
> The sun was rising at six,
> No longer a battered panache above snow . . .
> It would have been outside.
>
> It was not from the vast ventriloquism
> Of sleep's faded papier-mâché . . .
> The sun was coming from outside.
>
> That scrawny cry—it was
> A chorister whose c preceded the choir.
> It was part of the colossal sun,
>
> Surrounded by its choral rings,
> Still far away. It was like
> A new knowledge of reality.

Here the poet figures himself as being waked by a sound, and then gradually figures that sound—coming at the end of winter, out of the hard, bright morning—as being part of a reality which is absolutely "outside" him. The reward is something "like a new knowledge of reality," as bird and sun are discovered to be colossally present. The cost is the acknowledgment that it is all "far away," "outside." Here the effect of the poet's imaging is to see that, if the image is true to the reality which it bodies forth, it is not the poet's image but its own. The "Seemed" in "Seemed like a sound in his mind" is, as the poem moves, the first, most facile, therefore most mistaken, attempt of the poet to satisfy his mind. But once the mind begins its act, it acts to dissatisfy itself, so as far as it can to be true to the reality of that bright early spring morning. Even so, it cannot be entirely true to that reality. Its mediating presence is registered quite minimally, by that "like" in the next-to-last line. Inside the mind the cry is "scrawny." Outside, it *is*—not is *of*—"A chorister whose c preceded the choir." (The repetition of " *c* "-" pre*c*eded " makes for a kind of pun in which subject is incorporated into verb, all the more to identify it in its absoluteness.) The terrible knowledge earned here is, in the words of one of the *Adagia*, that "What reality lacks is a *noeud vital* with life." The poet's *noeud vital*, which is with himself, at least lets him be the first to face this as a fact.

And, thinking back to "The Rock," we may ask: Did "Night's hymn of the rock" also issue "from the vast ventriloquism / Of sleep's faded papier-mâché . . ."? No. But then "The Rock" is an old man's poem. The first section is called "*Seventy Years Later*" and begins by questioning the kind and range of certitude which are celebrated in "Not Ideas . . .":

> It is an illusion that we were ever alive,
> Lived in the houses of mothers, arranged ourselves
> By our own motions in a freedom of air.
>
> Regard the freedom of seventy years ago,
> It is no longer air. The houses still stand,
> Though they are rigid in rigid emptiness.
>
> Even our shadows, their shadows, no longer remain.
> The lives these lived in the mind are at an end.
> They never were . . . The sounds of the guitar
>
> Were not and are not. Absurd. The words spoken
> Were not and are not.

Of course, "Not Ideas . . ." is an old man's poem too. But it is not a matter of chronology; for there is no proper sense of history in Stevens' conception of the poet's work. ("All history is modern history," he wrote in the *Adagia*, and meant it.) Instead there is, especially in the later work, a sense of a pure, a-temporal dialectical movement, a fateful opting for one of a pair of radically opposed alternatives. And so in "Not Ideas . . ." sounds like those of Stevens' blue guitar "are" again, as in "The Rock" they "are not."

I have cited "The Rock" and "Not Ideas . . ." because Stevens placed them in the *Collected Poems* where they would mark the extreme, dialectically opposed tendencies in his work—tendencies which, as we shall see, he began to resolve only at the very end of his life in a handful of poems in the *Opus Posthumous*. His later poems (I mean those from the *Transport to Summer* collection through "The Rock" and "Not Ideas . . .") characteristically begin by showing us how we may catch ourselves in the act of reaching out toward some segment of reality—a place, a person, anything that is an "other" and therefore may seem to be merely an "object." The goal is that knowledge in whose perfection we may rest secure. As the poems develop, we are made to realize that what we do in fact know is not a segment of reality but ourselves in the act of reaching out. A segment then is the result of segmenting; reaching out is grasping and seizing upon, shaping. At this point, the poems may move toward one of two ends: toward celebrating the power of the subject, the mind which not only wills but makes its knowledge; or toward celebrating the givenness of the object, the reality which is unchanging and unchangeable, perdurably out there.

Moving toward the first end, the poems stop short and turn back upon themselves. Moving toward the second end, the poems strive to strike against what ultimately must be discovered to be (by virtue of the very act of striving) the blank wall of reality. The utopian alternatives are pure introspection and pure abstraction—knowledge of pure act as against knowledge of pure substance. In the one mode, we would know ourselves as knowing; in the other, we would know the "object" so completely that we would not be aware of ourselves as knowing. The radical disjunction is, as I have said, between act and substance, and marks the extreme development of Stevens' abiding concern with the relationship between "imagination" and "reality." Neither mode is altogether possible for us—since we have not the power to conceive of abstracting (to use Stevens' word) knowing from the known, or the known from knowing. But, at this stage of his work, Stevens was convinced that by the same token at any given time, in any given poem, the two modes could never adequately co-exist, except perhaps in theory, or in what he called the "ultimate poem." And for him theory—at least so far as poetry was concerned—involved an abuse of the power of abstract thinking, and the ultimate poem would necessarily be characterized by a kind of never-to-be-attained perfection by which are measured one's actual attainments. At most we are given, or give ourselves, intimations of subjectivity and of objectivity. And the task of poetry, thus its form and function, is somehow to transform intimations into convictions, to see the dilemma all the way through to an end triumphant in its very bitterness. This was, in words of "The Well Dressed Man with a Beard," the "final no." And it was the necessary condition for whatever "final yes" might be possible:

> . . . the yes of the realist spoken because he must
> Say yes, spoken because under every no
> Lay a passion for yes that had never been broken.
> ("Esthétique du Mal")

2

As philosophizing all this may well seem to be a naive treatment of the subject-object problem which is at the heart of Romantic poetry. For even non-philosophers expect something more than this from philosophical discourse. But it seems naive only on first glance—as it seems to be philosophizing only on first glance. Still, we must not be so timid as to refuse to take the first glance: to avoid the philosophy and to seek the poetry. For Stevens habitually began with a specifically philosophical problem and yet insisted on a specifically poetic solution for it. Indeed, in a late essay, "A Collect of Philosophy," he concluded that both philosopher and poet seek to "form concepts"—the "integration" of thought. "The philosopher," he said, "intends his integration to be fateful; the poet intends his to be effective." We may extend this to say that "effectiveness" implies that never-to-be-perfect sense of the complex denied to "fatefulness," which in turn implies the perfection of thought to the point where it is inevitable enough to seem simple. Thus it is of the essence of Stevens' later poetry that it explicate the simple in such a way that its complexity be totally revealed. (His philosophical counterpart—let us think of Wittgenstein—would explicate the complex in such a way that its simplicity be totally revealed.) "The poem," Stevens wrote in "Man Carrying Thing," "must resist the intelligence / Almost successfully." (His philosophical counterpart might well demand that the intelligence resist the poem almost successfully.)

Stevens concern for the subject-object problem is then continuous from that of his Romantic forebears. But for him, particularly in the poems from *Transport to Summer* through *The Rock* group, the solution of the problem is not to be authorized by any special poetic (imaginative, intuitive) access to myth or structure of symbolic correspondences. (This would be too "intelligent," too "philosophical.") If he must, he will say NO! in thunder. The poetic power has access only to itself; it controls only itself; its relation to the reality on which it is operative is that it "resists" (a word he uses in a critical essay)—and in resisting, shapes, and in shaping, seems to control. Surely, at times Stevens hoped for more than this. Explaining some lines in "The Man with the Blue Guitar," he wrote to his Italian translator: "Nature is a monster . . . which I desire to reduce: master, subjugate, acquire complete control over and use freely for my own purposes as a poet. I want, as a poet, to be that in nature which constitutes nature's very self." He would be "natural." His poetry after "The Man with the Blue Guitar," however, betrays his wishes. For in discovering his "naturalness," he cuts himself off from the substantial and contingent things which make up the rest of nature. Reducing, subjugating, controlling, he can never know. Or rather, he can know that there is a reality whose complexity of existence he cannot know, yet a reality which in his very ignorance he can acknowledge as existing, if only as something so "abstract" that he can say of it no more than that in its self-sufficiency (a counterpart of his own) it exists. He can bring himself to affirm that it will be his fate ever to say that "It can never be satisfied, the mind, never." He can say, "I am." Or he can say, "It is," even "You are." But he can never connect one proposition to the other with a "therefore."

Hence, philosophically speaking, the apparent naiveté. But again and again he remarked in effect that it is the philosopher's "therefore" which is naive, poetically speaking, as is the "therefore" of ordinary language. What happens in his most difficult, often most rewarding, poems of his penultimate period is that philosophy resists the poet almost successfully.

For in "The Man with the Blue Guitar" (1937), he had, even as he hoped against hope to resolve it, written of what he was ever more clearly to see as the poet's characteristic dilemma:

> I cannot bring a world quite round,
> Although I patch it as I can.
>
> I sing a hero's head, large eye,
> And bearded bronze, but not a man,
>
> Although I patch him as I can
> And reach through him almost to man.
>
> If to serenade almost to man
> Is to miss, by that, things as they are,
>
> Say that it is the serenade
> Of a man that plays a blue guitar.

Here the poem is remarked as a kind of inevitably necessary compromise between man and the world he knows. Strive to celebrate man, and you miss things as they are—as elsewhere in the poem what Stevens says amounts to: Strive to celebrate things as they are, and you miss man. "Man," of course, and "things as they are" are names for what Stevens most generally called mind (or imagination) and reality. And the record of his life's work is of a struggle to learn to do something more than "patch" as he could. The end of the struggle is recorded in "The Rock," "Not ideas . . .," and all the poems which surround them in *The Rock* section of the *Collected Poems*. What has happened is that the dialectical compromise, although it is still wished for, is no longer conceivable. The poet will do one thing or the other. He will celebrate mind or celebrate things themselves, be either the poet of night or the poet of day, an old man or a young man. He can, that is to say, take his position on either side of the dialectical movement which sets the rhythm of "creativity." He belongs to both sides of his universe, but never to both sides at once.

This is, I suggest, because in Stevens' deepest thought, his universe belonged too much to him. And the division was within him, so that he was not divided but dividing. The greatness of his poetry is a product of the greatness of his spirit, of a mind striving so terribly hard to perfect its knowledge of the world, to do something more than patch the reality it confronted day-to-day, that it never, until it was almost too late, found time to consider that it might well have first to perfect itself, and then see how the world looked. Then it might well discover that the world looked at it, even as it looked at the world. It would find its place, that is to say, in the middle of things, always in the middle of its dialectical journey. We can say this of Stevens, I suggest, because he finally said it of himself. The intelligence which his poetry resisted almost successfully was his own. And it was a great, honest intelligence.

> And one trembles to be so understood and, at last,
> To understand, as if to know became
> The fatality of seeing things too well.

3

At the very end of his life, Stevens seems to have had some suspicion that the world his mind had revealed to him, and likewise the kind of mind he had revealed to himself in the revealing, was not quite enough, because not true enough to the facts of the matter as in making poems he could discover them. Thus this poem, first published in 1956, the year after his death—"The Region November":

> It is hard to hear the north wind again,
> And watch the treetops, as they sway.
>
> They sway, deeply and loudly, in an effort,
> So much less than feeling, so much less than speech,
>
> Saying and saying, the way things say
> On the level of that which is not yet knowledge:
>
> A revelation not yet intended.
> It is like a critic of God, the world
>
> And human nature, pensively seated
> On the waste throne of his own wilderness.
>
> Deeplier, deeplier, loudlier, loudlier,
> The trees are swaying, swaying, swaying.

In all his profundity, Stevens had always to be ironic at his own expense. This, to paraphrase a notorious claim of his, is a gentle kind of violence which he employed to protect himself from the violence, the voracious violence, of his own mind. He finds that he is, like all of us, a "critic of God, the world / And human nature." The word "critic" supplies the irony which makes this bearable, especially as it helps us to bear the burden of "the waste throne of [our] own wilderness." This is, as they say, to supply a point of view. But what is seen? Something that is heard, or almost heard. The poem see-saws between "sway" and "say"—the movement of meter and sensibility being enforced by the outrageous adverbs, "deeplier" and "loudlier." The treetops are making an effort; and it is an effort which somehow the poet does not merely imagine. This is no matter of the pathetic fallacy, a too-muted version of "What are the wild waves saying?" For the poet cannot conceive of asking such a simple-mindedly overweening question. The effort of the treetops is "So much less than feeling, so much less than speech." Yet it proves a feeling and speech of some sort; and the poet can suppose that they "say / On the level of that which is not yet knowledge." "On the level of . . ." is "philosophic" diction, and so bids us think with this lyric, not sing mournfully with it. The "not yet intended" of the seventh line is in fact a bit of technical language out of Stevens' dabbling in phenomenology, in whose logic all revelations are nothing if not "intended." Now he decides that, spontaneously, without intention, to be is to say: to say what "It is hard to hear." In short, Stevens is claiming that if the treetops do "say," it is not in the language of any "speech." Thus he will not be caught imputing "humanity," much less "deity," to the treetops—both to be implicated in that "meaning" derivable from myth or a structure of symbolic correspondences. He will not let himself be trapped in the anthropocentricism, as often as not masked as theocentrism, of his "romantic" forebears and contemporaries. He will be a radical humanist to the end. But his humanism now forces him to acknowledge both the virtual life of the non-human and its virtual capacity to "say."

And anyhow: The poet has admitted at the outset that "It is hard to hear the north wind again"—after all those years, all those poems, when if nature did speak to the poet, it was in the end only his own voice coming back to him, as though from a synaesthetic mirror. The point is that the "critic of God, the world / And human nature" has at long last begun to understand what he has so long listened to. There are, it would seem, other kinds of saying than the poet's. And perhaps, just perhaps, he is beginning to wonder if there might not in the end prove to be a continuing dialogue between " mind " and " reality ": expressive of the ineluctable continuity between night and day, old man and young—between God, if He exists, and man.

One ventures to guess, because Stevens ventured to guess. And one wonders about those " true poems," which at the National Book Award dinner, he said he would " like to have written." I think that " The Region November " is one of them and that this, " As You Leave the Room " (1955), is another. (It is a doubly retrospective poem, being an enlargement of " First Warmth," written in 1947 and, because later enlarged upon, never intended for publication.)

> *You speak. You say*: Today's character is not
> A skeleton out of its cabinet. Nor am I.
>
> The poem about the pineapple, the one
> About the mind as never satisfied,
>
> The one about the credible hero, the one
> About summer, are not what skeletons think about.
>
> I wonder, have I lived a skeleton's life,
> As a disbeliever in reality,
>
> A countryman of all the bones in the world?
> Now, here, the snow I had forgotten becomes
>
> Part of a major reality, part of
> An appreciation of a reality
>
> And thus an elevation, as if I left
> With something I could touch, touch every way.
>
> And yet nothing has been changed except what is
> Unreal, as if nothing had been changed at all.

Now the poet can look at his own work and see that, even as it argued for the division between mind and reality, it manifested the poet's central involvement in both. He refers in turn to " Someone Puts a Pineapple Together " (1947), where he had seen it as the poet's categorical imperative " to defy / The metaphor that murders metaphor "; to " The Well Dressed Man with a Beard," cited above; to " Asides on the Oboe " (1940), " Examination of the Hero in a Time of War " (1942), and other related poems; and to " Credences of Summer " (1947), where he had put down his most concise statement as to the function of poetry:

> Three times the concentred self takes hold, three times
> The thrice concentred self, having possessed
>
> The object, grips it in savage scrutiny,
> Once to make captive, once to subjugate
> Or yield to subjugation, once to proclaim
> The meaning of the capture . . . .

"As You Leave the Room" is in effect a survey of Stevens' poetry during precisely that period when he began to push it into its most "philosophical" mode. It was in this period that he had begun to try to solve the problems of belief and commitment raised so variously and movingly in "Sunday Morning," "A High-Toned Old Christian Woman," "The Emperor of Ice-Cream," and the rest. From "Notes toward a Supreme Fiction" through the poems grouped in the *Collected Poems* under the title *The Rock* the solutions he achieved served only to make the problems more difficult. And, as I have tried to show in my notes on the title poem in *The Rock* group and on "Not Ideas . . ." (also included in that group), he had come to believe that the solution of the problem was that it was insoluble. Acknowledging the fact of the insolubility, the poet—as surrogate for Stevens' Common Reader, "the man of imagination" whom he saluted so often—might learn to rejoice in both his day- and his night-time powers, but alternatively. Yet now, as he leaves the (lecture?) room, it occurs to him that he is not the sort of "skeleton" that his critics have latterly made him out to be. (We ask: has he lectured? or been lectured upon?) He puts the question flatly: Has he been a "disbeliever in reality"?—or, one must add by way of recalling Stevens' thinking here, a disbeliever in the mind's capacity to relate directly to the "thing itself," therefore a believer only in mind, therefore a believer in the "unreal," therefore a disbeliever in reality? Again: No. The poet is certain: Somehow he has in fact accommodated the mind to reality, the unreal to the real. Even the snow (which, when it became a snowman, in the 1921 poem of that name, bodied forth nothingness, "uncreated" reality as against "pure" mind) has become an "appreciation" of reality. "Appreciation" is used with etymological exactness. The mind has *grown* by at once adding itself to, and being added to by, "major reality." Reality has been enlarged; and mind, for all its "unreality," has been changed. As has the poet. Now, in a kind of afterthought, he can claim that he has been at the center of things all along—as poet, not a divided but a whole man: or at least one capable of imagining himself as being at the center of his world and thereby being, in fact, potentially whole. The glance all the way back to "The Snow Man" makes this poem, for all its emphasis on the work of the forties, an exercise in retrospect become an exercise in redefinition.

The greatest victory in the poem is that Stevens, after a good number of stabbing attempts (see, for example, "The Motive for Metaphor" [1943]), can see himself not only as actually "I" but as possibly "you," and so find his place in the world. It is as though he were now beginning to conceive of the poem not as an "act of the mind" but as the "mind of an act" and to admit to himself—as a kind of "invention"—that "acts" are not all necessarily either of man or an imagined God, that "reality" is characterized by something resembling "mind." Perhaps what is involved is a form of panpsychism. If so, there was for Stevens not one but an infinite number of psyches. In any case, for the last Stevens the world of imagination and reality was not only alive and fragmented but in the very life of its fragmentation capable, when conceived of in poems, of being one.

Retrospection and redefinition on the whole characterize the poems which Stevens wrote in his last years. (There is no clearly chronological development here—just hard-won variations on a theme central to the last years. I date the poems only to place them thus.) Twice, surely in a recollection of Tennyson in the same mood, Stevens makes Ulysses his spokesman, calling him in the title of one of the poems "An External Master of Knowledge" (1954). (The other is "The Sail of Ulysses," a Phi Beta Kappa poem of the same year.) In the first-named poem Ulysses soliloquizes:

> "Here I feel the human loneliness
> And that, in space and solitude,
> Which knowledge is: the world and fate,
> The right within me and about me,
> Joined in a triumphant vigor,
> Like a direction on which I depend . . . ."

In "Conversation with Three Women of New England" (1954),

Stevens remarks three "modes" of understanding—what we can categorize as idealism, naturalism, and a kind of humanistic personalism; and he refuses to opt for any, imagining himself capable of comprehending them all, saying that it might be "enough to realize / That the sense of being changes as we talk, / That talk shifts the cycle of the scenes of kings." He is modest in "Local Objects" (1955):

> Little existed for him but the few things
> For which a fresh name always occurred, as if
> He wanted to make them, keep them from perishing,
>
> The few things, the objects of insight, the integrations
> Of feeling, the things that came of their own accord,
> Because he desired without knowing quite what . . . .

The key phrases in the poems from which I have just quoted are: "direction on which I depend"; "sense of being changes"; and "things that came of their own accord."

The feeling registered by the first two of these phrases is, of course, characteristic of Stevens' work almost from the beginning. But the feeling registered in the third is new; accordingly, the sense of direction and of being is surer, for it is no longer only his own direction and being which the poet can conceive of himself as possibly knowing. Whereas before he had known the other only by a kind of heroic inference (cf. the dialectic of "Notes toward a Supreme Fiction"), now he may know it directly as it is revealed to him. Thus in "Artificial Populations" (1954), he can go so far as to admit quite casually that "a state of mind" is no longer enough for him who would find his proper center:

> The center that he sought was a state of mind,
> Nothing more, like weather after it has cleared—
> Well, more than that, like weather when it has cleared
> And the two poles continue to maintain it
>
> And the Orient and Occident embrace
> To form that weather's appropriate people. . . .

We can read "weather" as a specifying, inclusive term for "ambiance"—or even "culture" or "world"; and then note that the "populations" which are formed by the "embrace" are "artificial" only as they are not the product of "pure" mind or "pure" reality—"Orient and Occident"—but the result of the conjoining of both, a conjoining in which the poet may take

part and then acknowledge and celebrate, but still one which he
by no means may bring about himself. There is a "making," that
is to say, beyond human will, but not beyond human understanding. Indeed, human understanding is, in necessary part, a product
of such making. Man must will himself toward such understanding—a condition of his situation as man. In his earlier poetry,
Stevens had hoped entirely on his own to manage such conjunc-
tions, thus such understanding; yet by the time of *The Rock*
group, he had despaired of the managing, and triumphed in the
honesty of his despair. Now he is sure of himself as he had
never been; for "This artificial population is like / A healing-
point in the sickness of the mind. . . ."

   The poet now watches and waits, as in "July Mountain"
(1955):

> We live in a constellation
> Of patches and of pitches,
> Not in a single world,
> In things said well in music,
> On the piano, and in speech,
> As in a page of poetry—
> Thinkers without final thoughts
> In an always incipient cosmos,
> The way, when we climb a mountain,
> Vermont throws itself together.

Again, retrospection and redefinition. "We live in a constellation
. . ." recalls "Sunday Morning": "We live in an old chaos of the
sun," "Patches and . . . pitches," and " single world " recall " The
Man with the Blue Guitar,": "I cannot bring a world quite round,
/ Although I patch it as I can." The fragmented sequence of
"music," "piano," "speech," and "poetry" recalls their intended
fusion in "Peter Quince at the Clavier." "Thinkers without final
thoughts" recalls the iterated motif of the never-to-be-satisfied
mind. "Always incipient cosmos" recalls the continuing emphasis
on change and process in the earlier poems. And then: "The way
. . . / Vermont throws itself together" recalls "Anecdote of the
Jar," in which whatever order given the Tennessee wilderness
derives from what Stevens came to call the "act of the mind."
The earlier observations are not so much contradicted as accommodated, each to the other. The poet in effect re-figures his role
as observer. Taken together, all that he may observe are so many

facts of life—not only his but their own. Again he finds a " heal-ing-point in the sickness of the mind."

4

"Poetry is a cure of the mind," wrote Stevens in one of the *Adagia*. His work through *The Rock* group constitutes, as I have maintained elsewhere, a magnificent series of attempts to work toward realizing the implications of this statement. That, as its implications are realized, the statement is proved wrong does not lessen the magnificence of his achievement. For it is given to the poet to do the right things for the wrong reason. We can ask only that the poems be right, right as poems—let the reasons be what they may. If the poems are right enough, in their right-ness they will eventually expose the wrongness of the reasons which inform them. If the reasons by chance are ours, then as we see them fully extended in poems, we shall see how wrong we have been. A means of measuring our wrongness is the rightness of the poetry which exposes it. For, as Stevens said in another note, "Poetry seeks out the relation of men to facts." There is an element of psychic distance here—or better, cultural distance—which often confuses not the issue but us. Our relation to some facts is such as to be beyond poetry's seeking out. *The Cantos* are in many places too strong medicine to work as art; but *The Merchant of Venice* is not. Likewise for some of his readers, Stevens' invention of " a cure of the mind " and the meditative and philosophical poetic modes it called forth were too strong medicine to work as art. Such readers were threatened at the very core of their being; and so they longed for more "Sunday Mornings," in which Stevens would assure them that they might yet be safely distanced, on the outside looking in. (They mistook mode for substance.) More fortunate readers, hoping that Stevens' reasons were perhaps the right ones, that poetry might indeed be a cure of the mind, were able to follow him ever inward, until, with him, they found themselves trapped on the inside looking out. (They were willing to be taken in by the mode, so to discover substance.) Outside there was something, and it was real. But the truest domain of man was on the inside, with the unreal—which proved to be the non-real, the imagination, the mind: at best, conscious-ness fully released; at worst, the power of sympathy with oneself.

For this self, at best or at worst, there was in the final analysis no time, no history, no living-in-the-world, except in imaginative acts which, when carried all the way, first transformed and then annulled time, history, and the world. The mind, the self, however, could maintain to the end its powers of postulation.

Thereby it might earn its salvation. For thereby it might imagine that whatever lay outside it was out there looking in, and then it might seek to verify this fact. "Swaying" might well be "saying," as the very act of making such poems might be an "appreciation of reality." "Poetry," Stevens wrote in another of the *Adagia,* "is health." And at the end as at the beginning he was seeking that health. The lesson of his life is surely that it could not come exclusively from "a cure of the mind." Yet it could not be a cure of something from which the mind was utterly cut off—reality, or "the thing itself," or even God. Moreover, were he to remain even minimally himself, man in his capacity as poet could not be derived from "things themselves"—or even from God. In the end, as I think these last poems show, for Stevens poetry must be expressive of a continuing dialogue between mind and reality. So far Stevens was able to go in his old age, and only so far. How much farther he would have gone, "what [he] should like to have written" (to recall a phrase from the speech I quoted at the beginning), we of course have no way of knowing. The trouble is—and it is always the trouble!—there are too few poems.

5

What would it be like for the mind to enter a dialogue with reality, the "thing itself"? It would be

> . . . hard to hear the north wind again,
> And to watch the treetops, as they sway.
>
> They sway, deeply and loudly, in an effort,
> So much less than feeling, so much less than speech,
>
> Saying and saying, the way things say
> On the level of that which is not yet knowledge:
>
> A revelation not yet intended.

At issue is the "appreciation" of reality. And, taken in the context of the continuity of Stevens' life's work, the inevitability of this last phase is such as to tempt us to believe that achieving it should somehow have been easier than in fact it was. We may, as are so many of our younger poets, look at the work of one of his Spanish contemporaries and say: But this is how it has always been! The " cure " has been with us, available to us, all the time! Seeking after the cure was itself a kind of disease—an unnecessary complication (to echo a phrase of Stevens') in the journey of the modern spirit as it seeks to find a home in its world! I think of Jorge Guillén's " Más Allá " (" Beyond "), in which there is fully realized the kind of perfected relationship of man and his world which in Stevens' last poems we can only catch a glimpse of. Some stanzas (from Parts I, II, and VI) read:

> Todo me comunica,
> Vencedor, hecho mundo,
> Su brío para ser
> De veras real, en triunfo.
>
> Soy, más, estoy. Respiro.
> Lo profundo es el aire.
> La realidad me inventa,
> Soy su leyenda; Salve!
>
> * * *
>
> No, no sueño. Vigor
> De creación concluye
> Su paráiso aqui . . .
>
> * * *
>
> Y con empuje henchido
> De afluencias amantes
> Se ahinca en el sagrado
> Presente perdurable
>
> Toda la creación,
> Que al despertarse un hombre
> Lanza la soledad
> A un tumulto de acordes.[1]

[1] In Stephen Gilman's literal rendering:

All communicates to me—the conqueror, transformed into the world, its elan for being truly real, triumphant.

I am, but even more, I am here, I breathe. What is profound is the air. Reality invents me: I am its legend. All hail!

*   *   *

No, I am not dreaming. Creation's vigor concludes its paradise here. . . .

*   *   *

And, its impetus swollen with loving tributaries, all creation fixes itself in the sacred everlasting present. For when a man wakes up, creation launches solitude into a tumult of harmonies. (*Cántico* [Buenos Aires, 1962], pp. 16-25.)

At most Stevens can do no more than discover the conditions which may make possible an affirmation such as this: of all-suffusing incorporeality. The poet in " Más Allá " wakes up not to something " like a new knowledge of realty," but to that " new knowledge " itself; and he is a necessary part of it. On principle, we may say, Stevens' journey toward this discovery should not have been so long or so difficult. But a poet in a world like ours travels not on principle but on fact. Indeed, he would discover the principle-generating, principle-incorporating facts of our lives (and his) in our culture. He can move only so fast and so surely as the facts of the case will let him. The facts of the case have, in the history of our culture, generated principles (of understanding, communication, relationship, community, identity . . .) which have, it seems, so far barred us from access to the world of " Más Allá "—even as in the bareness and purity of what they do offer us, they can be made (by a Stevens) to suggest that such a world must exist, because only in such a world might we be at long last truly at home. Those for whom a sense of the world of " Más Allá " comes from a struggle less difficult than Stevens' are fortunate—although I should guess that in truth the struggle is not less difficult, only different. I am insisting here only that Stevens' struggle, as his life's work outlines it, is, for well and for ill, an American struggle. Surely, his younger peers, of whatever literary persuasion, can more readily conceive of a world like that of " Más Allá " than he could. But this is to say no more than that they have somehow learned his last lesson—often better than they know.

6

" Whilst the world is a spectacle," Emerson wrote in " Nature," " something in [us] is stable "—and thus in good part set the American poet off on his phase of that romantic adventure which is the history of modern Western European thought. And he went on:

In a higher manner the poet communicates the same pleasure. By a few strokes he delineates, as on air, the sun, the mountain, the camp, the city, the hero, the maiden, not different from what we know them, but only lifted from the ground and afloat before the eye. He unfixes the land and the sea, makes them revolve around the axis of his primary thought, and disposes them anew. Possessed himself by a heroic passion, he uses matter as symbols of it.

. . . .

. . . the poet confirms things to his thoughts. . . . To him, the refractory world is ductile and flexible; he invests dust and stones with humanity, and makes them the words of the Reason. The Imagination may be defined to be the use which the Reason [i. e., Vernunft/ creative intuition] makes of the material world.

Stevens' version of this in the *Adagia* was: "The imagination is man's power over nature." His life-work was a monument to that "heroic passion"—only in him the passion was so heroic as to force him to deny that his "primary thought" partook, even transcendentally, of God's. If anything, he came to say God's primary thought was a product of his, a Supreme Fiction. A note in the *Adagia* reads:

The relation of art to life is of the first importance especially in a skeptical age since, in the absence of a belief in God, the mind turns to its own creations and examines them, not alone from the aesthetic point of view, but for what they reveal, for what they validate and invalidate, for the support that they give.

At the end, or almost at the end, as we have seen, the mind's sole creation was the mind, the revelation that its sole creation was itself. Outside there was yet the "thing itself." Man's power over nature was frustrated in its very exercise. We should recall again, but now exactly, Stevens' notorious "the mind . . . is a violence within which protects us from a violence without."

But another note in the *Adagia* reads:

Feed my lambs (on the bread of living) . . . the glory of god is the glory of the world . . . To find the spiritual in reality . . . To be concerned with reality.

The *Adagia* are, so Stevens' editor indicates, undatable. But most of them certainly belong to Stevens' later life. And as certainly they record not only his sense of what he had achieved but his attempt to reach beyond the limits which, in his achievement, he seemed so triumphantly to have set about himself in the poems through *The Rock*. There is in this *Adagia* note I have just quoted a hint of the concerns of the last poems: "to hear the north wind again." The revelations of Stevens' poetry through *The Rock*, I am suggesting, in all their power invalidated the propositions which informed them and so no longer gave support. But the relation of art to life as Stevens had defined it in the next-to-last *Adagia* note I have quoted still held; and the poet was bound to create new poems, seek for new revelations, discover new validations and invalidations. In the seeking itself lay the source of support. The revelation in the last poems is flickering but sure. At long last, the Emersonian paradox is taken to work both ways. But it is stripped of its resolution in the idea that subject and object, imagination and reality, man and nature are all unified in a God-ordained and God-containing system of symbolic correspondences, to which the poet, by virtue of his being poet, has access. Even in imagination the poet is neither God, nor shares in God's world. He cannot be; so he no longer needs to be. Now the Emersonian paradox is kept ever true to the facts of the case as the poet's creations discover them: the Imagination may be defined as at once the use which the Reason makes of the material world and the use which the material world makes of the Reason. Poetry is Reason's dialogue with reality, and must begin "On the level of that which is not yet knowledge: / A revelation not yet intended." The poet must master a speech which is not his own, must learn first to listen—then, if he can, to ask as well as to answer, to give as well as to take. Knowing what he knows—himself in "the act of the mind"—he must thereby know more. So Stevens began to learn, and so he began to teach—in his own way moving "Más Allá." As he wrote in the *Adagia*, "One's ignorance is one's chief asset." At the outset.

VII

WALLACE STEVENS' POETRY OF BEING

BY J. HILLIS MILLER

> We were as Danes in Denmark all day long
> And knew each other well, hale-hearted landsmen,
> For whom the outlandish was another day
>
> Of the week, queerer than Sunday. We thought alike
> And that made brothers of us in a home
> In which we fed on being brothers, fed
>
> And fattened as on a decorous honeycomb.[1]

There was once a time when man lived in harmony with his fellows and his surroundings. This harmony was a unified culture, a single view of the world. All men thought alike and understood each other perfectly, like the most intimate of brothers. Since they all shared an interpretation of the world they did not think of it as one perspective among many possible ones. Any other interpretation was queer, outlandish, something wild, ignorant, barbarian. Each man felt at home. He was a Dane in Denmark, not a Dane in Greece or Patagonia. Just as he possessed his fellows in the brotherhood of a single culture, so he possessed nature through their collective interpretation of it. He was a landsman, an inlander, someone dwelling close to the earth. Since man, society, and environment made one inextricable unity, as of Danes in Denmark, no one was aware of himself as a separate mind. Each man was like the bee in the honeycomb, the dwelling-place which he has exuded from his own body, and which now forms his food. All self-consciousness was lost in this reflexive feeding and fattening, and man "lay sticky with sleep" (*CP*, 419).

So enduring and beneficent did this order seem that it was impossible to believe that man himself could have made it. Surely, we thought, our happy world must be the gift of some supernatural beings, and these gods must guarantee its rightness and

---

[1] *The Collected Poems of Wallace Stevens* (New York, 1954), p. 419. This volume will hereafter be cited as *CP*.

143

permanence. They seemed outside of or beyond our world, " speechless, invisible " (*CP*, 262). They ruled us and sustained us " by / Our merest apprehension of their will " (*CP*, 262). Our culture was revelation of the invisible and speech of the speechless gods.

Suddenly something catastrophic happened, and all our happy order was destroyed:

> A tempest cracked on the theatre. Quickly,
> The wind beat in the roof and half the walls.
> The ruin stood still in an external world.
>
> *   *   *
>
> It had been real. It was not now. The rip
> Of the wind and the glittering were real now,
> In the spectacle of a new reality. (*CP*, 306)

Once the theater is destroyed it can never be rebuilt. The fact that it can be destroyed proves that even when it existed it was not what is seemed. It seemed a divine gift, something as solid as the earth itself. Now man discovers that all along it was a painted scene. The true reality has always been the wind and the indifferent glittering of an external world, a world in which man can never feel at home.

When the tempest cracks on the theater the whole thing disintegrates: " exit the whole / Shebang " (*CP*, 37). Men are no longer brothers, but strange to one another. The land withdraws to a distance and comes to be seen as no longer included in man's interpretations of it. When nature becomes outlandish the gods disappear. They do not withdraw for a time to an unattainable distance, as they did for De Quincey or Matthew Arnold. They vanish altogether, leaving nothing behind. They reveal themselves to be fictions, aesthetic projections of man's gratuitous values. Having seen the gods of one culture disappear man can never again believe in any god: " The death of one god is the death of all " (*CP*, 381).[2]

This evaporation of the gods, leaving a barren man in a barren land, is the basis of all Stevens' thought and poetry. The death of the gods coincides with a radical transformation in the way man sees the world. What had been a warm home takes on a look of hardness and emptiness, like the walls, floors, and banisters of

---

[2] See also Wallace Stevens, *Opus Posthumous* (New York, 1957), p. 165. This volume will hereafter be cited as *OP*.

a vacant house. Instead of being intimately possessed by man,
things appear to close themselves within themselves. They become mute, static presences:

To see the gods dispelled in mid-air and dissolve like clouds is one
of the great human experiences. It is not as if they had gone over the
horizon to disappear for a time; nor as if they had been overcome by
other gods of greater power and profounder knowledge. It is simply
that they came to nothing. Since we have always shared all things
with them and have always had a part of their strength and, certainly,
all of their knowledge, we shared likewise this experience of annihilation. It was their annihilation, not ours, and yet it left us feeling that
in a measure, we, too, had been annihilated. It left us feeling dispossessed and alone in a solitude, like children without parents, in a
home that seemed deserted, in which the amical rooms and halls had
taken on a look of hardness and emptiness. What was most extraordinary is that they left no mementoes behind, no thrones, no mystic
rings, no texts either of the soil or of the soul. It was as if they had
never inhabited the earth. There was no crying out for their return.
(*OP*, 206, 207).

There was no crying out for their return because we knew
they would never come back. They would never come back because they had never been there at all.

In this impoverishing of the world when the gods disappear man
discovers himself, orphaned and dispossessed, a solitary consciousness. Then are we truly " natives of poverty, children of malheur "
(*CP*, 322). The moment of self-awareness in Stevens coincides
with the moment of the death of the gods. God is dead, therefore
I am. But I am nothing. I am nothing because I have nothing,
nothing but awareness of the barrenness within and without.
When the gods dissolve like clouds they " come to nothing." When
the gods come to nothing, man is " nothing himself," and, since
this is so, he " beholds / Nothing that is not there and the nothing
that is " (*CP*, 10).

After the death of the gods and the discovery of nothingness
Stevens is left in a world made of two elements: subject and
object, mind and matter, imagination and reality. Imagination is
the inner nothingness, while reality is the barren external world
with which imagination carries on its endless intercourse. Stevens'
problem is to reconcile the two. But such a reconciliation turns
out to be impossible. This way and that vibrates his thought,
seeking to absorb imagination by reality, to engulf reality in
imagination, or to marry them in metaphor. Nothing will suffice,

and Stevens is driven to search on tirelessly for some escape from conflict. This endless seeking is the motive and life of his poetry. The human self, for him, is divided against itself. One part is committed to the brute substance of earth, things as they are, and the other just as tenaciously holds to its need for imaginative grandeur. Self-division, contradiction, perpetual oscillation of thought—these are the constants in Stevens' work. Is it possible, as some critics have thought, that he is just confused? Is it from mere absence of mind that he affirms on one page of his *Adagia* that reality is the only genius (*OP*, 177), only to reverse himself two pages later and declare just as categorically that imagination is the only genius (*OP*, 179)?

The critic can develop radically different notions of Stevens' aims as a poet, and for each of these it is easy to find apposite passages from the text. It can be shown that Stevens believes poetry is metaphor, and that he believes all metaphors are factitious. At times he is unequivocally committed to bare reality. At other times he repudiates reality and sings the praises of imagination. Nor is it just a question of contradictions in the logical statements of the prose which are reconciled in the poetry. For each position and for its antithesis there are fully elaborated poems or parts of poems. It is impossible to find a single one-dimensional theory of poetry and life in Stevens. His poetry defines a realm in which everything " is not what it is " (*OP*, 178). Such poetry is not dialectical, if that means a series of stages which build on one another, each transcending the last and moving on to a higher stage, in some version of the Hegelian sequence of thesis, antithesis, synthesis. At the beginning Stevens is already as far as he ever goes. After the disappearance of the gods the poet finds himself in a place where opposites are simultaneously true. It seems that this situation can be dealt with in poetry only by a succession of wild swings to one extreme or another, giving first one limit of the truth, then the other. To escape such oscillation Stevens must find a way to write poetry which will possess simultaneously both extremes.

The elaboration of such a mode of poetry is Stevens' chief contribution to literature. In the meditative poems of his later years he takes possession of a new domain. The finished unity of his early poems, which makes many of them seem like elaborately wrought pieces of jewelry, is gradually replaced by poems which

are open-ended improvisations. Such poems are not a neat en-
closure of words forming a complex organic unity. They begin
in the middle of a thought, and their ending is arbitrary. "The
Man with the Blue Guitar" has a special place in Stevens' canon.
It marks his turning to the new style. The reader has the feeling
that the poem has been going on for some time when he hears the
first words, and the last verses are not really an ending. The
twanging of the strings continues interminably. Such a poem
could be endless, and indeed three more "Stanzas for 'The Man
with the Blue Guitar'" are given in *Opus Posthumous* (72, 73).
The man with the guitar is described in "An Ordinary Evening in
New Haven" as a permanent presence, some one always there in
the mind's eye, watching the poet, and reminding him of his
obligation to a faithful thinking of things as they are (*CP*, 483).

Life, for Stevens, is a series of states of consciousness with
neither start nor finish. If the poem is to be true to life it must
be a constant flowing of images which come as they come, and are
not distorted by the logical mind in its eagerness for order. "One's
grand flights," says Stevens, "one's Sunday baths, / One's tootings
at the weddings of the soul / Occur as they occur" (*CP*, 222).
Just as "The Man with the Blue Guitar" refuses to round itself
off formally with beginning, middle, and end, so the parts which
are given do not organize themselves into a whole, or even into
part of a whole. There is no coherent pattern of symbols and
metaphors, each one referring to all the others. One metaphor
or symbol is introduced, developed for a while, then dropped.
Another motif appears, is developed in its turn, disappears, is
replaced by another which has no connection with the other two,
and so on. "The Man with the Blue Guitar" proceeds in a series
of disconnected short flights, each persisting for only a brief span
of time. Each short flight, while it lasts, is like a "half-arc
hanging in mid-air / Composed, appropriate to the incomplete"
(*CP*, 309).

The same thing is true of Stevens' other long poems, "Esthétique
du Mal," or "Notes toward a Supreme Fiction," or "An Ordinary
Evening in New Haven." These poems keep close to the quality
of life as it is. Such poems, like life, proceed in a series of momentary crystallizations or globulations of thought, followed by dissolution, and then re-conglomeration in another form. "Thought,"
says Stevens, "tends to collect in pools" (*OP*, 170). A man's

mental energy tends to organize itself momentarily in a certain shape, but life flows on, and a new pattern is called for. The mind has a powerful resistance to doing the same thing twice, and "originality is an escape from repetition" (*OP*, 177). "As a man becomes familiar with his own poetry," says Stevens, "it becomes as obsolete for himself as for anyone else. From this it follows that one of the motives in writing is renewal" (*OP*, 220). Stevens always emphasizes the evanescence of poetry. Poetry is like a snowflake fluttering through the air and dissolving in the sea. It is radically bound to a time experienced as a sequence of present moments, each real and valid only so long as it is present. "Poetry," says Stevens, "is a finikin thing of air / That lives uncertainly and not for long" (*CP*, 155). In the *Adagia*, "Poetry is a pheasant disappearing in the brush" (*OP*, 173). Most succinctly: "A poem is a meteor" (*OP*, 158).

This fragmentary quality is evident in Stevens' titles, both those for individual poems and those for books. Each poem by itself, like the whole mass of them together, is a hesitant and uncertain movement toward a goal which is never reached. He calls a poem "Prelude to Objects," or "Asides on the Oboe," or "Extracts from Addresses to the Academy of Fine Ideas," or "Debris of Life and Mind," or "Notes toward a Supreme Fiction," or "Prologues to What is Possible," in each case emphasizing the broken, partial nature of the poem, the way it is a piece of something larger, or is only an indirect and incomplete movement toward its object, something preliminary and unfinished. The titles of his books of poetry suggest the same qualities. The harmonium is a small key-board organ used in the home. The book of poems called *Harmonium* seems to be a series of improvisations on this amateur's instrument. But Stevens wanted to call his first book "The Grand Poem: Preliminary Minutiae." [3] This title would have been a perfect expression of the nature of all his poems. "Harmonium" too suggests something of this notion of tentative fragments. Stevens may have been remembering this, as well as trying to affirm the unity of his work, when he wanted to call his collected poems *The Whole of Harmonium* (*OP*, xiv). The titles of his other books are just as tentative: *Ideas of Order, Parts of a World,*

[3] *Poems by Wallace Stevens,* selected, and with an Introduction, by Samuel French Morse (New York, 1961), p. viii.

Transport to Summer (in which one side of the pun gives the idea of motion in the direction of summer), and *The Auroras of Autumn* (an apt phrase to describe poems which are a flickering continuum of light). Only *The Rock* suggests something final and stable, but that title was affixed after Stevens had attained the ultimate immobility of death. All his poems taken together form a single poem. This poem is a long series of provisional pools of imagery, each drawn toward a goal which can never be named directly or embodied in any poem. Man can never live again in a unified homeland. "We live in a constellation / Of patches and of pitches, / Not in a single world," and we are therefore always "Thinkers without final thoughts / In an always incipient cosmos" (*OP*, 114, 115).

Within the "endlessly elaborating poem" (*CP*, 486) which is life, the same sequence of events is constantly happening over and over again. First something happens which "decreates," which destroys an earlier imagination of the world. Then man is left face to face with the bare rock of reality. This happens every year in autumn. When the leaves have all fallen, "we return / To a plain sense of things," and "it is as if / We had come to an end of the imagination" (*CP*, 502). This clearing away is experienced not as a loss but as a gain. What is removed was a fictive covering of the rock, and what is exposed is the real in all its clarity:

> The barrenness that appears is an exposing.
> It is not part of what is absent, a halt
> For farewells, a sad hanging on for remembrances.
>
> It is a coming on and a coming forth.
> The pines that were fans and fragrances emerge,
> Staked solidly in a gusty grappling with rocks. (*CP*, 487)

The autumnal experience of decreation, as of leaves turning brown and falling, gives man a sense of "cold and earliness and bright origin" (*CP*, 481). It is as if the poet were like the first man facing an "uncreated" world, with everything still to be imagined.

This experience of coldness and earliness is only the start. The poet is not satisfied to confront a bare and unimagined world. He wants to possess it, and it can only be possessed by being imagined well. Man is inhabited by a "will to change" (*CP*, 397) which is just as unappeasable as his will to see the rock of reality exposed in all its bareness. The experience of decreation is followed by the reconstruction of a new imagination of the world. Spring follows winter, the rock is covered with leaves which are the icon of the poem, and what had been the simplicity of beginning becomes the ornate complexity of the end. The poet moves from "naked Alpha," "the infant A standing on infant legs" to "hierophant Omega," "twisted, stooping, polymathic Z" (*CP*, 469). If the beginning is bare and simple, the end is multiple and encrusted with color, like an illuminated manuscript, or like a splendid robe of state, "adorned with cryptic stones and sliding shines, . . . / With the whole spirit sparkling in its cloth, / Generations of the imagination piled / In the manner of its stitchings, of its thread" (*CP*, 434).

No sooner has the mind created a new fictive world than this "recent imagining of reality" (*CP*, 465) becomes obsolete in its turn, and must be rejected. This rejection is the act of decreation, and returns man once more to unadorned reality. The cycle then begins again: imagining followed by decreation followed by imagining and so on for as long as life lasts. In this rhythmic alternation lies our only hope to possess reality. Each moment is born in newness and freedom, with no connections to the past. Man must match the ever-renewed freedom of time with an equally radical freedom on his own part, a willed disencumbering of himself of all the corpses of the past. This is the sense in which "all men are murderers" (*OP*, 168), for "Freedom is like a man who kills himself / Each night, an incessant butcher, whose knife / Grows sharp in blood" (*CP*, 292), and "All things destroy themselves or are destroyed" (*OP*, 46). So Stevens cries: "what good were yesterday's devotions?" (*CP*, 264). This refusal of the past gives him a possession of the present moment in all its instantaneous vitality: "I affirm and then at midnight the great cat / Leaps quickly from the fireside and is gone" (*CP*, 264).

The present is the great cat who leaps from the fireside and is gone. It can never be seized or held and it lasts only for the blink of an eye. But if life is a series of such moments, how is it possible to justify even the cycle of decreation followed by a re-imagining of reality? This cycle seems to move with a slow and stately turning, like the sequence of the seasons which is so often its image. If the poet pauses long enough to write the poem of winter it will already be part of the dead past long before he has finished it, and so for the poems of the other seasons. It seems that the poet will make sterile vibrations back and forth between one spiritual season and the other, always a little behind the perpetual flowing of reality.

There is one way to escape this impasse, and the discovery of this way gives its special character to all Stevens' later poetry. He can move so fast from one season to another that all the extreme postures of the spirit are present in a single moment. If he can do this he will never pause long enough at any extreme for it to freeze into dead fixity, and he will appease at last his longing to have both imagination and reality at once. An oscillation rapid enough becomes a blur in which opposites are touched simultaneously, as alternating current produces a steady beam of light, and the cycle of decreation and imagining, hopelessly false if the poet goes through it at leisure, becomes true at last to things as they are if he moves through it fast enough. Each tick of the clock is " the starting point of the human and the end " (*CP*, 528). In " this present " there is a " dizzle-dazzle of being new / And of becoming," " an air of freshness, clearness, greenness, blueness, / That which is always beginning because it is part / Of that which is always beginning, over and over " (*CP*, 530). The present is always beginning over and over because it has no sooner begun than it has gone all the way to the end, and has moved so rapidly that " this end and this beginning are one " (*CP*, 506). All the possible elements of experience are always present in every instant of time, and in every season or weather of the mind: consciousness in its emptiness detached from reality and seeking it in bare impoverishment, the imagination covering the rock with leaves, flowers, and fruit, the drying and falling of the leaves in autumn.

Stevens' *Collected Poems* moves in a stately round through the whole cycle of the seasons, from the gaudy, spring-like poems of *Harmonium*, like new buds on the rock, through *Transport to Summer* and *The Auroras of Autumn*, and then back again to winter's bareness with *The Rock*. Every authentic image, from one end of his poetry to the other, recapitulates this sequence in a breath. In " Notes toward a Supreme Fiction " Stevens says that a true poem allows the reader to share, for a moment, the " first idea." This means having a vision of things in the radiance of their presence, without any intervening film between man and the pure sensation of things as they are. To do this, Stevens says, is to see things in "living changingness" (*CP*, 380), to go in a moment from the white candor of the beginning in its original freshness to the white candor of the end in its multiplicity of imaginative enhancements. "We move between these points: / From that ever-early candor to its late plural" (*CP*, 382).

In "The Owl in the Sarcophagus" (*CP*, 431-436) Stevens gives his fullest dramatization of the way time moves from beginning to end in a moment. The poem is about "the forms of thought," that is, about the universal limits between which human thought moves, and in terms of which man lives, for "we live in the mind." If man lives in the mind he dies there too:

> It is a child that sings itself to sleep,
> The mind, among the creatures that it makes,
> The people, those by which it lives and dies. (*CP*, 436)

Man dies in the mind because the mind too is bound by time. This means that it is defined by the fact that it will one day die. Life dwells within death, is constantly coming from and returning to death, as its origin, home, and end. The owl, Minerva, the mind, lives in a sarcophagus, and the poem describes "the mythology of modern death" (*CP*, 435). It embodies the forces which determine the mind's activity, "the creatures that it makes." These forces are "death's own supremest images, / The pure perfections of parental space, / The children of a desire that is the will, / Even of death, the beings of the mind / In the light-bound space of the mind, the floreate flare . . ." (*CP*, 436).

Since the figures of the poem live in the perpetual present of mental space, they live "in an element not the heaviness of time" (*CP*, 432), that is, in "a time / That of itself [stands] still, perennial" (*CP*, 432). The moment is "less time than place" (*CP*, 433) because it is outside of time, though it is the only living part of time.

The figures of the mythology of modern death are three: sleep, peace, and "she that says / Good-by in the darkness" (*CP*, 431). Sleep is the beginning, the radiant candor of pure mind without any content, mind as it is when it faces a bare unimagined reality, or mind as it is when it has completed the work of decreation, and is ready "in an ever-changing, calmest unity" (*CP*, 433) to begin imagining again: "Sleep realized / Was the whiteness that is the ultimate intellect, / A diamond jubilance beyond the fire" (*CP*, 433).

If sleep is the beginning, peace is the end, "the brother of sleep," "the prince of shither-shade and tinsel lights" (*CP*, 434). "Peace after death" is the end in the sense that it represents a fulfillment of imagination. Sleep is prior to life, since ultimate intellect cannot even be called consciousness, or is consciousness with no content. Peace is the death at the end of life, the death of a consummation of the imagination. Peace, like sleep, is that death man touches in every moment as he moves all the way from the immaculate beginning to its late plural. Peace is "that figure stationed at our end, / Always, in brilliance, fatal, final, formed / Out of our lives to keep us in our death" (*CP*, 434).

What of the third figure, "she that says good-by," who is she? She broods over the moment of life, the infinitesimally brief flash between start and finish which is living reality, surrounded on all sides by death. She dwells in what Stevens calls in another poem "the mobile and the immobile flickering / In the area between is and was" (*CP*, 474). This moment, evanescent as it is, is the only reality, and it is only in the moment, a moment which changes and evaporates with the utmost rapidity, that man can glimpse things as they are. Things exist only in the time they are moving from is to was, and the third figure is the embodiment of this presence of the present, a presence which is like that of a glow in molten iron, such a glow as fades even as we watch it.

How is it possible to write poetry which will match the mobility of the moment? It would seem that any image or form of words would be too fixed to move with a time which changes so instantaneously. A poem of any length would be far too long to be a meteor. It would transform the living flow of reality into a clumsy machine wholly unable to keep up with time. Such a poem would be a dead relic of the past long before the reader had reached the last line.

Stevens gradually develops, as his poetry progresses, a way of matching the fluidity of time. He comes to write a poetry of flickering mobility, a poetry in which each phrase moves so rapidly it has beginning and ending at once. Instead of being fixed and unyielding, a solid piece of language interacting with other words, each image recapitulates within itself the coming into being of the moment and its disappearance. The fluctuation between beginning and ending has become so rapid that it takes place in a single phrase, or in a "syllable between life / And death" (*CP*, 432). Each image in a poem of such phrases is a meteor. "An Ordinary Evening in New Haven," for example, constantly generates itself out of its own annihilation, ending and beginning again indefatigably. It expresses, in its "flickings from finikin to fine finikin," "the edgings and inchings of final form, / The swarming activities of the formulae / Of statement, directly and indirectly getting at" (*CP*, 488).

At first, after the dissolution of the gods, it seemed that Stevens was left, like post-Cartesian man in general, in a world riven in two, split irreparably into subject and object, imagination and reality. All his work seems based on this dualism. Any attempt to escape it by affirming the priority of one or the other power leads to falsehood. But as his work progresses, Stevens comes more and more to discover that there is after all only one realm, always and everywhere the realm of some new conjunction of imagination and reality. Imagination is still present in the most absolute commitment of the mind to reality, and reality is still there in the wildest imaginary fiction. The later Stevens is beyond metaphysical dualism, and beyond representational thinking. In his late poems it is no longer a question of some reality which already exists out there in the world, and of which the poet then makes an image. The image is inextricably part of the thing, and the most extreme imaginative "distortion" is still based on reality. There is only one ever-present existence: consciousness *of* some reality. Imagination is reality, or, as Stevens says: "poetry and reality are one."[4] In another formulation: "the structure of poetry and the structure of reality are one" (*NA*, 81). If this is the case, then there is no real thing which is transformed into various imaginary aspects. The real thing is already imagined, and "imaginative transcripts" are as much a part of reality as anything else is. "What our eyes behold," says Stevens, "may well be the text of life but one's meditations on the text and the disclosures of these meditations are no less a part of the structure of reality" (*NA*, 76). As he puts it in the title of a very late poem: "Reality Is an Activity of the Most August Imagination" (*OP*, 110).

[4] Wallace Stevens, *The Necessary Angel: Essays on Reality and the Imagination* (New York, 1951), p. 81. This volume will hereafter be cited as *NA*.

This discovery of the identity of all the elements of life means a redefinition of poetry. Words are not pictures of reality. They are part of the thing, tangled inextricably with the event they describe. " The poem is the cry of its occasion,/ Part of the res itself and not about it " (*CP*, 473) , and therefore " description is revelation " (*CP*, 344) . Words are the vortex of the whirlpool, where imagination and reality merge, for " words of the world are the life of the world " (*CP*, 474) .

This seems to be Stevens' ultimate position: a resolution of imagination and reality in a theory of the identity of poetry and life, and the development of a poetry of flickering mobility to sustain this identity. But there is one more aspect of his thought, and this is the most difficult to see or to say.

It begins with an increasing movement toward nothingness in Stevens' later poetry. Along with the phrases expressing the swarming plenitude of the moment there is something different. At the same time as its tensions are resolved, Stevens' poetry gets more and more disembodied, more and more a matter of " the spirit's alchemicana," and less and less a matter of the solid and tangible, the pears on their dish, the round peaches with their fuzz and juice. It seems as if the poetry becomes more and more intangible as the oscillations between imagination and reality get more and more rapid, until, at the limit, the poem evaporates altogether. At the extreme of speed all solidity disappears. It is as if the same speed which allows beginning and ending to merge also releases something else: a glimpse of the nothingness which underlies all existence.

The word or the idea of nothingness comes back more and more often. Nothingness appears as early as *Harmonium*, but there it is associated with the bareness of winter. Only the snow man, the man who is " nothing himself," is free of imagination's fictions and can behold "nothing that is not there and the nothing that is." Stevens' later poetry is continuous with this early intuition of nothing, but the theme of nothingness gradually becomes more dominant. In the later poetry nothingness appears to be the source and end of everything, and to underlie everything as its present reality. Imagination is nothing. Reality is nothing. The mind is nothing. Words are nothing. God is nothing. Perhaps it is the fact that all these things are equivalent to nothing which makes them all equivalents of one another. All things come

together in the nothing. Stevens speaks of "the priest of nothingness who intones" on the rock of reality (*OP*, 88). In another
poem the wind "intones its single emptiness" (*CP*, 294). He tells
of a room "emptier than nothingness" (*CP*, 286), or of a moon
which is "a lustred nothingness" (*CP*, 320). He asks for a "god
in the house" who will be so insubstantial that he will be "a
coolness, / A vermilioned nothingness" (*CP*, 328), and speaks
of metaphysical presences which are like "beasts that one never
sees, / Moving so that the foot-falls are slight and almost nothing" (*CP*, 337). Again and again he says that all things, "seen
and unseen," are "created from nothingness" (*CP*, 486; *OP*,
100), or "forced up from nothing" (*CP*, 363). The growth of
leaves on the rock of reality comes from nothing, "as if," says
Stevens, "nothingness contained a métier" (*CP*, 526). In another poem, the first breath of spring "creates a fresh universe
out of nothingness" (*CP*, 517).

The rock of reality seems not to be a substantial reality,
material and present before the poet's eyes. It seems to have
come from nothingness. If it has come from nothingness, its
source still defines it, and all things dwell in the "stale grandeur
of annihilation" (*CP*, 505). As Stevens says in a striking phrase:
"Reality is a vacuum" (*OP*, 168).

A number of his poems attempt to express the way reality is a
vacuum. In such poems "we breathe / An odor evoking nothing,
absolute" (*CP*, 394, 395). "A Clear Day and No Memories"
(*OP*, 113) describes a weather in which "the air is clear of
everything," "has no knowledge except of nothingness," and
"flows over us without meanings" in an "invisible activity."
"Chocorua to Its Neighbor" (*CP*, 296-302) is an extraordinarily
disembodied poem, the subject of which is a strange shadow, "an
eminence, / But of nothing" (*CP*, 300). In *The Auroras of
Autumn* a serpent is present everywhere in the landscape, and
yet present as form disappearing into formlessness:

> This is where the serpent lives, the bodiless.
> His head is air. . . .
>
>   *   *   *
>
> This is where the serpent lives. This is his nest,
> These fields, these hills, these tinted distances,
> And the pines above and along and beside the sea.

This is form gulping after formlessness,
Skin flashing to wished-for disappearances
And the serpent body flashing without the skin. (*CP*, 411)

Such poems accomplish a hollowing out or subtilizing of reality. They give the reader the feeling of what it is like to see reality not as a solid substance, but as something less tangible than the finest mist. They attempt to make visible something which is "always too heavy for the sense / To seize, the obscurest as, the distant was" (*CP*, 441). They are based on the presupposition that the center of reality is a nothingness which is "a nakedness, a point, / Beyond which fact could not progress as fact. / . . . Beyond which thought could not progress as thought" (*CP*, 402, 403). If it is true that the underlying substance of reality is a vacuum, "the dominant blank, the unapproachable" (*CP*, 477), then we must give up the idea that reality is a solid rock, and see it as a nameless, evanescent flowing, something hovering on the edge of oblivion. "It is not in the premise that reality / Is a solid," says Stevens in the last words of "An Ordinary Evening in New Haven." "It may be a shade that traverses / A dust, a force that traverses a shade" (*CP*, 489).

If reality is a vacuum, imagination is no less empty. It is the "nothing" of "Imago" (*CP*, 439), which lifts all things. Man in a world where reality is nonentity "has his poverty and nothing more" (*CP*, 427). Such a man is defined as "desire," and is "always in emptiness that would be filled" (*CP*, 467).

It seemed that Stevens was moving closer and closer to a full possession of the plenitude of things, but as the tension between imagination and reality diminishes there is an unperceived emptying out of both, until, at the moment they touch, in the brevity of a poem which includes beginning and ending in a breath, the poet finds himself face to face with a universal nothing.

Nevertheless, this apparent defeat is the supreme victory, for the nothing is not nothing. It is. It is being. Being is the universal power, visible nowhere in itself, and yet visible everywhere in all things. It is what all things share through the fact that they are. Being is not a thing like other things, and therefore can appear to man only as nothing, yet it is what all things participate in if they are to exist at all. All Stevens' later poetry has as its goal the releasing of the evanescent glimpse of being which is as close as man can come to a possession of the ground of things. The para-

doxical appearance to man of being in the form of nothing is the
true cause of the ambiguity of his poetry. Man's inability to see
being as being causes the poet to say of it: "It is and it / Is not
and, therefore, is" (*CP*, 440), and yet in the supreme moments
of insight he can speak directly of it, in lines which are a cry of
ecstatic discovery:

> It is like a thing of ether that exists
> Almost as predicate. But it exists,
> It exists, it is visible, it is, it is. (*CP*, 418)

The nothing is, but it is not merely the nothingness of consciousness. Human nature participates in being, but so do all
other existences. Wherever the poet thinks to catch it, it disappears, melting into the landscape and leaving just the pines
and rock and water which are there, or being absorbed into the
mind and taking the mind's own shape: "If in the mind, he
vanished, taking there / The mind's own limits, like a tragic thing
/ Without existence, existing everywhere" (*CP*, 298). Being is
released in the flash of time from is to was, just as it is released
in the expansion of perception to occupy space. Being is the presentness of things present, the radiance of things as they are, and
is therefore "physical if the eye is quick enough" (*CP*, 301).

In two late poems, "Metaphor as Degeneration" (*CP*, 444)
and "The River of Rivers in Connecticut" (*CP*, 533) Stevens
sees being as a river, hidden behind all the appearances that tell
of it, and yet flowing everywhere, through all space and time,
and through all the contents of space and time. In these two
poems he gives his most succinct expression of his apprehension
of being:

> It is certain that the river
>
> Is not Swatara. The swarthy water
> That flows round the earth and through the skies,
> Twisting among the universal spaces,
>
> Is not Swatara. It is being. (*CP*, 444)
>
> It is not to be seen beneath the appearances
> That tell of it. The steeple at Farmington
> Stands glistening and Haddam shines and sways.
>
> It is the third commonness with light and air,
> A curriculum, a vigor, a local abstraction . . .
> Call it, once more, a river, an unnamed flowing,

Space-filled, reflecting the seasons, the folk-lore
Of each of the senses; call it, again and again,
The river that flows nowhere, like a sea. (*CP*, 533)

At the heart of Stevens' poetry there is a precise metaphysical experience. Or, rather, this experience is beyond metaphysics, since the tradition of metaphysics is based on a dualism putting ultimate being in some transcendent realm, above and beyond what man can see. Being, for Stevens, is within things as they are, here and now, revealed in the glistening of the steeple at Farmington, in the flowing of time, in the presentness of things present, in the interior fons of man.

Stevens' experience of being is " a difficult apperception," " disposed and re-disposed / By such slight genii in such pale air" (*CP*, 440). To speak directly of this apperception, to analyze it, is almost inevitably to falsify it, to fix it in some abstraction, and therefore to kill it. Though man participates in being, he does not confront it directly. It is the center of which each man is an eccentric particle, for he is always " helplessly at the edge " (*CP*, 430). When he tries to grasp it, it disappears. Man can never possess " the bouquet of being " (*OP*, 109), that fugitive aroma. The best we can do is " to realize / That the sense of being changes as we talk" (*OP*, 109), and go on talking in the hope that if we are careful to see that " nothing [is] fixed by a single word " (*OP*, 114), nothing will be, in another sense, fixed momentarily in a word, and we shall have another evanescent insight into being.

The only passage in Stevens' prose which speaks directly of his perception of being, " that nobility which is our spiritual height and depth " (*NA*, 33, 34), is curiously evasive. It is evasive because its subject is evasive. There is *something* there, Stevens says, but it can only be described negatively, for to define it is to fix it, and it must not be fixed:

I mean that nobility which is our spiritual height and depth; and while I know how difficult it is to express it, nevertheless I am bound to give a sense of it. Nothing could be more evasive and inaccessible. Nothing distorts itself and seeks disguise more quickly. There is a shame of disclosing it and in its definite presentations a horror of it. But there it is. The fact that it is there is what makes it possible to invite to the reading and writing of poetry men of intelligence and desire for life. I am not thinking of the ethical or the sonorous or at all of the manner of it. The manner of it is, in fact, its difficulty, which each man must feel each day differently, for himself. I am not thinking of the solemn, the portentous or demoded. On the other hand, I am evading a definition. If it is defined, it will be fixed and it must not be fixed. As in the case of an external thing, nobility resolves itself into an enormous number of vibrations, movements, changes. To fix it is to put an end to it. (*NA*, 33, 34)

To fix it is to put an end to it, but in poetry it can be caught unfixed. The mobile, flickering poetry of Stevens' later style, poetry which fears stillness beyond anything, is more than a revelation of the impossibility of escaping the war of the mind and sky. It is a revelation of being. The poem names being, the human-like figure which the mind is always confronting at every extreme, but which it is never able to catch and immobilize in words. The nothing which makes it impossible ever to rest, which makes nonsense of any attempt to express things rationally, and which always drives the poet on to another effort to seize the nothing by marrying imagination and reality—this nothing turns out to be being. The poetry of flittering metamorphosis is the only poetry which is simultaneously true to both imagination and reality, and it is the only poetry which will catch being. Being is "the dominant blank, the unapproachable," but it is nevertheless the source of everything, all man sees and all he is. The ultimate tragedy is that being is transformed instantaneously into nothing, and therefore though the poet has it he has it as an absence. Only a poetry of iridescent frettings will remain in touch with it, for "life / Itself is like a poverty in the space of life, / So that the flapping of wind . . . / Is something in tatters that [man] cannot hold" (*CP*, 298, 299). Being is inherent in human nature, but it is inherent as a center which can never be embraced. In the process of going in a moment through the whole cycle from A to Z something is released, glimpsed, and annihilated, like those atomic particles which live only a millionth of a second. This something is being. As soon as it is named, it disappears, takes the limits of the mind, or melts into the limited existence of the object. But for a moment it is seen. "It is and it / Is not and, therefore, is."

The motive for rapid motion in Stevens' poetry is not only that speed reconciles imagination and reality. Speed also makes possible a vision of being—in the moment of its disappearance. After reading one of Stevens' poems the reader has the feeling that, after all, nothing has happened, no change of the world such as science or technology can perform: " And yet nothing has been changed except what is / Unreal, as if nothing had been changed at all " (*OP*, 117). At the end it *was* there. It is already part of the past. Poetry is a pheasant disappearing in the brush. So Santayana, in " To an Old Philosopher in Rome," lives " on the threshold of heaven," and sees things double, things and the presence of being in things, " The extreme of the known in the presence of the extreme / Of the unknown " (*CP*, 508). To see things transfigured in this way is still to see them just as they are, in all their barrenness and poverty. This world and the other are " two alike in the make of the mind " (*CP*, 508), and the old philosopher's ultimate insight, like Stevens' own, is not at all a vision of things beyond this world:

> It is a kind of total grandeur at the end,
> With every visible thing enlarged and yet
> No more than a bed, a chair and moving nuns,
> The immensest theatre, the pillared porch,
> The book and candle in your ambered room . . . .
>
> (*CP*, 510)

But merely to see being in things is not enough. Being must be spoken. The speaking of poetry liberates being in the presence of things. Through words man participates in being, for words of the world are the life of the world, and " the word is the making of the world, / The buzzing world and lisping firmament " (*CP*, 345). Poetry does not name something which has already been perceived, or put in words a pre-existent mental conception. The act of naming brings things together, gathers them into one, and makes present the things which are present. Speaking belongs to being, and in naming things in their presence poetry releases a glimpse of being.

From De Quincey through Arnold and Browning to Hopkins, Yeats, and Stevens the absence of God is starting point and basis. Various poets, Browning or Yeats for example, beginning in this situation are able to make a recovery of immanence. Perhaps it is Stevens' way, the movement from the dissolution of the gods to the difficult apperception of being, which represents the next step forward in the spiritual history of man. Stevens may be in the vanguard of a movement " toward the end of ontology," as

Jean Wahl calls it.[5] Central in this movement is the idea that all our spiritual height and depth is available here and now or nowhere. The last stanza of "A Primitive like an Orb" is one of Stevens' most eloquent statements of his belief that all the words and all the experiences of man are part of being, eccentric particles of the giant "at the centre on the horizon," the giant who can never be fully possessed or spoken in any words, but who is shared by all. If this is the case, then the simplest phrase, in all its limitation, is indeed "the human end in the spirit's greatest reach" (*CP*, 508):

> That's it. The lover writes, the believer hears,
> The poet mumbles and the painter sees,
> Each one, his fated eccentricity,
> As a part, but part, but tenacious particle,
> Of the skeleton of the ether, the total
> Of letters, prophecies, perceptions, clods
> Of color, the giant of nothingness, each one
> And the giant ever changing, living in change. (*CP*, 443)

[5] See *Vers la Fin de L'Ontologie* (Paris, 1956).

VIII

THE QUALIFIED ASSERTIONS
OF WALLACE STEVENS

BY HELEN HENNESSY VENDLER

Wallace Stevens has often been written about in terms of his doctrine, but his words suffer odd mutations as they are paraphrased, and what was a diffident suggestion in the poetry becomes bold assertion as his " doctrine " is condensed and solidified in the hands of his critics. Stevens' own irony and playfulness in toying with the mechanism of logical statement are ignored as chaff to the kernel of " thought." It is quite true that Stevens has ideas, and that in some way he is one of the " dependent heirs," of the great Romantics, but the Romantic assertions, whether of anguish or of trust, are in every way mitigated and qualified in Stevens' verse, both semantically and syntactically, as well as in his stance as a poet, and in the images to which he has recourse. The deliberate irony of Stevens' personae and of his imagery has been remarked on often, but the irony of diction and syntax, equally pervasive in the poetry, goes unremarked.

Though Stevens does make unqualified assertions, whether of ecstasy or of despair, from time to time, he more naturally tends to a middle ground, looking for an accommodation, a sensible ecstasy of pauvred color, to use his own terms. Interpretations of the world become so many hypotheses, interesting to entertain but of questionable solidity:

> Suppose these couriers brought amid their train
> A damsel heightened by eternal bloom. (p. 15)[1]

> Say that the hero is his nation,
> In him made one, . . . (p. 279)

> Perhaps these forms are seeking to escape
> Cadaverous undulations. (p. 355)

Stevens' usual method is not to depend on such overt semantic

---

[1] Numbers in parentheses refer to pages in *The Collected Poems of Wallace Stevens* (New York, 1957), except when prefaced by *OP*, in which case they refer to *Opus Posthumous* (New York, 1957).

163

tokens of uncertainty as "suppose," "say that" or "perhaps";
more often than not, he relies on syntactic manipulations, and
it is by these, appearing in his poetry of mixed regret and hope,
that he can be usefully distinguished from the other poets who
share his themes.[2]

The resolution of any poem is always a critical point, and
Stevens is, I think, unique in English poetry in the frequency
with which he closes his poems on a tentative note. He resorts
repeatedly to some of the modal auxiliaries—may, might, and
must, could, should, and would—to conclude his "statement."
Examples can be found on almost any page of the *Collected
Poems*:

> . . . If we propose
> A large-sculptured, platonic person, free from time,
> And imagine for him the speech he cannot speak,
>
> A form, then, protected from the battering, may
> Mature: A capable being may replace
> Dark horse and walker walking rapidly. (p. 330)

The "may" of final probability depends on an antecedent hypothesis, and the whole construct is a nebulous one, a predictive
statement of the utmost reservation. If "may" is congenial to
Stevens, "might" is even more so, since his constant sense of
disparity between the thing and its name is bridged only by his
notion of possibility, that perhaps one name might be accurate:
"How close / To the unstated theme each variation comes . . ."
(pp. 356-57) he reflects and then wonders:

> In that one ear it might strike perfectly:
>
> State the disclosure. In that one eye the dove
> Might spring to sight and yet remain a dove.
>
> The fisherman might be the single man
> In whose breast, the dove, alighting, would grow still. (p. 357)

The almost imperceptible shift from one mood or tense to another,
as in the poem just quoted, is one of Stevens' hallmarks. Usually
the passage is from the less certain to the more certain; here
Stevens substitutes for the expected "might" in the final line
the far more conclusive "would," as the poem passes from the

---

[2] I notice here chiefly the endings of poems, since in them Stevens' indeterminacy
is most striking, but the tendencies described appear throughout the body of his poetry.

possible to the probable. In the same way, the third section of
"Description without Place" leads us from "might" to "would"
and then, by sleight of hand, into the present tense, moving from
possible to probable to actual (or almost so; we tend to forget
that these present tenses are shorthand for conditionals, that they
depend on the principal verbs which are conditional):

> There might be, too, a change immenser than
> A poet's metaphors in which being would
>
> Come true, a point in the fire of music where
> Dazzle yields to a clarity and we observe,
>
> And observing is completing and we are content,
> In a world that shrinks to an immediate whole,
>
> That we do not need to understand, complete
> Without secret arrangements of it in the mind. (p. 341)

Such untoward modulations of tense are simply not available to
the critic who tries to paraphrase Stevens in prose, and so an
apprehension becomes a statement, an intuition becomes a dogma.
Often, where an earlier "Romantic" might make a confident
assertion, Stevens temporizes, either by "might" or by "may":

> It may be that the ignorant man, alone,
> Has any chance to mate his life with life
> That is the sensual, pearly spouse, . . . (p. 222)
>
> . . . Crow is realist. But, then,
> Oriole, also, may be realist. (p. 154)

Though "might" and "may" recur in special ways in Stevens'
poems, they are common poetic property; his use of "must" (and
its related forms "had to" and "cannot" or "could not") seems
to me his most distinctive appropriation of a modal auxiliary.
Usually it is found in conjunction with some other mood, often
in a very moving way:

> She must come now. The grass is in seed and high.
> Come now. . . . (p. 119)
>
>   . . . But see him for yourself,
> The fictive man. He may be seated in
> A café. There may be a dish of country cheese
> And a pineapple on the table. It must be so. (p. 335)

From "must come" to "come," from "may be" to "must be"—
this fluidity of mood, though not peculiar to Stevens' "must"

constructions, is characteristic of them. The constraint, the sad-
ness, the attempts at self-conviction, the enforced nobility—all
of these are missing from critical portraits of Stevens in the indicative mood. "A necessary function of the imagination," we might
represent Stevens as saying, "is to imagine its own absence." But
that condensation is false to the poetic "statement" of that
aphorism:

> Yet the absence of the imagination had
> Itself to be imagined. . . .
>
> . . . .
>
> The great pond and its waste of the lilies, all this
> Had to be imagined as an inevitable knowledge,
> Required, as a necessity requires. (p. 503)

The pathos in this passage comes from the desolate imagery and
deliberate repetition as well as from the mood, but the hard
necessity is in the strange phrase "had to be imagined." We rarely
use "must" or its variants except in cases of clear obligation;
Stevens implies in these lines obligations or destinies of a less
voluntary sort.

Diffident or tenuous statement gives way in many poems to
a spate of questions, which serve as a qualified way to put an
argument. Stevens is not prepared to make downright assevera-
tions, and yet we know from the questions the statements toward
which his mind is tending. These are not exactly rhetorical questions, since the answer to a rhetorical question is usually supposed
to be a ringing "yes" or "no": these questions function as
suggestions:

> One sits and beats an old tin can, lard pail.
> One beats and beats for that which one believes.
> That's what one wants to get near. Could it after all
> Be merely oneself, as superior as the ear
> To a crow's voice? Did the nightingale torture the ear,
> Pack the heart and scratch the mind? And does the ear
> Solace itself in peevish birds? Is it peace,
> Is it a philosopher's honeymoon, one finds
> On the dump? Is it to sit among mattresses of the dead,
> Bottles, pots, shoes and grass and murmur *aptest eve:*
> Is it to hear the blatter of grackles and say
> *Invisible priest*; is it to eject, to pull
> The day to pieces and cry *stanza my stone?*
> Where was it one first heard of the truth? The the. (pp. 202-3)

Oneself, as Stevens has said elsewhere, is the *the*: "There was that difference between the and an, / The difference between himself and no man" (p. 255). All the questions preceding the final two words of the poem suggest the notion that a poet's object is himself and his own world, not an absolute, but they suggest it as hints, not as dogmatic statements. There are enough questions at crucial points throughout Stevens' work to make us see the question as one of the natural forms into which his mind casts its observations. The evasion of direct statement continues,[3] and even the past, whether of personal history or of myth, is not safe from questions. Stevens is full of forms half-glimpsed, whose meaning he debates:

> Who was it passed her there on a horse all will,
> What figure of capable imagination?
>
> .   .   .   .
>
>   Was it a rider intent on the sun,
> A youth, a lover with phosphorescent hair,
> Dressed poorly, arrogant of his streaming forces,
> Lost in an integration of the martyrs' bones,
> Rushing from what was real; and capable? (p. 249)

We can take our choice of answers: perhaps it was a rider, a lover, and perhaps not; the figure remains in a sense undefined, since the definition is interrogative.

The mood of questioning in Stevens, whether marked by direct interrogation or by implicit qualification, frequently shifts to a mood of desperate assertion, where the insistence is based on fear, on the apprehension of chaos and disintegration if the assertions are not valid:

> To discover winter and know it well, to find,
> Not to impose, not to have reasoned at all,
> Out of nothing to have come on major weather,
>
> It is possible, possible, possible. It must
> Be possible. It must be that in time
> The real will from its crude compoundings come,
>
> Seeming, at first, a beast disgorged, unlike,
> Warmed by a desperate milk. . . . (p. 404)

---

[3] Although "evasion" is a pejorative word, I use it because Stevens himself regarded it as the nature of poetry to evade, in a special sense. "Metaphor" and "evasion" become synonyms in the *Collected Poems*: see, for instance, pp. 199, 272, 373, 388, 486.

This is anything but serene didacticism; it is not even a passionate creed. Creeds and beliefs are not voiced in these fevered phrasings. "Must" is not a word of faith, but a word of doubt, implying as it does an unbearable otherwise. In spite of his intent to remain the poet of reality, to hasp on the surviving form of "shall" or "ought to be" in "is," to assert that "For realist, what is is what should be" (p. 41), Stevens is seduced away again and again to what ought to be. He is not primarily at all a hedonist poet, describing the satisfactions of the life that is; he is a normative or optative poet, forsaking the reportive tenses, present and past, in favor of all the shifting moods of desire. His poems are resolved frequently by one of the clauses of desire—"he wanted," "he sought," "he needed," or a variant on these—which lead to the inevitable syntactic form of the infinitive as complement:

> He wanted to feel the same way over and over.
>
> He wanted the river to go on flowing the same way,
> To keep on flowing. He wanted to walk beside it,
>
> .   .   .   .
>
> He wanted his heart to stop beating . . . . (p. 425)

The peculiar, timeless, unqualified nature of infinitives suits Stevens' purposes exactly, since infinitives imply a future, usually, but without reminding us that it is a future and not yet accomplished:

> Bastard chateaux and smoky demoiselles,
> No more. I can build towers of my own,
> There to behold, there to proclaim, the grace
>
> And free requiting of responsive fact,
> To project the naked man . . . . (p. 263)

These are programs for action, not descriptions of action; manifestos, not reports; potentialities, not completions; views forward to something evermore about to be, to a place "where we have yet to live" (p. 336).

When Stevens appears to be asserting unconditionally in the simple present tense, not using the common modal auxiliaries, not using questions, not using infinitives, he nevertheless tends to avoid being final, often by recourse to the aspectual "seems": "It is possible that to seem—it is to be, / As the sun is something seeming and it is" (p. 339). Where we might expect "is," especially at the end of a poem, we find the mitigating "seems":

> So that this cold, a children's tale of ice,
> Seems like a sheen of heat romanticized. (p. 468)

> How good it was at home again at night
> To prepare for bed, in the frame of the house, and move
> Round the rooms, which do not ever seem to change . . . (p. 372)

"Seems" introduces the uncertainty of knowing, and qualifies by its hesitation the suggestions of heat in the first quotation, of unchangingness in the second. Stevens is also likely to end a poem with a verb[4] which semantically implies a future, though cast in the present tense; of these verbs, "become" is his favorite, though he also uses "promise," "foretell," and "must":

> . . . The blue guitar
> Becomes the place of things as they are. (p. 168)

> The yellow grassman's mind is still immense,
> Still promises perfections cast away. (p. 318)

> And Juda becomes New Haven or else must. (p. 473)

> The clouds foretell a swampy rain. (p. 161)

Corresponding in the realm of syntax to these "future-like" phrases is of course the future or future-perfect tense used to resolve a poem, one of the commonest forms of poetic resolution, and in fact one of the most satisfactory ways to make a poetic assertion, since the future is always a fiction. But Stevens, though he uses the simple future tense as resolution, prefers a more devious syntactic form of the future, the sort expressed in English by "when" or "until" followed by the present tense, a future in disguise, so to speak. For instance, he adjures the Muses to repeat the magic phrase *"To Be Itself"* until an apocalypse of some sort occurs:

> Until the sharply-colored glass transforms
> Itself into the speech of the spirit, until
> The porcelain bell-borrowings become
> Implicit clarities in the way you cry
> And are your feelings changed to sound, without
> A change, until the waterish ditherings turn
> To the tense, the maudlin, true meridian

---

[4] It is not only verbs which can imply a future although not used in a future tense; all nouns and adjectives of potentiality do the same. Stevens' poetry is full of words like possible, accessible, capable. "Our affair," he says, "is the affair of the possible" (p. 342), and like Emily Dickinson he considers possibility a fairer house than prose.

> That is yourselves, when, at last, you are yourselves,
> Speaking and strutting broadly, fair and bloomed,
> No longer of air but of the breathing earth,
> Impassioned seducers and seduced, the pale
> Pitched into swelling bodies, upward, drift
> In a storm blown into glittering shapes, and flames
> Wind-beaten into freshest, brightest fire. (*OP*, p. 52)

This passage, the conclusion to one of the poems in " Owl's Clover,"
is a statement of apotheosis, but it is far from being a direct
future statement of apotheosis like Milton's " Attired with stars,
we shall forever sit / Triumphing over Death and Chance and
Thee, O Time." Stevens' apotheosis is hypothetical, beginning as
it does with " until " followed by his present-tense " futures "—
" transform," " become," and " turn," modulating into " when "
followed by " are." Even in the cluster of appositions closing the
poem the implicit futurity is remarkable: the pale Muses are to
be " pitched into swelling bodies," they are to be " drift . . . blown
into glittering shapes," and " flames / Wind-beaten into . . . fire,"
a second-order futurity: they *will be* X which *will be transformed*
into Y. And the final superlatives (" freshest, brightest fire "),
Stevens' commonest reflection of the ecstatic moment, obscure
too the possible delineation of this projected time; they simply
ask us to imagine the unimaginable, the brightness and freshness
beyond which there is no better brightness and freshness. The
sleight-of-hand man is working rapidly here.

When Stevens is reluctant to assert even an unequivocal past,
present, or future, he resorts to hypothesis and supposition, chiefly
by using his indispensable conjunction " if," which takes away
with one hand what the poet has already given with the other:

> Or if the music sticks, if the anecdote
> Is false, if Crispin is a profitless
> Philosopher, . . .
>
> . . . .
>
>   what can all this matter since
> The relation comes, benignly, to its end?
>
> So may the relation of each man be clipped. (pp. 45-46)

This is one of the most satisfying of Stevens' shrugs of disavowal,
coming as it does in a witty and comic poem. Other instances
seem merely evidence of a repetitive trick: " the summer came, /
If ever, whisked and wet " (p. 34) ; these " ifs " are like marks

of punctuation, like small question marks inserted in the sentence.
More powerful are the ampler hypotheses of desire:

> The malady of the quotidian. . . .
> Perhaps, if winter once could penetrate
> Through all its purples to the final slate,
> Persisting bleakly in an icy haze,
>
> One might in turn become less diffident,
> Out of such mildew plucking neater mould
> And spouting new orations of the cold.
> One might. One might. But time will not relent. (p. 96)
>
> If they could gather their theses into one,
> Collect their thoughts together into one,
> Into a single thought, thus: into a queen,
> An intercessor by innate rapport,
>
> . . . .
>
> If they could! (p. 254)

These remain hypotheses, not facts, and they are denied, in the
first case by the obstructive "But time will not relent," and in
the second case by the violence of the final optative. Sometimes
there is no such denial present, and the hypothesis becomes a
softened way of assertion:

> If it should be true that reality exists
> In the mind: the tin plate, the loaf of bread on it,
>
> . . . .
>
> . . . it follows that
> Real and unreal are two in one. . . . (p. 485)

These "ifs" of uncommitted assertion serve as pegs from which
Stevens can suspend long deductions, making us disregard the
shaky status of the antecedent in the accretion of apparent logic
that follows. In the eighth section of "It Must Give Pleasure"
from the "Notes toward a Supreme Fiction" the central hypothetical structure is clear:

> What am I to believe? If the angel in his cloud,
>
> . . . .
>
> Leaps downward through evening's revelations, and
>
> . . . .
>
> Forgets the gold centre, the golden destiny,
>
> . . . .
>
> Am I that imagine this angel less satisfied?
>
> . . . .

> Is it he or is it I that experience this?
> Is it I then that keep saying there is an hour
> Filled with expressible bliss,
>
> . . . .
>
> And if there is an hour there is a day,
>
> There is a month, a year, there is a time
> In which majesty is a mirror of the self. (pp. 404-5)

The odd and individual combination of hypothesis and question reveals the poet's need to convince himself of the possibility of " expressible bliss," and prepares us for his final bitter turning on himself as he dismisses his edifice of " logic " with yet another question:

> These external regions, what do we fill them with
> Except reflections, the escapades of death,
> Cinderella fulfilling herself beneath the roof? (p. 405)

The angel, the angelic leap, the majestic hour, all that has been constructed on the central hypotheses, collapse as the critical mind strikes Cinderella's midnight.

A poetic statement can be left indeterminate by being phrased as a hypothesis, or as I have said earlier, as a question, a future event, or a tenseless event (by means of the infinitive). The use of the imperative is another way of manipulating the verb without " asserting " something, and Stevens takes full advantage of it. The imperative is by no means an unusual mood in which to resolve poems (all poems that end in prayers end this way, and poems of social or moral exhortation do too, if we include the jussive and hortatory varieties of the mood). It is only remarkable in Stevens in conjunction with his other handling of moods, and remarkable too insofar as it imitates the tradition of prayer. Stevens' divinities have a shadowy *ad hoc* existence, materializing momentarily as an interior paramour, a rabbi, a green queen, or even an unnamed presence:

> Oh! Rabbi, rabbi, fend my soul for me
> And true savant of this dark nature be. (p. 134)
>
> Unreal, give back to us what once you gave:
> The imagination that we spurned and crave. (p. 88)

Nothing in an imperative implies that it will be complied with, and the poem retains the same unsettled sort of ending that

Stevens has accomplished elsewhere by other means: the action invoked remains as yet unperformed.

When an ending escapes confident formulation, Stevens modulates into conjecture, with his characteristic " as if." [5] Currents of feeling have usually become so entangled by the end of any poem resolved on " as if " that the logical sense of the conclusion is lost in the affective result of the comparison. So it is in the eighth poem of *The Auroras of Autumn* where the poet, faced with the terrifying aurora, must decide whether it is malign or innocent, grim or benevolent. In accents of description he insists on the reality of innocence, " But it exists, / It exists, it is visible, it is, it is." The conclusion follows:

> So, then, these lights are not a spell of light,
> A saying out of a cloud, but innocence.
> An innocence of the earth and no false sign
>
> Or symbol of malice. That we partake thereof,
> Lie down like children in this holiness,
> As if, awake, we lay in the quiet of sleep,
>
> As if the innocent mother sang in the dark
> Of the room and on an accordion, half-heard,
> Created the time and place in which we breathed . . .
>
> (pp. 418-19)

The last four lines attempt to soothe by conjuring up a nursery peace, a retreat to the comforts of childhood; not " let us lie down as if we were lying in the quiet of sleep," but rather " as if we lay," in which the past tense invokes recollection of a real experience of such quiet. There is no innocent mother singing in the present, but Stevens' lines evoke her presence as a counterforce to his apprehensions, even though she exists only in his shadowy " as if."

" As if " forms a bridge between perception and reflection: we

---

[5] The recent *Concordance to the Poetry of Wallace Stevens* by Thomas Walsh (University Park, Pa., 1963) lists over 100 uses of " as if " in this conjectural sense; the frequency increases in the later poetry. The optative, not descriptive function of " as if " in Stevens appears most clearly in " Study of Images II ":

> As if, as if, as if the disparate halves
> Of things were waiting in a betrothal known
> To none, awaiting espousal to the sound
>
> Of right joining, a music of ideas, the burning
> And breeding and bearing birth of harmony,
> The final relation, the marriage of the rest. (pp. 464-65)

stop the film to analyze it. This analysis often goes unremarked unless we sense a departure from the expected tense and mood, as we so often do in Stevens. The texture of Stevens' language is such that it shifts from "reality" to the realm of "as if" very easily, making the two almost interchangeable at times; one poem begins, "All night I sat reading a book, / Sat reading as if in a book / Of sombre pages" (p. 146). In the second line we are "let in" on the metaphorical nature of this "book" (which turns out to be the heavens filled with falling stars) but after this momentary withdrawal from the fiction, we once again re-enter, and the sombre pages remain pages. The effect is of something half-glimpsed, half-seen, and that is, finally, what Stevens achieves over and over: if he has a dogma, it is the dogma of the shadowy, the ephemeral, the barely-perceived, the iridescent: "It is not in the premise that reality / Is a solid. It may be a shade that traverses / A dust, a force that traverses a shade" (p. 489).

In his witty moments, Stevens practices legerdemain with the world's "reality" and produces a fantasia of shifting possibles, the exhilarating and brilliant changes of "Sea Surface Full of Clouds." In the more reflective poems, he juggles with logic as he juggles with colors and shapes, often less successfully, but sometimes with the confident disposition of alternatives he commands in "The Idea of Order at Key West":

> She sang beyond the genius of the sea.
>
> · · · · · · · · · · · · · ·
>
> The sea was not a mask. No more was she.
> The song and water were not medleyed sound
> Even if what she sang was what she heard,
> Since what she sang was uttered word by word.
> It may be that in all her phrases stirred
> The grinding water and the gasping wind;
> But it was she and not the sea we heard.
>
>   *　　*　　*
>
> If it was only the dark voice of the sea
> That rose, or even colored by many waves;
> If it was only the outer voice of sky
> And cloud, of the sunken coral water-walled,
> However clear, it would have been deep air,
> The heaving speech of air, a summer sound
> Repeated in a summer without end
> And sound alone. But it was more than that,
> More even than her voice, and ours, among

> The meaningless plungings of water and the wind,
> Theatrical distances, bronze shadows heaped
> On high horizons, mountainous atmospheres
> Of sky and sea. (pp. 128-29)

The structure of the poem is ostensibly one of logical discrimination, but actually the complicated progressions ("even if . . . since . . . it may be . . . if . . . or . . .") simply serve to implicate the various alternatives ever more deeply with each other so that the sea, the girl, the water, the song, the wind, the air, the sky and cloud, the voices of the spectators, all become indistinguishable from each other, as Stevens wants them to be. To separate out his inferences and insist on the demarcations his logic would seem to be making would be to run counter to the intent of the poem. Stevens uses logical form here not as a logician but as a sleight-of-hand man, making assertion appear in different guises and from different angles, delighting in paradoxical logic, and sometimes defying logic entirely: "In the little of his voice, or the like, / Or less, he found a man, or more, against / Calamity, proclaimed himself, was proclaimed" (p. 230). Such passages can be parsed into sense, but not very rewardingly. Stevens' use of "or" in this way is one more device for hovering over the statement rather than making it. The atmosphere of false precision sometimes conferred by this language of logical discrimination is deceptive: Stevens is not at pains to distinguish between the little, the like, and the less in the passage above, but to merge them.

In Stevens' poems there are many voices speaking, and it is a limitation of the poet to isolate one, as I have done here, even though it is the prevalent voice of hesitation and qualification, of apathy lightened by a flash of hope, of happiness flickered with irony, of any feeling shadowed by its opposite. Still, Stevens' nuances are better sensed by a habitual knowledge of the patterns into which his voice falls. Even in the simplest and shortest poems the characteristic grammar and syntax, the characteristic logic, the characteristic resolutions appear. The last poem in the *Collected Poems* will serve as an example of Stevens' manner; it is called, bravely enough, "Not Ideas about the Thing but the Thing Itself." Even the title embodies one of Stevens' typical formulas, "not X but Y," which appears in a frequency far beyond the normal throughout Stevens' work, and seems to be another case of the left hand subtracting what the right hand gives. (We are reminded by the "not-but" formula that what we might be impelled to call The Thing has been said on imposing authority to be merely Ideas About The Thing, a fact we might not have recalled if we were not so reminded.) The poem is about the most meager evidence of spring, a faintly-heard bird's cry, and the poem is deliberately meager in reflecting it:

NOT IDEAS ABOUT THE THING BUT THE THING ITSELF

At the earliest ending of winter,
In March, a scrawny cry from outside
Seemed like a sound in his mind.

He knew that he heard it,
A bird's cry, at daylight or before,
In the early March wind.

The sun was rising at six,
No longer a battered panache above snow . . .
It would have been outside.

It was not from the vast ventriloquism
Of sleep's faded papier-mâché . . .
The sun was coming from outside.

That scrawny cry—it was
A chorister whose c preceded the choir.
It was part of the colossal sun,

Surrounded by its choral rings,
Still far away. It was like
A new knowledge of reality. (p. 534)

Was the bird's cry a new knowledge of reality, the *ding-an-sich?* We are not told; the epistemological question is begged by the final simile. It is what we would *call* (perhaps deludedly) a new knowledge of reality, but the poet, ironically aware of human shortcomings in seeing "reality," is content to leave the feeling of revelation intact, but with the intellectual justification for the feeling impugned. The poem, though in a diminished and minor key, resembles Herbert's "The Flower": "Who would have thought my shrivel'd heart / Could have recover'd greennesse?" Who could have thought that the birds would return? But Stevens' poem is not phrased in that astonished wonder; it is the most tentative of rejoicings, the most hesitant admission of the presence of spring, the most wintry supposition of refreshment. He hardly dares anticipate his own realization: not "at the earliest beginning of spring," but " at the earliest ending of winter," the poet hears, or seems to hear, or thinks he hears, or wonders if he did hear, a scrawny cry, unbeautiful but *there*. The phases in his realization of spring are gradually unfolded, and we follow his uncertainty in his phrasing. First, the cry " seemed like a sound in his mind," not in the world, though " he knew that he heard it." The question is, where did it come from—from his mind, from a dream, or from outside? " It would have been outside," he conjectures, not yet sure. " It was not," he concludes, "from the vast ventriloquism " of sleep's artifice. Finally he decides (by what logic we are not immediately sure) that it was truly a bird's cry, but the uncertainty of his perception (when did he hear it? " at daylight or before? ") still makes the sound only the barest perceptible token. " Seemed," " would have been," " not X," " or," " like,"—all of these, reflecting the conjectural, half-awake state of the speaker, are familiar signs of Stevens' mitigated assertion.

But there is another presence in the poem besides the equivocal bird's cry, and that is the sun, equally equivocal at first, but later an undeniable object. Like the definition of the weather (not spring but the " earliest ending of winter ") the definition of the sun is fatigued and negative: it is " no longer a battered panache above snow," but what it now *is* is not yet revealed. It is the presence of the spring sun, a visible, felt presence, which somehow proves to the spectator, according to the strange logic of the poem, that the bird cry was not imagined, or dreamed, but real:

> The sun was rising at six,
> No longer a battered panache above snow . . .
> It [the bird's cry] would have been outside.

> It was not from the vast ventriloquism
> Of sleep's faded papier-mâché . . .
> The sun was coming from outside.

The speaker knew, even before the sunrise, that it was March, a logical time to hear the first bird of spring; he even knew the time of sunrise (it was getting earlier, the sun was rising at six, not seven or eight), from which he might conclude to the reality of the bird's cry. But in fact, it is not by these logical links that the realization comes; it is by the concrete fact, the sunlight coming in his window: he *sees* the sunlight, and *knows* the bird is real. This conviction by concomitance, not by deduction, is emphasized by the "rhyme" of the third and sixth lines in the excerpt just quoted; the bird cry must have come from outside because the sun is outside. The two presences harmoniously converge in the poet's mind, one explaining the other, and he immediately conceives a metaphor to express their relation: the colossal sun is the episcopal figure surrounded by a choir which is led by the bird-chorister, the tone-giver who precedes the choir. Just as the faint c of the chorister is, to the trained ear, the signal of the imminent *Ecce sacerdos magnus* of the choir, so all the spectator needs to confirm the barely audible cry is a sense, given by the first faint beams of the sun, of the whole of which it is a part. Even so, the realization is not a jubilant one, since the *colossal* sun, like all of Stevens' apocalyptic entities, is "still far away." The only guarantee of its coming, in fact, is the faint bird note. There is a circular process here: the (faint) sun confirms the reality of the (scrawny) bird cry, which in turn, by its relation to the (expected) choir, guarantees the reality of the (colossal) sun. And in fact, after the initial strongly-felt identification of the cry, the tone dwindles from "it was a chorister" to "it was part of" to "still far away" to "it was like X." The tone is no doubt still affirmative, but in a chastened way; the entrance of the sun in glory will be celebrated by some poet of more ecstatic bent. Stevens has constructed something upon which to rejoice—a scrawny cry—as his version of those larks and nightingales of his Romantic ancestors, inaccessible forever in his later day, or, more truthfully perhaps, uncongenial to his wintry temperament.

IX

ON THE GRAMMAR OF WALLACE STEVENS

BY MAC HAMMOND

Many readers of modern poetry find themselves baffled by the late poems of Wallace Stevens. Not only are the poems almost exclusively about poetry itself but, after the gorgeous vocabulary of the 1923 *Harmonium* volume, the bareness of vocabulary in poems beginning with "The Man with the Blue Guitar" (1937) seems something of a desert. The same music is there but the bright flowers are gone. Of what does this desert music consist?

The most obvious structural characteristic of Stevens' late poems is the repetition of words and phrases in proximity. The primary result of the device is to lay bare the grammatical structure of the speech and to place a heavy burden on the grammar in respect to the communication of meaning. The late poetry of Stevens is, in short, a poetry of grammar. Stanza XX of "The Man with the Blue Guitar" provides a typical illustration:

> What is there in life except one's ideas,
> Good air, good friend, what is there in life?
>
> Is it ideas that I believe?
> Good air, my only friend, believe,
>
> Believe would be a brother full
> Of love, believe would be a friend,
>
> Friendlier than my only friend,
> Good air. Poor pale, poor pale guitar . . .

Readers of this stanza, baffled by difficulty to discover ordinary meanings, may find comfort in the remarks and questions that the late Renato Poggioli addressed to Stevens when he was translating "The Man with the Blue Guitar" into Italian. Of this particular stanza he wrote to Stevens:

Only a long paraphrase could solve for me all the problems presented in this section by the function and relations of the often repeated words *good air, good friend*. Is the first a vocative? Or is it the second that is one? Is the second an apposition of the first? I am full of doubts also concerning the sentences containing the word *believe*.[1]

---

[1] In an unpublished letter from Poggioli to Stevens dated July 4, 1953, in Houghton

179

But Poggioli was on the wrong track; mere lexical paraphrase is not the avenue to understanding grammatical functions. One must scrutinize the grammar itself and make resolutions about it. Rhetoric provides something of a guide to this endeavor.

In rhetorical terminology the repetition of a word or phrase in the same grammatical situation is known as *repetitio*, as in "good air" (lines 2 and 4)—both vocative. Also in rhetoric the repetition of a word or phrase in a different grammatical situation is known as *traductio*, as in "believe" (lines 3 and 4)—the first, a third person, present tense, indicative verb; the second, an imperative. The particular figures of both *repetitio* and *traductio* in poetry are classified according to where repetition occurs in respect to beginnings and endings of lines (or syntactic units in prose). Thus the repetition of the phrase "What is there in life" (lines 1 and 2) is an instance of *kyklos*; the occurrences of "Good air" (lines 2, 4, and 8) is an instance of *anaphor*; the repetition of "believe" (lines 4 and 5) is an instance of *anadiplose*, as is the stem repetition "friend" / "Friendlier" (lines 6 and 7); and the continguous repetition of "poor pale" (line 8) is an instance of *epanalepse*.[2] These highly symmetrical repetitions seem of course largely decorative when viewed simply under the nomenclature of rhetoric; but, considered in terms of their shifting grammatical functions, they reveal important components of the meaning of the stanza.

Take for instance the grammatical shifts in the four times repeated word "believe." It first occurs in line 3 as a first person, present tense, indicative verb; then, in line 4, as an imperative; and, finally, in lines 5 and 6, still as an imperative but hypostatized, that is, spoken of as a word, and made to serve as noun subject. *Each time the word appears the concept that it evokes becomes progressively more tenuous.* The first occurrence of "believe" in line 3 as an indicative verb describes an actual state of mind; then, at the end of line 4, the imperative form posits the concept more distantly as a desired attitude of mind rather than as an actuality; and, finally, when the imperative is presented in lines 5 and 6 merely as a linguistic consideration, merely as a

---

Library, Harvard University. I wish to thank Mrs. Renata Poggioli for permission to quote from her husband's correspondence.

[2] These classifications are made according to Heinrich Lausberg, *Elemente der literarischen Rhetorik* (Munich, 1949).

linguistic symbol stripped by hypostatization of its direct force as a command, the concept it evokes achieves the limits of abstraction. This progressive grammatical detachment of the word "believe" is a major force in communicating the addressee's sense of disoriented confidence, first indicated by his questions in the first three lines and reinforced by his indications of isolation ("my *only* friend") and expectation ("believe *would be*").

The transformation of the twice repeated vocative "Good air" (lines 2 and 4) into an appositional object of a comparison (line 8) fosters a similar sense of detachment. The air is invoked as the *addressee* of the message to follow, but then in the message itself this same addressee becomes *a topic of discussion*. This transposition of "good air" is definitely from the conative to the cognitive.[3]

Accompanying the great amount of *repetitio* and *traductio* in Stevens' late poems are extraordinary accumulations of different words with the same or with ambiguous grammatical functions. Thus, for example, the grammatical texture of Stanza XIII of "The Man with the Blue Guitar" is determined predominantly by adjectives and nouns.

> The pale intrusions into blue
> Are corrupting pallors . . . ay di mi,
>
> Blue buds or pitchy blooms. Be content—
> Expansions, diffusions—content to be
>
> The unspotted imbecile revery,
> The heraldic center of the world
>
> Of blue, blue sleek with a hundred chins,
> The amorist Adjective aflame . . .

Twelve adjectives and fourteen nouns account for over half of the forty-five words in this stanza. This extraordinary balance in favor of adjectives and nouns is thrown into particular prominence by the complete absence of concrete verbs expressing action; there are only three verbs in this stanza, and they are either copular or forms of the existential "to be." In spite of

---

[3] Compare the use of the usual intimate conative pronoun "you" in "Janet, Alice would be more friendly than you" *vs.* the peculiarly distancing cognitive in "Janet, Alice would be more friendly than Janet." We frequently have recourse to this distancing cognitive device when addressing children who have not yet acquired the distinction between personal pronouns and with whom we have fairly tenuous verbal communication, e.g., "Would Anna like her dinner?"

this absence of concrete verbs, the stanza is redolent with action—
"intrusions," "corrupting," "expansions," "diffusions," "revery."
No action, however, is considered grammatically as an action but
rather as an entity or as a quality.

The usual grammatical distinction between nouns and adjectives obscures a very important linguistic fact: nouns and adjectives have more in common than mere endocentricity. It is well
known that many words can function without morphological
alteration as nouns or as adjectives or even as verbs. Indeed, in
many languages there is no formal distinction between nouns
and adjectives. Quine, concerned with problems of reference, has
remarked: "Grammatical contrasts among substantive, adjective, and verb . . . are contrasts in grammatical role, with associated distinction in word form; but it happens that the separation
of roles into those that call for substantial form, those that call
for the adjectival, and those that call for the verbal has little
bearing on questions of reference."[4] This observation must be
somewhat shocking to those schooled in traditional grammar,
but it is very telling upon reflection. Consider some of the adjectives and nouns from Stanza XIII: the references of the noun
"expansions" are clearly actions; those of the noun "pallors"
clearly qualities. And it is clear even in this stanza that many
of the words, such as "imbecile," could assume substantival or
adjectival functions without change of form. Indeed, in this stanza
there is an important instance of a word changing function without changing form: "blue" (line 1) is a noun; "blue" (line 3)
is an adjective. Quine is particularly illuminating about this particular kind of duplication of roles, on which so much of the sense
of this stanza depends. He says that "adjectives that are cumulative in reference even double as mass substantives—as when
we say 'Red is a color' or 'Add a little more red'. In such cases
English agrees with us in making light of the distinction between
substantive and adjective."[5]

The preponderance of nouns and adjectives in Stanza XIII,
together with the absence of concrete, active verbs seems, then,
less than accidental, seems rather to be founded in a natural condition of the language: the interchangeability of referential and
sometimes grammatical roles of nouns, adjectives, and verbs.

[4] Willard Van Orman Quine, *Word and Object* (New York, 1960), p. 96.
[5] *Ibid.*, p. 97.

How does this fact of language operate in Stanza XIII of "The Man with the Blue Guitar"? Stevens simply plays linguistic sleight-of-hand with the potentiality of an adjective that is cumulative in reference to double as a mass substantive. A paraphrase of the stanza, *with particular attention to grammatical categories,* may render the trick in slow motion.

The following paraphrase is based on the premise that the color blue is a symbol for the imagination.[6]

Paraphrase of Stanza XIII: Reality thrusts itself into the imagination ("blue" a noun, line 1) and reduces the imagination, alas, to a dependent status ("blue" in line 3 is merely an adjective modifying "buds"). Be satisfied, while the imagination expands and diffuses itself, to be imaginative revery untouched by reality, to be the noble center (because producer) of the imagination ("blue," a noun, first occurrence, line 7), to be the imagination ("blue", a noun, second occurrence, line 7) enormously fat with potential, to be "the amorist Adjective aflame" ("Adjective" line 8 is a noun apposition to the last occurrence in line 7 of the noun "blue," symbol for the imagination) which, as it flames, reaches out to embrace reality as an adjective embraces a noun (as, indeed, it does in line 3).

Or, again, to speed up the trick with focus only on the grammar: there are four occurrences of the word "blue," three (lines 1 and 7) as a noun and one (line 3) as an adjective. At its final occurrence as a noun, in line 7, "blue" is the appositional antecedent of the noun "Adjective" in line 8.

By this last apposition a quality "blue," already substantivized, is hypostatized, i.e., spoken about as a word by the grammatical categorization of it as an "Adjective." Hence Stevens' own explanation of the meaning of this last line: ". . . amorist Adjective means blue (the amorist Adjective) as a word metamorphosed

---

[6] This premise is drawn from Stevens' notes to Poggioli on this stanza. He wrote about the last and crucial line as follows: ". . . the amorist Adjective means blue (the amorist Adjective) as a word metamorphosed into blue as a reality." Dissatisfied with this explanation, he wrote again: "The other day I commented on 'amorist Adjective aflame.' Perhaps my explanation was a bit too expansive. The poem in which this appears, Blue Guitar XIII, is a poem that deals with the intensity of the imagination unmodified by contacts with reality, if such a thing is possible. Intensity becomes something incandescent. I took a look at this poem after I had written to you and thought that the metamorphosis into reality, while a good illustration, was misleading. The poem has to do with pure imagination." See Stevens, *Mattino Domenicale ed Altre Poesie,* trans. Renato Poggioli (Torino, 1954), pp. 177-78.

into blue as a reality "—which (see note 6) he called a "good illustration" of what the line means but a "misleading" one. He might have said more simply: "Adjective," a noun denoting an entity, means "blue," a noun denoting a quality.

The imagination is, after all, not an entity, even though spoken of in nominal form; it is not—to use the traditional terminology for a noun—a person, place, or thing. The imagination is rather a quality or an action. But Stanza XIII of "The Man with the Blue Guitar" entertains, through a kind of linguistic trickery, the notion that the imagination is an entity. Such hypostatization is a typical result of metalanguage or of metapoetry—speech about speech.

Poetry about poetry (metapoetry) is the key phrase to describe all of Stevens' poetry, especially the late poems culminating in "Notes toward a Supreme Fiction" and "An Ordinary Evening in New Haven"—and metapoetry presents, of necessity, a highly grammatical drama, for it consists of *concepts about poetic language itself* of which grammar makes up a large part of the story.

X

THE CLIMATES OF WALLACE STEVENS

BY RICHARD A. MACKSEY

1

> . . . dichterisch, wohnet
> Der Mensch auf dieser Erde . . .
> Hölderlin

> To speak humanly from the height or from the depth
> Of human things, that is acutest speech.
> " Chocorua to Its Neighbor "

The world of Wallace Stevens is a universe of particulars. His poet, "any man of the imagination," inhabits the center, surrounded by the vast disorder and richness of the physical world. It is not yet a universe, but rather " a constellation / Of patches and of pitches." [1] He is alone, unsponsored, free—dispossessed of his gods, his myths, his essences, and even his own past. In poetry he achieves endless temporary alliances with his world, lives in the instant finality of experience. In this " immensest theater," time is represented by images of flowing away, of water, of wind, and of human life from sleep to death. Although certain cycles recur, change is endless both in the world and in the reflecting mind passing, like Leibniz's monad, from perception to perception.

And from the welter of things in flight the poet " measures the velocities of change." [2] He marks the ascents and declensions of both the world and his imagination:

> A blue pigeon it is, that circles the blue sky,
> On sidelong wing, around and round and round.
> A white pigeon it is, that flutters to the ground. (*CP*, 17)

The " ambiguous undulations " of things " as they sink, / Downward to darkness " and ultimate extinction command the poet's

---

[1] Wallace Stevens, *Opus Posthumous* (New York, 1957), p. 114. This volume will be hereafter cited as *OP*.

[2] *The Collected Poems of Wallace Stevens* (New York, 1954), p. 414. This volume will be hereafter cited as *CP*.

rapt attention and restore his imagination (*CP*, 70). The imagination, which suffuses and transforms his world like the light of
the " Augusta " moon or " the hermit's candle," seizes upon fleeting
congruences, images, what Stevens calls " these casual exfoliations . . . / Of the tropic of resemblance." [3] The imagination is a
way of apprehending the world in its nicest particularity, but it
is a translation and transformation of the world in the alembic of
his consciousness, what Stevens calls with lingering affection " the
fiction that results from feeling . . . my green, my fluent mundo "
(*CP*, 406, 407). And language, which is endlessly coming to be
and passing away like all else, is the sovereign instrument of the
imagination:

> A flick which added to what was real and its vocabulary,
> The way some first thing coming into Northern trees
> Adds to them the whole vocabulary of the South,
> The way the earliest single light in the evening sky, in spring,
> Creates a fresh universe out of nothingness by adding itself,
> The way a look or a touch reveals its unexpected magnitudes.
>
> (*CP*, 517)

The change wrought here on the Northern landscape by the

[3] Wallace Stevens, *The Necessary Angel: Essays on Reality and the Imagination*
(New York, 1951), p. 86. This volume will be hereafter cited as *NA*. Stevens' doctrine
of " resemblance," as elaborated in the lecture on " The Effects of Analogy " (*NA*,
105-30), bears a curious similarity to the attempt of Petrus Aureoli (d. 1322) to
work out a theory rooted in the perception of concrete, existing things, a theory which
argues the " fabricating " power of the mind to form concepts from the quality of
" likeness " in material things—a middle way between extreme realism and extreme
nominalism. At first Aureoli seems to suggest immediate apprehension of the thing
itself; there is no argument about individuation: " omnis res est se ipsa singularis
et per nihil aliud " (*In II Librum Sententiarum* [Rome, 1605], 9, 3, 3, p. 114, a A).
Cognition, however, is still mediated. Because of resemblance (*similitudo*), a *quality*
of being and not being, the intellect is able to form a concept, by which it is made
similar to the thing. The concept has only " phenomenal being " (*esse apparens*),
i. e. being as an object of knowledge; to that extent, it is different from the thing
known; on the other hand, it is the thing known itself, in the only way in which it can
be present in the mind, and, in this sense, it has " intentional being " (*esse intentionale*).
The concept of the rose, as Aureoli says in an example which provoked Ockham and
may have inspired Mallarmé, is, by the conceptualizing power of the mind, an
" appearance " in the intellect alone, ". . . but that form which we are conscious
of beholding when we know the rose as such or the flower as such is not something
real impressed subjectively on the intellect, or on the imagination; nor is it a real
subsistent thing; it is the thing itself as possessing *esse intentionale* " (*Commentariorum
in I Sententiarum, pars prima* [Rome, 1596], 9, I, p. 319, a B). Aureoli consequently
stresses the primacy of adhering to the particulars of experience; but the thing itself
has its phenomenal being only in the mind which assimilates resemblance.

Southern light of the imagination suggests one change which is
cyclic and self-renewing in Stevens' poetry: the succession of the
seasons. For Stevens, man lives in the weather as he lives in the
changing light of his moods and new redactions of reality; and,
like the weather, he can be described only from day to day. For
him, as for Baudelaire, the climates of his landscapes are also the
climates of his consciousness. Man lives in *ecstatic* identities
(where the adjective has much of the weight with which Heidegger
invests it)—man "stands out" in the changing elements:

> . . . Ecstatic identities
> Between one's self and the weather and the things
> Of the weather are the belief in one's element,
> The casual reunions, the long-pondered
> Surrenders, the repeated sayings that
> There is nothing more and that it is enough
> To believe in the weather and in the things and men
> Of the weather and in one's self, as part of that
> And nothing more. . . . (*CP*, 258)

These ambiguous marriages of mind and environment, here
heightened to the pitch of poetry, constitute our conscious life.
For Stevens, as for primitive man, utterance is neither a question
of discursive form nor of presentational form. If immediate knowledge is denied, there is still a sufficiency and peace in the momentary identity between the "finding mind" and its surroundings;
the climate which the "major man" thus recovers is neither
wholly of the earth nor of the mind, but a human creation rooted
in the weather: "half earth, half mind; / Half sun, half thinking
of the sun" (*CP*, 257).

And this fictional unity is open to change from both quarters,
the turning seasons and the spinning mind. As the mind returns
to familiar points in the cycle, a fusion of the past already lived
and a present never lived before, it experiences both recognition
and discovery symbolized by what Novalis celebrated as "the
marriage of the seasons." The poet can move with the speed of
light from the bare "winter branch" to "the bough of summer"
(*CP*, 67).

In the weather of Stevens' sensibility, then, the consciousness
describes a cycle analogous to the seasons, though it admits of
rapid shifts and sudden transformations (as in the poem above).
Early and late in Wallace Stevens' development certain moments

recur which enact for the poet his continuing dialogue of central self and circling nature. The drama is always a return to his grandest theater of the imagination where the mind exists and changes alone in the flux of the circumambient weather. The first of these moments—rare in the tropics of *Harmonium* and dominant in the northern world of *The Rock*—is represented by the nothingness of winter, the "basic slate" (*CP*, 15), "the bare spaces of our skies" (*CP*, 108) to which the perceiving poet lies open, empty "in an elemental freedom, sharp and cold" (*CP*, 297). The experience is one of immense clarity and intense poverty, an abandonment to pure content of consciousness unrefracted by convention or individuality. It is a moment which cannot be long sustained.

> . . . naked of any illusion, in poverty,
> In the exactest poverty, if then
> One breathed the cold evening, the deepest inhalation
> Would come from that return to the subtle centre. (*CP*, 258)

In this moment of contraction he returns without baggage or clothing to the bare fact of the world, "to the final slate, / Persisting bleakly in an icy haze" (*CP*, 96), a winter world of unmediated perception. In the physical and mental poverty of this winter, man is "nothing," the innocent eye of Bergson, which Stevens amends to the "ignorant eye" (*CP*, 380). And the world without, too, is "nothing," untransformed by the vivifying imagination, a "hoard / Of destructions" (*CP*, 173) which were grounded, as Stevens asserts explicitly in "A Primitive like an Orb," in nothingness. The world is ice and snow and vacancy; the man of winter is a glass lens or a diamond or simply an emptiness, "air collected in a deep essay" (*CP*, 297).

The evolving imagination expands from this primitive moment; the green leaves come and cover the high rock, "the gray particular of man's life, / The stone from which he rises" (*CP*, 528). The world blooms and the "habit of analogy" flourishes as the seasons turn:

> . . . The pearled chaplet of spring,
> The magnum wreath of summer, time's autumn snood,
>
> Its copy of the sun, these cover the rock.
> These leaves are the poem, the icon and the man.
>
> (*CP*, 526-27)

As the sun warms the earth of Crispin's tropics or Florida's "venereal soil," the earth proliferates its imagery and the imagination discovers resemblances and correspondences. The autumnal leaves harvest the last flamboyant extremities of color and whisper of the final contraction and mortality to come.

"It Must Change." Reality appears at every point in the cycle: "the imagination loses vitality as it ceases to adhere to what is real." But Stevens adds that "the world about us would be desolate except for the world within us." Like the fluent world without, this interior "seeming" place must change; the return to the nothing of winter is the very act of perception for a man of glass, a crystal, transparent to perception. In "The Man on the Dump" the poet sits amid the extravagant waste of outworn images which reality has left behind, but just at the moment when all has been tossed on the dump," "the moon creeps up," the recurrent emblem of the imagination, and with it "the bubbling of bassoons" (*CP*, 202). "It is desire at the end of winter, when / It observes the effortless weather turning blue / And sees the myosotis on its bush" (*CP*, 382).

The poet, then, is always at the center of his changing weather, open to his double environment of mind and sky; he is

> The central man, the human globe, responsive
> As a mirror with a voice, the man of glass,
> Who in a million diamonds sums us up.
>
> He is the transparence of the place in which
> He is and in his poems we find peace. (*CP*, 250-51)

And, transparent and central, he wrestles with "the giant of nothingness" to win the central poem, a version of the world, "The essential poem at the centre of things" (*CP*, 440). In his essay, "Effects of Analogy," Stevens contrasts what he calls a "marginal poetry" ("the attempt to live on the verge of consciousness") with a second theory of poetry which "relates to the imagination as a power within [the poet] to have such insights into reality as will make it possible for him to be sufficient as a poet in the very center of consciousness" (*NA*, 115). He identifies himself with this second, "central," poetry, and adds:

The proponents of the second theory believe that to create the poetry of the present is an incalculable difficulty, which rarely is achieved, fully and robustly, by anyone. They think that there is enough and more than enough to do with what faces us and concerns us directly and that in poetry as an art, and, for that matter, in any art, the central problem is always the problem of reality. (*NA*, 115-16)

The earth is the text of every "central poem" and man sits perilously in "The Hermitage at the Centre" like a studious ghost. The lesson is

> A text of intelligent men
> At the centre of the unintelligible,
> As in a hermitage, for us to think,
> Writing and reading the rigid inscription. (*CP*, 495)

The poet is an inquisitor of the structures of reality, but from his central vantage as transparent consciousness. This "man of glass" is always open to the play of experience—most purely in the "winter phase" of his cycle. This primitive central monad, empty of ideas or preconceptions, is precisely non-Leibnizian, not windowless and regulated by the calculus, but vitreous and emptied of all opacity, a poetic vacuum tube. The glass is clearly not that of Valéry's mirror or of Mallarmé's glacier, self-reflecting or static, but a transparent and fluent medium.

This concept of the *emptiness* of the *central man* in his first moment introduces the second general theme of winter which relates the three poems to be discussed—the cluster of words Stevens uses in each to indicate nothingness: the ice, the empty air, the successive negations, finally, the last words of the first two poems, echoing "nothing" and "no one." Just as the world and the consciousness are revealed as vacancy, the poem for Stevens must become an "abstraction," a fiction erected over the void and an invention without inventor. The sensing self grows aware of the fiction of his own sensing, the word-picturing, and, in the root sense of the word, is *abstracted* further from the data of the initial impulse; in the nothing of the imagination he can construct possibles.

Behind the abstracted nothing of the fictive imagination is the relation of the self to itself in a successful moment of contemplation. This is the experience of "*la conscience de la conscience*" which Valéry so sedulously courts. The self experiences a moment of otherness; life is turned into a pure act of awareness and the mind, transported, regards itself as nothing. Chocorua, speaking through the airy distances, is a personification of the perfect state of spiritual nothingness which transcends metaphor. Finally, the constant change which is the fate of every particular in the world, and of every consciousness exploring it, moves between nothing and nothing like the "river that flows nowhere," between "not yet" and "was," between sleep and death.

Despite "the dumfoundering abyss / Between us and the object" which torments the romantic poet in every generation, the air between the two is, for Stevens, of crystalline clarity, and change on the far side has its reflex within (*CP*, 437). And paralleling this merely epiphenomenal change the poet's mind displays the creative change of dialectical process. The poetic dialogue moves from the givenness of the object to the annihilating power of subject and is resolved in the synthesis of the poem itself. Stevens begins, as did Hegel in the *Logik*, by confronting pure Being; it vanishes before his attention and is displaced by its antithesis, the nothingness which is to play an increasingly vital role in his thought. He finds the concrete synthesis of Being and Not-Being in Becoming, the dynamism of both his worlds which saves the one from the curse of changelessness and propels the other ceaselessly toward the "ultimate poem" which is always the next poem. And the dialectical process itself, the passage from one concept to its contrary, from thesis to antithesis, and then to union, illustrates how change is always in our thought and how the poem which imitates this thought must be founded on change and movement.

To say this much about the dialectical life of Stevens' central man is not to suggest that he fails, with Hegel, to blink that abyss which separates him from the object. He refuses the idealist's reduction. His way of bridging the distance is much closer to the patient "description" of the phenomenologist, who refuses to founder his project on one brink or the other.

There is a peculiar temptation to enlist analogies from the philosophers in reading Wallace Stevens' poetry—and a peculiar danger. The temptation and the danger spring from the uninterrupted concern of the poetry itself where theory and practice are one:

> This endlessly elaborating poem
> Displays the theory of poetry,
> As the life of poetry. . . . (*CP*, 486)

And, exploring the New Haven of his mind, Stevens extemporizes " more urgent proof that the theory / Of poetry is the theory of life, / As it is " (*CP*, 486). His patient interrogations of his environment and his consciousness would seem to be a quest for an adequate theory of knowledge to support both. Yet no one saw more clearly than Stevens the radical differences between the trade of the philosophers he enjoyed reading and his vocation as a poet. Despite the unity of his work which is revealed in retrospect, he wrote individual poems, each " the cry of its occasion," which live in the richness of their particularity and the uniqueness of utterance. The concept or the image drawn from the philosopher was frequently a point of departure for an individual poem, but it was never its justification. The interest in the three poems which follow is in no way based on an argument for the originality or adequacy of Stevens' theory of knowledge. The poems are more simply and more successfully " the mind in the act of finding / What will suffice " (*CP*, 239). The reader is immediately concerned with the *way* in which the poet's epistemological situation is *enacted*, in that perilous space where the affective and the discursive however briefly coincide.

Although much given to his own kind of " abstraction " and " generalization," Stevens instinctively distrusted any system of thought which discredited the particulars of experience; he had much fun in his notes, and in occasional poems, at the expense of the excesses of subjective idealism. But one development of twentieth-century philosophy which " brackets " systematic metaphysical speculation, does in its point of departure and its method suggest a means of looking at his poetics. Enmeshed in the world, open to the future and the concreteness of experience, the phenomenologist choses Husserl's " third way " between the dangers of absolute realism or idealism. His cry of " to the things themselves " and his insistence that all consciousness is intentional, that every *cogito* is an act, reveal fundamental aspects of Stevens' approach to writing poetry; the poems, ultimately, have to reveal themselves. In " Credences of Summer " Stevens echoes the watchword: " Let's see the very thing and nothing else " (*CP*, 373). For Stevens as for Husserl " the world " is an irreducible component of the given; consciousness is relational and not substantial, not so much mental as " *weltlich*." Moods suffuse and penetrate the moving chaos of the world around one, an enormous field of intentional relations. Stevens perhaps never goes as far as Heidegger in completely dissolving the transparent, porous sphere of the central consciousness, but like master and pupil he is committed to the unity of experience, the interpretation of "mind and sky." Husserl might be describing the initial moment of Stevens' man, open to experience:

Ich bin mir einer Welt bewust, endlos ausgebreitet im Raum, endlos werdend und geworden in der Zeit. Ich bin mir ihrer bewust, das sagt vor allem: ich finde sie unmittelbar anschaulich vor, als daseiende, ich erfahre sie.[4]

. . . .

Auf diese Welt, *die Welt, in der ich mich finde und die zugleich meine Umwelt ist,* beziehen sich denn die Komplexe meiner mannigfach wechselnden *Spontaneitäten* des Bewustseins.[5]

This central commitment is the point of departure of each of the three poems which follow, stages in the winter cycle of phenomenal openness. And despite the announced intention of each poem in its title, all three return to the intrinsic difference between modes of tuition which Husserl elaborates: although there is always a correlation between the intentional unity and the description, the sensory data always differ from (and in a sense displace) the thing itself:

. . . in *schlechthin unbedingter* Allgemeinheit, bzw. Notwendigkeit kann ein Ding in keiner möglichen Wahrnehmung, in keinem möglichen Bewustsein überhaupt, als reell immanentes gegeben sein. Ein grundwesentlicher Unterschied tritt also hervor zwischen *Sein als Erlebnis* und *Sein als Ding.*[6]

Thus consciousness and reality in a way cancel each other out in the very unity of perception, a simultaneous creation and decreation which opens the way to the speculations of Heidegger and Sartre, but which also suggests the essential oscillations of Stevens' poetry, from winter to summer, day to night, and from world to imagination. But, as Stevens adds, "the theory of description matters most"—it is the point of departure for phenomenologist and for poet (*CP*, 345).

[4] Edmund Husserl, *Ideen zu einer reinen Phänomenologie und phänomenologischen Philosophie,* ed. Walter Biemel, in *Husserliana* (The Hague, 1950), III, 57.
[5] Husserl, p. 60.
[6] Husserl, p. 95.

Despite the extraordinary evolution of styles which occupied Wallace Stevens for over forty years, his poetry displays a rigorous unity of impulse and purpose; a limited number of themes, situations, characters, and images reappear and build their private resonances. This unity can perhaps be traced only in retrospect, with the gathering urgency of the late poems as gloss for the tentative vocabulary of *Harmonium*. In his meditation on the poem beyond poetry, "A Primitive like an Orb," he argues that "One poem proves another and the whole" (*CP*, 441). All the metamorphoses of style ultimately become the shadow of a single purpose. Marianne Moore has written eloquently of "the interacting veins of life between the early and the late poems."[7]

Yet to read Stevens as the poet of a single poem is as dangerous as it is to reduce him to the role of a repetitious amateur epistemologist. Any attempt to "construct" a Stevens of the endlessly fresh slices of his poems is reminiscent of the solemn discourse by the pedagogue in "Someone Puts a Pineapple Together." The odor of the particular escapes.

>   . . . the odor of this fruit,
> That steeps the room, quickly, then not at all,
>
> It is more than the odor of this core of earth
> And water. It is that which is distilled
> In the prolific ellipses that we know. (*NA*, 87)

It is in the "prolific ellipses" of the particular poems that we must learn to know Stevens. It is fairer, then, to his achievement in its flexibility and variety to examine a few texts, poems which first establish their own identity and then suggest their creator's continuity. Such an approach is responsive to Stevens' Heraclitean axiom that the imagination never touches the same cheek twice in the same way.

The three poems cover a third of a century in the poet's development, from "The Snow Man" (which first appeared in *Poetry* as part of the 1921 collection, "Sur Ma Guzzla Gracile") to the short meditation which Stevens elected to conclude his *Collected Poems*. Yet each poem begins at a point in the "winter phase" of the imagination and begins from the same transparent center. Each poem explores an aspect of the vocabulary of negation: the nothingness of perception, the nothingness of death, and the

---

[7] Quoted in Marius Bewley, *The Complex Fate* (London, 1952), p. 171.

nothingness of the burgeoning poetic invention. Each poem "captures" its title, contemplates it, and ultimately transforms its meaning, "this hard prize, / Fully made, fully apparent, fully found" (*CP*, 376). Finally, each poem enacts a familiar strategy: the bare statement elaborated through "resemblance," and its self-cancellings. Each poem moves, in the terms of "An Ordinary Evening in New Haven," between the "naked Alpha" of bare fact and the "hierophant Omega" of the sovereign imagination; each moves between the nothingness of being or of death or of sleep and the plenitude of its poetic realization.

2

THE SNOW MAN

One must have a mind of winter
To regard the frost and the boughs
Of the pine-trees crusted with snow;

And have been cold a long time
To behold the junipers shagged with ice,
The spruces rough in the distant glitter

Of the January sun; and not to think
Of any misery in the sound of the wind,
In the sound of a few leaves,

Which is the sound of the land
Full of the same wind
That is blowing in the same bare place

For the listener, who listens in the snow,
And, nothing himself, beholds
Nothing that is not there and the nothing that is.

"The Snow Man" occupies a privileged place in the Stevens canon. It serves as a point of departure for the luxuriant cycle of the seasons in *Harmonium*; it represents (with "Domination of Black") the initial encounter with nothingness which animates his "central man of glass"; it reveals the "emptiness within" which the poet discovers in the face of this radical contingency. Below the first, perceptual poverty, beneath winter's chastity, we can detect Santayana's definition of skepticism: "the chastity of the intellect." Stevens' later giant heroes, "the oldest and coldest philosopher" of "The Auroras of Autumn" and "Chocorua to Its Neighbor" open to the season and chilled through by it, are here economically prefigured. The poem projects a world of light; distance is transparent; objects glitter in the January sun (the sun of a new year).

The poem is both one of Stevens' most successful experiments in a free verse of extraordinary flexibility and a demonstration of his power of sustained syntax. One measure of its achievement is the various resources of rhythm and sound which have been brought into play in a relatively short lyric. According to Yvor Winters' suggestions for the scansion of free verse, indicating major and minor stresses only, the poem is organized on a three-beat norm. Two lines, the first and the tenth (which contrast the "mind" and the "land"), fall one stress short of this, while two others, the fifth and the last, have four beats. The line-sense is strong, with a moment of arrest before each new movement begins. In the fifth, sixth, and seventh lines where the visual phenomena are being described, the secondary stresses serve to accelerate the rhythm with the free movement of the eye. In the lines immediately following, where the fullness of sound is suggested, the pace sobers and slows markedly. The last lines resolve these elements and balance the final paradox of perception. Throughout the poem the *sounds* of winter are evoked by the recurrent, stopped sibilants ("the frost and the boughs / Of the pine-trees crusted with snow"). The stanzaic units are open tercets which, in the later poetry, are increasingly to bear the weight of the poet's meditations. Mr. Winters summarizes the resources of feeling which Stevens develops within such narrow limits: "There is complete repose between the lines, great speed and great slowness within the line, and all in a very short poem." [8]

Syntactically, the range of the meditation is entirely confined within the limits of a single sentence, the shortest intelligible unit in discourse. And yet the impersonal "One" of the first line is dissolved into the "nothing" which concludes the poem.

The title is deceptively simple; its ambivalence can be read

---

[8] Yvor Winters, *In Defense of Reason* (New York, 1947), pp. 126-27. In the reading which follows I must question Mr. Winters scansion of the final line, which he renders "Nothing that is not there . . ." I take the sense of the adage to require the rhythmic notation with a heavy stress on *each* of the negatives, as follows: "Nothing that is not there and the nothing that is."

only in the light of the last line. The argument of the poem moves irresistibly from imagistic detail to phenomenological "description." It moves first in the finite space of the observer's perceptual horizon and then enters the world of the perceiver as the wind bleakly penetrates the observer's consciousness. The initial poverty of this world has been succinctly described by Valéry:

L'observateur est pris dans une sphère qui ne se brise jamais; où il y a des différences qui seront les mouvements et les objets, et dont la surface se conserve close, bien que toutes les portions s'en renouvellent et s'y déplacent. L'observateur n'est d'abord que la condition de cet espace fini: à chaque instant il est cet espace fini. Nul souvenir, aucun pouvoir ne le trouble tant qu'il s'égale à ce qu'il regarde.[9]

For Valéry as for Stevens one "universe" (the mind) reflects the other (the world); the two are bound together. The empty place where the "same" wind blows is unaltered by any human conceits, by any human "misery," and yet it is completely realized by the human consciousness. There are two "empty places," the one without and the one within, and yet they are mirror images— "the same bare place." The bareness through which the wind blows is the bareness of the perceiver (who has evolved in stanza three from viewer to listener, becoming even more passive before the landscape as the poem moves from a spatial to a temporal dimension). The poverty of the scene and the purity of the observer achieve that algebraic "zero" which Valéry in his "Lettre-Préface" to Père Emile Rideau reserves for his reflexive consciousness: "le refus d'être quoi que ce soit":

Je ne me suis jamais référé qu'à mon MOI PUR, par quoi j'entends l'absolu de la conscience, qui est l'opération unique et uniforme de se dégager automatiquement de *tout*, et dans ce tout figure notre personne même avec son histoire, ses singularités, ses puissances diverses et ses complaisants propres. Je compare volontiers ce MOI PUR à ce précieux zéro de l'écriture mathématique, auquel toute expression algébrique s'égale. . . . Cette manière de voir m'est, en quelque sorte, consubstantielle. Elle s'impose à ma pensée depuis un demi-siècle . . .[10]

One must be cold a long time to reach an absolute zero, whether open to the weather or to self-reflection. In abandoning the consciousness to a chaos of particulars which surround it, in identi-

[9] Paul Valéry, *Oeuvres*, ed. Jean Hytier (Paris, 1957), I, 298.
[10] Paul Valéry, "Lettre-Préface," in *Introduction à la Pensée de Paul Valéry* by Emile Rideau (Paris, 1944).

fying the observer with what he beholds, Stevens' man is trapped in a continuous present of Bergsonian flux like that of Valéry's succession of instants which he termed the "*moi instantané.*" Georges Poulet diagnoses the latter's predicament:

S'abandonner au présent transitif et au flux seul de la durée, c'est s'abandonner à *un double néant*: néant de l'objet qui n'est jamais ce qu'il est; et néant de la pensée qui par sa spontanéité même se fait à chaque instant ce qu'elle pense, devient l'objet et participe ainsi de son éphémérité.[11]

Although Stevens and Valéry differ, as the former clearly saw, in their ultimate definition of the constructive power of the imagination, they share this radical point of departure. From it Valéry sees composition as "proliferation," and Stevens sees it as "concentration."

Stevens closes his meditation with the paradox which has the ring of an adage: "And, nothing himself, beholds / Nothing that is not there and the nothing that is." The listener is *nothing* as he opens himself to the brute inhumanity of the scene; he beholds (seeing again) nothing that is not there because he intrudes nothing from his own veritable past, neither memories, nor sympathies, nor illusions; further, he tries to read no meaning, no pathos, into the *facts*—the wind, the leaves, the ice—which live only in his perception. He himself lives homeless in the *nunc stans*. But finally, this perceiving instant expanding to its epistemic limits is itself a fiction, a private world, incontemporaneous with the world about and refracted by and fragilely confined in the interior distance of the consciousness. The poem thus becomes a dialogue with the self where mood, understanding, and language (Heidegger's formula) allow man, standing in the "no-thingness" of being, to reveal nothingness. Heidegger speaks of the alien voice which "calls" man to this recognition: "Der Rufer ist in seinem Wer 'weltlich' durch nichts bestimmbar. Er ist das Dasein in seiner Unheimlichkeit, das ursprüngliche geworfene In-der-Welt-sein als Un-zuhause, das nackte 'Dass' im Nichts der Welt." [12] This homeless voice exposes for Stevens the nothingness at the center of human existence, the nothingness behind entities

---

[11] Georges Poulet, *Etudes sur le Temps Humain* (Edinburgh, 1949), pp. 357-58.

[12] Martin Heidegger, *Sein und Zeit* (Tübingen, 1949), pp. 276-77. This volume will be hereafter cited as *SuZ*.

and the nothingness that annihilates the external world as an object of direct connatural knowledge in the very act of apprehending it. Yet this realization makes possible the endless creation of pseudo-objects, ambiguous marriages of nothingness and being, neither wholly real nor wholly unreal. "The theory of poetry," Stevens adds

> is the theory of life,
>
> As it is, in the intricate evasions of as,
> In things seen and unseen, created from nothingness,
> The heavens, the hells, the worlds, the longed-for lands. (*CP*, 486)

Merleau-Ponty speaks of the "zones of emptiness" that are produced in being, as bubbles are formed in the density of a boiling liquid and displace themselves outward. But he adds that it is in this area that language works its magical transformation of the world: "La dénomination des objets ne vient pas après la reconnaissance, elle est la reconnaissance même." [13] It is in this ambiguous space that "the snow man" finally takes shape, not as an object in the world but as a creation of the poet. And in this activity the poet recognizes himself.

It is this act of achieving one's own identity before the object which suggests the parallel of Stevens' poetics with the achievement of his cherished Impressionists. Ramon Fernandez defines the importance of the quest for the naïve impression:

> D'où vient donc ce sens de la réalité qui est incontestablement le don précieux de l'impressionisme? De ce que l'objet qui n'est plus perçu qu'à travers les lunettes du sens commun n'est plus senti par nous, nous sommes anesthésiés par l'habitude. Survienne une circonstance qui éveille en nous des impressions vives et naïves, aussitôt nous reprenons possession de notre sensibilité, *nous nous connaissons devant l'objet.*[14]

Stevens celebrates the achievement which goes beyond even the Canon Aspirin's heroism in "It Must Give Pleasure," Section VII. In place of the Canon's order bravely but impatiently *imposed* on sprawling chaos, the poet must seek order through discovery, that is, through an openness to the weather:

> To discover winter and know it well, to find,
> Not to impose, not to have reasoned at all,
> Out of nothing to have come on major weather,

---

[13] Maurice Merleau-Ponty, *Phénoménologie de la Perception* (Paris, 1945), p. 207.
[14] Ramon Fernandez, *Messages: Première Série* (Paris, 1926), p. 46.

It is possible, possible, possible. It must
Be possible. It must be that in time
The real will from its crude compoundings come,

Seeming, at first, a beast disgorged, unlike,
Warmed by a desperate milk. To find the real,
To be stripped of every fiction except one,

The fiction of an absolute—Angel,
Be silent in your luminous cloud and hear
The luminous melody of proper sound. (*CP*, 404)

This is the supreme activity of "The Snow Man." The experience is one which gives rise, for all its emptiness and its fictive realization, to a sense of power and plenitude. From this moment can flower Stevens' "blue bush of day," the extravaganzas of the imagination. Spring is not far behind.

3

THE COURSE OF A PARTICULAR

Today the leaves cry, hanging on branches swept by wind,
Yet the nothingness of winter becomes a little less.
It is still full of icy shades and shapen snow.

The leaves cry . . . One holds off and merely hears the cry.
It is a busy cry, concerning someone else.
And though one says that one is part of everything,

There is a conflict, there is a resistance involved;
And being part is an exertion that declines:
One feels the life of that which gives life as it is.

The leaves cry. It is not a cry of divine attention,
Nor the smoke-drift of puffed-out heroes, nor human cry.
It is the cry of leaves that do not transcend themselves,

In the absence of fantasia, without meaning more
Than they are in the final finding of the ear, in the thing
Itself, until, at last, the cry concerns no one at all.

"The Course of a Particular" marks a return to the wintry hero of "The Snow Man," but it also illustrates the evolution of the poet's style and the increasing urgency of his late concerns. It is a long way from the virtuoso prosodic effects of the earlier poem to the sustained iambic argument of "The Course of a Particular"; and it is a long way, too, from the deceptively imagistic title of "The Snow Man" to the bare notation of this title. Yet each poem enacts the "zero point" in the imaginative cycle:

> This is the last day of a certain year
> Beyond which there is nothing left of time.
> It comes to this and the imagination's life.
>
> There is nothing more inscribed nor thought nor felt. (*CP*, 372)

A few lines later in the same poem, "Credences of Summer," the poet supplies his impossible program: "Let's see the very thing and nothing else."

Yet "The Course of a Particular" describes a new dimension of absence not found in "The Snow Man." From the inescapable *nothing* which is the ground of being we are led to the inconceivable anonymity of *death*. Just as Heidegger finds *Dasein*'s existence, facticity, and falling revealed in the phenomenological analysis of death, Stevens grounds his poetics and defines his individuality in terms of a death which always *impends* even in "the genius of summer" (*CP*, 482). In Heidegger's analysis of the *Sein zum Tode* he argues that only in death can we achieve an ontological delimitation of *Dasein*'s totality; and when *Dasein* reaches its wholeness in death, it simultaneously loses the Being of its "there" (*SuZ*, 281). Consequently, he turns to the phenomenal analysis of the dying of Others as a possible route to comprehending the self. Death is the experience which *impends* for everyone, although always uniquely: "Der Tod ist kein noch nicht Vorhandenes, nicht der auf ein Minimum reduzierte letzte Ausstand, sondern eher ein Bevorstand." (*SuZ*, 250) Similarly, Stevens turns to the analysis of the impending annihilation of the least element in his spinning world of leaves and light to reveal the desolation which surrounds even his most ecstatic moments of celebration. Death in every manifestation makes possible change, the limit to every entity and every poem; thus, "Death is the mother of beauty," as his woman finally learns in "Sunday Morning"; poems "compounded and compounded" are "death's own supremest images" (*CP*, 69, 436). The "wide water" which surrounds each individual existence is not to be crossed, but remains a guarantee of our "island solitude" in a sea of other beings.

By way of cursory stylistic "definition" of the present poem, we can mark it as a fair, if condensed, representative of Stevens' late style, as studied by Frank Doggett and others.[15] Here there is little of the Fabergé work one finds on the auditory and rhetorical surface of, for example, "Le Monocle de Mon Oncle," where the poet's solution for the drabness and sterility in a waste of spirit is "bravura," "the music and manner of the paladins" (*CP*, 16). Laforgue's ironic parachute—never an adequate escape for Stevens, who distrusted escapes—has by now been packed away with the "essential gaudiness" of *Harmonium*. The development has been one of chastening and reduction. We are not confronted, as in the early poetry which Mr. Blackmur has glossed, with rare words used precisely, but with ordinary words given a new weight and urgency. Stevens here seems to have abandoned the doubtful protection of that studied carelessness which mars some of the poetry of the 'thirties, the shameless adlibbing which tried to make an imperfection into the rhetorical emblem of an honesty disdaining perfection. (And also, in the later poems he avoids the then popular contrived hesitancies and uncertainties in rhythm which were enlisted to similar rhetorical ends.) The words that matter in this poem are repeated, turned, and redefined: the "cry" becomes "no cry"; "someone" becomes "no one." These metamorphoses of crucial words in the action of the poem are familiar to all readers of the late poetry. The tactic is to let the poem become its own answer, to push the words toward their own antitheses; change for Stevens, as for Hegel, depends upon the dialectics of continuing negation.

One more characteristic element of the style of Stevens' later poetry is insistent here: the preference for the indefinite third person. Although the poem is deeply personal and consistently felt, the tone is regulated through the reciprocal interactions of "It" and "One." The lyric strategy is deceptively general; the topic may be expanded to read, in Stevens' words, as "formlessness gulping after form" and the reflux of the imagination; yet the central experience of the poem remains disturbingly particular, personal.

The poem enacts another familiar syntactic device of the later style through its development of a progression of predicate nom-

---

[15] Frank Doggett, "Wallace Stevens' Later Poetry," *ELH*, XXV (June, 1958), 137-54.

inatives. The interrogation of experience takes the form of equivalences. Again characteristically (echoing the syntax of Mallarmé here), the progress ends with a series of "is not's" which cancel the earlier assertions and remind us of the insistent negatives of "The Snow Man."

The repetitions, the vocabulary, the recurrent predicate nominative constructions are all directed at a deliberate courting of the commonplace, in both its senses. Even the directness of the title suggests this; it joins the quotidian litany of "The Plain Sense of Things," "Man Carrying Things," "Pieces," "Things of August," which lead to the muted ritual of "An Ordinary Evening." The theme of the poem suggests, of course, only the initial diastole of Stevens' circulation of the imagination through his "moving chaos that never ends" of impenetrable singulars (*OP*, 50). As so many other poems adumbrate, life is a continuous dialectic between this unmastered flux of *things* and the imagination; it involves, indeed requires, the constant attempt to arrive at a synthesis of the two in a state which Stevens, after Samuel Alexander, liked to call "compresence." In "The Course of a Particular," however, we have only the coldest phase of contraction and refusal, the return to the condition of aboriginal innocence "open" to sensation. Here Stevens' primitive lives on the edge between the moving chaos of things and the fragile inner world where he tries to order the refracted "pseudo-objects" he creates in the very act of apprehending. It is precisely in that act of violence, the consciousness *of* the object, that consciousness and object are inextricably intertwined. Stevens quotes from Alexander's *Space, Time and Deity* the exactest description of his notion whereby the individual both asserts himself and participates in things:

What is of importance is the recognition that in any experience the mind enjoys itself and contemplates its object or its object is contemplated, and that these two existences, *the act of the mind* and the *object* as they are in the experience, are distinct existences united by the relation of compresence. The experience is a piece of the world consisting of these two existences in their togetherness. The one existence, the enjoyed, enjoys itself, or experiences itself as an enjoyment; the other existence, the contemplated, is experienced by the enjoyed. The enjoyed and the contemplated are together. (*OP*, 193-94)

In "Les Plus Belles Pages" Stevens adds: "Nothing exists by

itself." And in the poem under consideration it is the perilous alliance between the object and its comprehending mind which is threatened by a declining *attention* on the part of the beholder and menaced ultimately by the prospect which the object affords of impending extinction. "There on the edges of oblivion" (*CP*, 435), between that which is not quite and that which was, the poem takes shape.

Although this poem is not directly concerned with the creative activity of the imagination and its language as are so many of the late poems, it is the necessary prelude to all these discussions. Stevens felt the absolute and recurrent need for a return to this prelude to refresh his work. In this tentativeness about the poet's utterance (and his attention) he would seem to differ from Mallarmé, who placed a so much greater faith in the transforming efficacy of language: "Je dis une fleur!" For Stevens there is finally no hierophant language of the poet nor any great natural syllable which comes to the singer from the sea or the sound of the wind; there is only the ever fresh " cry of the occasion " which implicates both the poet and his world. In "The Man on the Dump," a portrait of the artist surrounded by the gaudy litter of outworn images which have lost their relationship to experience, a world of stale convention that imagination must abandon every winter, Stevens would seem to suggest one danger of the symbolist adventure; the poem, however adequate to the moment, is not a formula to escape the contingencies of life and it has significance only in the present moment which it creates. For Stevens the poem begins (and in a sense ends) with the impingement of reality on the perceiving center, not with the Mallarméan flight beyond the hospital windows toward an atemporal *azur*.

Finally, in *form* "The Course of a Particular" has much in common with other poems of Stevens' last years. The poem is a single meditation closely argued and does not build the cumulative episodes and effects of the longer meditations on mortality and the imagination such as "The Owl in the Sarcophagus" and "A Primitive like an Orb." Like them, however, it is constructed of the familiar tercets of the later style (which may remind us of the meditative process of: experience + understanding = transformation). The iambic-based line is generally strongly drawn. Rather than the loosened pentameters, however, we have an unusually weighty unit, an Alexandrine with frequent ionic and anapestic substitutions. The line gives Stevens ample verge for his portentous pauses.

Increasingly, as the poem progresses, the language and the syntax of qualification insist on the bareness of the argument. The discourse is purged of anything which might suggest the "poetic" or the vividness of "human" speech. The poet resists what he calls "the habit of analogy" and any words which might provoke it.

The title serves as a gloss to the text of the poem, but, as in "The Snow Man," it has a double applicability. The word "course" suggests the double emphasis on the flux in the world of discrete particulars, and on the process of perceiving and transforming it which is the poem. Stevens sees both his world and his "mundo" of the mind in constant, coursing change "which exceeds all metaphor"—"Our sense of these things changes and they change" (*CP*, 431). To illustrate the fluency of imagination open to experience Stevens cites a rather unwieldy chapter-title from Henri Focillon: "Technique as the instrumentation of metamorphosis and as epistemological mode." The technique is for Stevens a poetics, a means of fixing change in language. As is clear from his Bergen lecture at Yale, the concept of discovering analogies out of an experience changing before his senses bears a striking resemblance to the "metaphoric" technique of Proust's Elstir; to perceive is to live in time even as the object is transformed in time.

Another element worthy of remark in the title is the indefinite article. The compulsive use of the *definite* article was for Rostrevor Hamilton the betraying device of the "modern verse" of his generation. Just as persistently Wallace Stevens in his later poetry settles on the *indefinite* article for his "major abstractions" growing from particular encounters. Thus, in his vision of mortal time "that flows nowhere," "The River of Rivers in Connecticut," he concludes:

> It is the third commonness with light and air,
> A curriculum, a vigor, a local abstraction . . .
> Call it, once more, a river, an unnamed flowing. (*CP*, 533)

To say "a vigor" instead of "vigor," to say "a Particular" instead of "the Particular," avoids personification and all the penumbra of conventional pathos. Stevens did not refuse personification, but it was always erected from those private mythologies he projected on his imagination, " A giant on the horizon, given arms / . . . A definition with an illustration " or " The personae of summer [who] play the characters / Of an inhuman author . . ." (*CP*, 443, 377). In this poem Stevens represents himself as still at the point of wintry poverty in his creative cycle; he is concerned with sensations at the very moment of impingement, before there is any imaginative activity, any human projection possible. Here the indefinite article, and all that it implies about a world of singularity empty of universals, touches the very topic of the poem. Another poem annotates the enormous distance between the unclaimed world of the indefinite article and a world where the poet names and projects himself again; the moment there is a windy Sunday in April after a long winter; the movement is from the anonymity of " The Snow Man " to the identity of the warmer seasons of resemblance:

> . . . The wind blew in the empty place.
> The winter wind blew in an empty place—
> There was that difference between the and an,
> The difference between himself and no man,
> No man that heard a wind in an empty place. (*CP*, 255)

Finally, the word " particular " runs its course, like one of Lucretius' atoms, down through the text. In the third section of " The Rock " Stevens celebrates " the gray particular of man's life," the irreducible stone from which he rises, " the starting point of the human and the end " (*CP*, 528). Just as Heidegger's privileged term for human existence, *Dasein*, implies an entity already projected " there " in the world (*In-der-Welt-sein*), Stevens' " parts of the immense detritus of a world," his " particles of nether-do," and " sprinklings of bright particulars " all suggest however chaotically the possibility of a *whole* to which these discrete elements may belong (*OP*, 49; *CP*, 509, 344). For Stevens, however, this cosmic suggestion can be realized only in the private world, the insubstantial mundo of every fictive imagination. And in " The Course of a Particular " the isolated entity, the leaf, faces the depletion of a world which flowered in another season and which can offer it little comfort in the flowerings to come. Change, the affront and the consolation of Stevens' poetry, here means a falling away into a private, unique oblivion—the silence into which the poem is uttered (" acutest at its vanishing ") and the silence which terminates the individual life.

Considering first the insistent image of the leaves crying—and in a sense it is the only image asserted in the poem, a pathetic image which will be destroyed "in the course of things"—we find two paradoxical sources. Although the sight of " a few leaves " in a winterscape animate early poems of Stevens' maturity such as "Domination of Black" and "The Snow Man," in the later poetry the whirlings of the leaves through the streets of New Haven define "the area between is and was" (*CP*, 474), while in the central poem of *The Rock*

> The fiction of the leaves is the icon
>
> Of the poem, the figuration of blessedness,
> And the icon is the man. . . . (*CP*, 526)

Finally, the life of the leaf can in the circle of seasons form the image of the life of man and the life of the poem. And yet the earliest appearance of this commonplace in Stevens' poetry is banal enough to remind the reader that much of the great work of the late poetry is the metamorphosis of the commonplace. The earliest "internal" source in Stevens' own career of the topos of mortal leaves appeared in his contribution to the *Harvard Monthly* in March, 1899; the lugubrious young student begins a sonnet: "If we are leaves that fall . . . ."

Still closer to the details and tone of the meditation, however, is the cry of a leaf which Stevens seems to have heard in his readings. The figure of the lamenting leaf would seem to have been rescued from the talus of notes and correspondence which he gathered for his "Collect of Philosophy" in 1951, the same year in which he published the poem. The essay, which was declined by a professional philosophic journal and remained unpublished at the poet's death, considers in what sense the concepts of philosophy may be called poetic; the leisurely remarks evidently grew from discussions of this question with Jean Wahl, Jean Paulhan, and other friends in Paris engaged in the analysis of conceptual creativity. The poet invokes images drawn from a considerable gallery of philosophers: Plato, Aristotle, Bonaventura, Aquinas, Bruno, Descartes, Pascal, Spinoza, Vico, Berkeley, Maine de Biran, Kant, Hegel, Nietzsche, Lequier, Husserl, Samuel Alexander, Bergson, James, Santayana, Russell, Whitehead, Planck, and so on. Many of the figurative examples which he cites appear, transformed, in a number of the later poems. He pauses, for instance, over Husserl's suggestion of the enormous *a priori* in our minds, an inexhaustible infinity of *a priori*; the suggestion disturbs Stevens; he finally, in two poems in *The Auroras of Autumn*, likens it to the idea of the infinity of the world. Stevens lingers longest, however, over two images: the busy, buzzing monads of Leibniz's universe (an idea he orchestrates in " The Woman That Had More Babies than That "); and over what he terms the " eccentric philosophic apparatus on the grand scale in the *World as Will* of Schopenhauer " OP, 190). He speaks of Schopenhauer's theory of perception, of his image of the blind man carrying on his shoulders the lame man who can see, as " a text of the grotesque, both human and inhuman." It is the text," he continues, " of a poem although not a happy one. It is, in a way, the same poem as the poem of Leibniz although the terms are different. It is," he concludes, " the cosmic poem of the ascent into heaven . . ." (*OP*, 193). Stevens generalizes that while the habit of forming concepts as images unites poets and philosophers, the use to which they put their ideas separates them. " The philosopher intends his integration to be fateful; the poet intends his to be effective " (*OP*, 197).

Professor Eucalyptus, the greeny academic of " An Ordinary Evening," notes the common quest of philosopher and poet; Stevens distinguishes their means:

> . . . " The search
> For reality is as momentous as
> The search for god." It is the philosopher's search
> For an interior made exterior
> And the poet's search for the same exterior made
> Interior. . . . (*CP*, 481)

He concludes, " To re-create, to use / The cold and earliness and bright origin / Is to search." The poet apprehends the exterior images to himself even as he " becomes " the snow man in his interior space; he continues the unending " dialogue between mind and sky."

> . . . Likewise to say of the evening star,
> The most ancient light in the most ancient sky,
>
> That it is wholly an inner light, that it shines
> From the sleepy bosom of the real, re-creates,
> Searches a possible for its possibleness. (*CP*, 481)

Every poem for Stevens was a new search for this translation and recreation of experience; yet in many poems of the winter cycle the initial images "do not transcend themselves," but only remind the poet of his own attempt to apprehend them, "the life of that which gives life as it is."

The conceit of the leaf crying in the wind which is ultimately rejected in the poem, appears explicitly in chapter 41 of the Supplement to the Fourth Book of *Die Welt als Wille und Vorstellung.* Schopenhauer in his analysis of what he calls "the indestructability of inner nature" exteriorizes the human datum in the predicament of the leaf; it speaks for "such common minds [as] are capable of knowing only the particular thing, simply and solely as such, and are strictly limited to knowledge of individuals"; Schopenhauer contrasts these stubborn nominalists with his Platonic elect who can "perceive of the universal in the particular." Moving to parable he speaks of his "deluded questioner," who, faced by his isolation and approaching extinction, "mistaking of his true nature is like the leaf on the tree." Although the image is sufficient for the philosopher's argument, it is precisely inadequate for Stevens' poem; and the action of the poem rests in the final finding, the interiorization, of the image's inadequacy and the poet's mortality. But Schopenhauer first sets up all the rhetorical apparatus which Stevens will test:

. . . Wo ist der reiche Schooss des weltenschwangeren Nichts, der sie noch birgt, die kommenden Geschlecter?—Wäre darauf nicht die lächelnde und wahre Antwort: Wo anders sollen sie sein, als dort, wo allein das Reale stets war und sein wird, in der Gegenwart und ihrem Inhalt, also bei Dir, dem bethörten Frager, der, in diesem Verkennen seines eigenen Wesens, dem Blatte am Baume gleicht, welches im Herbste welkend und im Begriff abzufallen, jammert über seinen Untergang und sich nicht trösten lassen will durch den Hinblick auf das frische Grün, welches im Frühling den Baum bekleiden wird, sondern klagend spricht: "Das bin ja Ich nicht! Das sind ganz andere Blätter!"—O thörichtes Blatt! Wohin willst du? Und woher sollen andere kommen? Wo ist das Nichts, dessen Schlund du fürchtest? —Erkenne doch dein eigenes Wesen, gerade Das, was vom Durst nach Dasein so erfüllt ist, erkenne es wieder in der innern, geheimen, treibenden Kraft des Baumes, welche, stets eine und dieselbe in allen Generationen von Blättern, unberührt bleibt vom Entstehen und Vergehen. Und nun

οἵη περ φύλλων γενεή, τοίη δὲ καὶ ἀνδρῶν.

(Qualis foliorum generatio, talis et hominum.) [16]

---

[16] Arthur Schopenhauer, *Die Welt als Wille und Vorstellung* (Munich, 1911), II, 544-45.

The Homeric allusion is to the fountainhead of the *topos*, Glaukos'
speech in *Iliad* VI: "As is the generation of leaves, so is that of
humanity. The wind scatters the leaves on the ground, but the
live timber burgeons with leaves again in the season of spring
returning."

The complaint of the "foolish leaf" suggests at once the essential solitude of Stevens' primitive man of glass, fixed like the leaf
in the center of his perceptual field; but it suggests too the sub-
sidiary sense of depletion, dilapidation, and impending death
which is the phase of winter in the poet's system. Thus, running
parallel to the announced topic of the poem, a meditation on a
most elemental impingement on the consciousness (like "The
Snow Man"), is the darker covert meditation on death and
extinction in a world of absolute isolation, an isolation so complete
that it resists the ordering powers of language (the cry is not a
"human cry"). Much of the ambiguous power of the poem
derives from this subtle multiplication (and canceling out) of
topics, a multiplication without confusion. Stevens is not digging
for old epistemological or theological bones; rather he is presenting
a mode of experience with all the affective commitment which
this implies. Like much meditative poetry, this is one form (a
preparatory one) of a contemplation of the inexplicable fact of
existence itself.

"After the leaves have fallen, we return / To a plain sense of
things," he says in the poem with that title. And yet, paradoxically, he demonstrates there that the plain sense of things
is a form of seeming, and thus is itself a way of feeling and sensing
the world. In his metaphor of the rundown mansion, he says
of his inert and inanimate world:

> It is difficult even to choose the adjective
> For this blank cold, this sadness without cause.
> The great structure has become a minor house. (*CP*, 502)

And so he finds that to experience the plain sense of things is
an attitude that includes the world and the mind of man, too,
the mind imagining, as in "The Snow Man" or "The Course
of a Particular," its own bare perception of the world, unem-
bellished and without meaning beyond the act of finding: "Yet
the absence of the imagination had / Itself to be imagined" (*CP*,
503). And then in the final vision Stevens represents reality by

the image of a great pond and the unthinking *awareness* of reality, its mere acceptance, by the image of a rat come out to see it and " its waste of the lilies " (echo of Eliot?), its proliferation of perishing forms of life. He erects a poem on the ruins of the poetic premise.

Between the nature of mind and the nature of the world it captures, Stevens sees irreconcilable differences. The first is mortal and limited in its prospect, while the second is endless in its variety and rebirth. Out of these differences come the variety and freshness of living, what Mr. Winters calls the poet's hedonism; out of these differences comes too the continual everlasting effort to comprehend which is the action of the present poem; and out of these differences comes, as well, continual human disintegration and mortality.

" The Course of a Particular " opens abruptly, in the present moment, with the sound of Schopenhauer's leaves. The repeated use of the caesura in the first line of each tercet, alternately as medial and variant, will serve to figure the break between the world of the leaves and that of the central poet. The transparent poet is at first little more than a sensing ear, although it is his temptation to hear a meaning in the cry which makes "the nothingness of winter" (the inhuman world of " The Snow Man ") " a little less." The vacuum at the center of the poet is filled with the cry (rather like Condillac's statue). The primeval elements then of the first tercet are simply the ear (which grows ultimately to the abstract status of " one "), and the litter of things dying (in this case the leaves), and finally the winter wind "which blows in the same bare place," traditionally an insubstantial mediator between the world and the genius of the poet, but here simply one more particular.

The wind which fails to animate the central mind of the poem is clearly not Coleridge's "mighty [natural] Poet " playing on the Aeolian strings of the human poet's sensibilities in the *Dejection Ode*. Nor is it Wordsworth's welcome winter winds and " corresponding mild creative breeze." Most especially this alien force is not Shelley's West Wind, which Stevens mocks in " Mozart, 1935 " and in the central section of " Notes toward a Supreme Fiction." While Earl Wasserman has persuasively developed in his precise reading of Shelley's snow-piece, *Mont Blanc*, a resolution of romantic mind-body paradoxes which in part parallels Stevens'

thoughts on creative perception, the latter sees a simpler and
more solipsistic Shelley. Thus Stevens, in quoting Whitehead on
"The Romantic Reaction," seems to find in the lines: "The everlasting universe of Things / Flows through the Mind . . ." a conventional idealism. He notes ironically in the poem on the reality
of flux and mutability in "It Must Change":

> Bethou me, said sparrow, to the crackled blade,
> And you, and you, bethou me as you blow,
> When in my coppice you behold *me* be.

> Ah, ké! the bloody wren, the felon jay,
> Ké-ké, the jug-throated robin pouring out,
> Bethou, bethou, bethou me in my glade. (*CP*, 393-94)

The ego song of each bird asserts that *it* is its "coppice" world;
the songs merge against their will into one insistent voice, and
the generations of birds like the generations of leaves merely
repeat the burden. Stevens finds in this "idiot minstrelsy" (a
phrase he consecrates elsewhere to Leibniz's "lisping monads")
only one more assurance that such natural choirs as "violets,
doves, girls, bees and hyacinths / Are inconstant objects of inconstant cause / In a universe of inconstancy" (*CP*, 389). He sees
the great specter of the romantic imaginations as solipsism and he
attempts to exorcise it in a hymn to mutability and mortality.

There is then no sense of any identification of the breath of
Nature and the living breath of the poet. Even in a poem of
artistic consummation, "The Idea of Order at Key West," a great
American seashore ode where the extremities of sea and sky and
land, of the inanimate and the animating, for a moment meet,
he sees the poet as "beyond the genius of the sea"; nature is
simply "a body wholly body, fluttering / Its empty sleeves" on
the line of the world (*CP*, 128-30). The "mimic motion" and
"constant cry" are not the song of his solitary maker:

> It may be that in all her phrases stirred
> The grinding water and the gasping wind;
> But it was she and not the sea we heard.

> For she was the maker of the song she sang. (*CP*, 129)

The singer, unlike the natural elements and like her song, is
mortal.

The wind furnishes the temporal dimension, then, of "The
Course of a Particular," its high-vowel [ī] and diphthong [ay]

("leaves cry") playing through every stanza; but it is no pineal gland uniting the consciousness and the world's body. Even when the wind stops in Stevens' poetry, and the line pauses, the clouds of the imagination continue—

> When the wind stops and, over the heavens,
> The clouds go, nevertheless,
> In their direction. (*CP*, 97)

(We recognize in this final stanza from an early meditation on death a similar mastery in the use of caesura to that which distinguishes the later poem.)

The visual details of the poem are barely sketched: icy shades and shapen snow. There is no sense of the imagist detail of "The Snow Man"; we have only the ice of death and the shapes of absence. This poem is entirely concerned with a primitive auditory phenomenon; the leaves themselves are never clearly seen. We are in that inner darkness and absence whence the little owl of the "imagination piece" hoots for joy (*CP*, 246). The "nothingness" of the chilly season is lessened only by the intervention of an ear and the pathetic image. In this sense nothing exists before the single, continuing, and unitary experience of the noise. The rhetorical suggestion that the noise is a "cry" (a suggestion ironically drawn from the depths of Schopenhauer's rhetoric) will ultimately be discredited: the brute sound to which the central poet at first submits, stripping himself to the nothingness of a sensorium, fails within the action of the poem to be apprehensible either as a cry *to* someone or as a cry *about* anything. We have opposed here to the fiction which the poet might make, not truth, but, as Stevens remarks, fact: in this case the fact of a single auditory sensation. Despite its starkness, this is precious to the poet; it is from this "winter" that his fiction must grow:

We have excluded absolute fact as an element of poetic truth. But this has been done arbitrarily and with a sense of absolute fact as fact destitute of any imaginative aspect whatever. Unhappily the more destitute it becomes the more it begins to be precious. (*NA*, 60)

But this winter world is, as Stevens reminds us, a chaos of particulars, completely nominalistic in the absence of any universals.

Here, as in "The Snow Man," or in the "icy Elysée" that concludes "Of Heaven Considered as a Tomb," or in "the region

of frost" where Rosenbloom is buried, the time of absence and
death in nature corresponds to the weather of the sensibility and
both in turn are the necessary point of departure for any new
beginning, any new flowering of images, any transport to summer.
Yesterday's superfluities are gone; the self is withered and shrunken
to its center, " the final dwarf of you," says Stevens (*CP*, 208).
There are none of Stevens' heroes, giants of generalization, on
the mental scene, none of "summer's smoke-drift of puffed-out
heroes," the "buffos" of the poet's swelling self. These are fig-
ments of a more sultry world of the imagination. The wind is
all outside and chilly. "On dit un poète inspiré, mais on dit aussi
une omelette souflée," as Paul Claudel remarked.

The next stage in the action of the poem is represented by the
words "conflict" and "resistance." The central self in the very
poverty of its sensation changes with the course of things. As
in the first poem of "Notes toward a Supreme Fiction," the self
tries to attain a pure image of external reality untouched by its
own wishes and attitudes and conceivings. There the object is
visual and the poet in the face of this sensation must be the
clearest crystal, uncrazed by the past. "Clear and, except for
the eye, without intrusion" (*CP*, 400). But the crucial effort to
attain such awareness, to take "life as it is," cannot be long
sustained without exhaustion. The poet finds that the adage
"one is a part of everything" cannot be enacted without a pressure against the other discrete particulars. (The word "particular" itself seems to suggest a linguistic trap implying a "whole.")
The verb "exert" suggests besides the sense of effort its etymological weight of "thrust forth." Stevens' central self, like Dryden's
star, "exerts his head." The implied effort is reinforced by the
difficulties of Stevens' meter, which has previously been almost
regular enough to satisfy Mr. Ransom. Finally we have a suggestion familiar from Maine de Biran's redaction of Condillac, which
Stevens exploits elsewhere, that self-consciousness itself rises from
just this sense of effort in the very act of sensing. As Stevens
puts it here, characteristically employing the repetition of a word
in order to turn it inside out: "One feels the life of that which
gives life as it is." The life which one "feels" is no longer the
sense-impression which possesses him, but his will to the possession of the sense of this. We have seen that the sensation itself
is only that of a "pseudo-object" (Stevens delighted in the obser-

vation that we never see the world until a moment after its enactment). The central self of the poem can, at one more remove
from the object, sense the effort "to be concerned," that is,
etymologically, *to mix, to mingle*, or, phenomenologically, *to care,
to attend*.

The self rejects, however, the few "possibles" tentatively presented to give relation to the cry: in repeating the word four
times in the fourth tercet he eliminates the stuff of fiction—a
Berkeleyan divinity, his own major men of airy abstractions, or
external human concern. He returns quite finally to the cry of
leaves. This is a fact in a nominalistic world of discrete singulars;
there is no question of self-transcendance. As the line runs over
into the last tercet, Stevens introduces the one possibility by
which all things *might* be possible. Characteristically, he introduces it negatively: "In the absence of fantasia . . ." As I scan
the line it would be necessary to stress this word after the Greek
accent (fantasía), emphasizing the privileged and technical use
of the term. Although the original word is generally a "making
visible, displaying, a parade" (reminding us of the time-sequence);
it is more strictly, as a term in philosophy, "the power of the
mind, *by which* it places *objects* before *itself*, a presentative
power." The word suggests a cluster of others: *phántasma,
phásma, epiphany*: all words out of the Indo-European root "to
shine," √BHA. From the same root Heidegger derives the crucial
word for his method of ontological analysis: phenomenology
(*SuZ*, 28-31). It is just this activity, of bringing to the light of
the imagination, which, in Stevens' poetics, gives a local, personal
meaning. Against the screen of the blue sky (or the blue reflected
in the sea), "the blue bush of day," the nothing of the imagination, Stevens' tropes of resemblance and correspondence can
flower. There, "absente de tous bouquets," can bloom his rose
of the possible, of as many possibles as there are poets and
moments.

Without the transforming power of the imagination, then, the
cry is simply noise devoid of meaning and concerning "no one
at all." The leaves "do not transcend themselves." The oblivion
which meets the cry of the leaf in this reduction is strikingly like
that described in Heidegger's analysis of the phrase "one dies,"
the everyday response to the death of the other:

Die Analyse des ' man stirbt' enthüllt unzweideutig die Seinsart des alltäglichen Seins zum Tode. Dieser wird in solcher Rede verstanden als ein unbestimmtes Etwas, das allererts irgendwoher eintressen muss, zunächst aber für einen selbst noch nicht vorhanden und daher unbedrohlich ist. Das ' man stirbt' verbreitet die Meinnung, der Tod treffe gleichsam das Man. Die öffentliche Daseinsauslegung sagt: ' man stirbt', weil damit jeder andere und man selbst sich einreden kann: je nicht gerade ich; denn dieses Man ist *das Niemand*. Das 'Sterben' wird auf ein Vorkommnis nivelliert, das zwar das Dasein trifft, aber niemandem eigens zugehört. . . . Das Sterben, das wesenhaft unvertretbar das meine ist, wird in ein öffentlich vorkommendes Ereignis verkehrt, das dem Man begegnet. (*SuZ*, 253)

The " one " of the phrase is thus *the nobody*. The death is an event which reaches our existence, but " belongs to nobody in particular." (This failure of attention parallels the initial response of Marcel to the death of his grandmother in *A la Recherche du Temps Perdu*: an evasive concealment in the face of death.)

And yet while the pathetic image of the leaves ultimately concerns no one at all, the action of the poem has prepared the way for the submerged theme to announce itself. From the conventional image of mortality the persona listening can move to the immediate reality of his own extinction, a concern which appears to have generated the poem.

We come at last to the unhappy misprint which mutilates the poem as it is printed in *Opus Posthumous*. I am grateful to Mr. Winters for calling this grotesque alteration to my attention during his visit to Hopkins in 1958.[17] Without his emendation I had been unable to make much sense of the argument of the poem. In the collected volume the penultimate line reads in part: " in the final finding of the *air* " (*OP*, 97). The point of the poem's drama has been to establish the poet and his impoverished senses at the very center of the action. The interrogation has not been one of divine attention; the air, whether in motion or not, is simply an element of the surrounding chaos of particulars, equally alien to leaf and poet, and certainly not a personified and elemental force which sentimentally judges the action.

The text as it originally appeared in the *Hudson Review*

---

[17] Since this essay was written Mr. Winters has recorded his crucial emendation in a " Postscript " to his 1943 essay, " Wallace Stevens, or the Hedonist's Progress," as it appears in the revised edition of *In Defense of Reason* (Denver, 1960), p. 459. Unfortunately, the paper-back selection, *Poems by Wallace Stevens*, preserves the mutilating typographical error.

(Spring, 1951) restores the sense and resolves the tension between the rejected drama of the leaf and the achieved tragedy of the central poet who hears, understands, and finds himself " in the final finding of the ear." It is he who senses the course and who at last accepts his own solitude, and out of this utters the poem. The poet has become for a moment at least (like Stevens' fisherman) a sensing *ear*. As the verb to represent the activity he has just " described," Stevens returns to a word familiar in his work and dense with history: " to find." He sometimes uses the verb with its connotation of " seeking after, flying towards " and again, as here, with the more passive and ancient sense of " falling " ($\pi\iota\pi\tau\epsilon\iota\nu$ / PAT). He says in " Of Modern Poetry ": " The poem of the mind in the act of finding / What will suffice. It has not always had / To find . . ." (*CP*, 239).

The note of finality struck, the poem moves through the rush of the hexameters to the exhaustion of the last line, a fourteener, ending in the choriambic negation of " no one at all," a negation echoing the close of " The Snow Man."

It is important finally to emphasize the vital difference between these two winter poems, a difference which can be detected in the words of negation. In the earlier poem the reader shares in one of those brief, " privileged moments " which support the poetic life of Stevens. From the blankness of transparent crystal the poet progresses through an *exposure* to the world to a sort of secular revelation: he mirrors in the inner space of his perception a possible picture of the world. After Rilke's image he is the bee of the invisible who " frantically plunders the visible of its honey, to accumulate it in the great golden hive of the invisible." (Or, in other terms from the Sonette an Orpheus which Stevens would recognize, " Sei—und wisse zugleich des Nichtseins Bedingung " [II, xiii].) This is the " Fiction " which Husserl called the vital element of all phenomenology. Here the world is redisposed anew and the alchemic activities of the imagination can begin. The word thrice repeated is *nothing*, a nothing which, paradoxically, precisely is and precisely is not there in the beholder. After the poet's ascesis the effect is transport (*ekstasis*).

In " The Course of a Particular " the emphasis is reversed. The search is not so much for a thing (or nothing) as for a someone which will give meaning. There is no escape from the absolute solitude and no suggestion of available meaning. The poem

ends not with the sufficiency of the thing itself, but with the
phrase (which metrically parallels " life as it is ") " no one at all "
echoing in absence. In the merciless stripping away of all that
would clothe particular object and the particular subject, all the
resources of language and imagination, we have a search for a
discourse before (or beyond) the poetry of *fantasía*. And in the
reciprocal fates of the two dying particulars, we have an integral
enactment of how death appears to *Das Man* and to *Dasein*. From
this double analysis arises the final paradox: out of his ultimate
solitude, the extremity of a less-than-human extinction, Stevens
has built his most " human " poem.

4

NOT IDEAS ABOUT THE THING
BUT THE THING ITSELF

At the earliest ending of winter,
In March, a scrawny cry from outside
Seemed like a sound in his mind.

He knew that he heard it,
A bird's cry, at daylight or before,
In the early March wind.

The sun was rising at six,
No longer a battered panache above snow . . .
It would have been outside.

It was not from the vast ventriloquism
Of sleep's faded papier-mâché . . .
The sun was coming from outside.

That scrawny cry—it was
A chorister whose c preceded the choir.
It was part of the colossal sun,

Surrounded by its choral rings,
Still far away. It was like
A new knowledge of reality.

In the spring of 1954 the students of Trinity College, Hartford,
invited Wallace Stevens to contribute to an issue of *The Trinity
Review* celebrating (a few months before the fact) his seventy-
fifth birthday. He sent his maturest sequence on the vocation
of the poet contained within (and containing) the seasons of his

years, *The Rock*, which had already appeared abroad. To this he added a poem for the occasion, " Not Ideas About the Thing But the Thing Itself." And when, later in the same year, he carefully arranged the " total edifice " of his *Collected Poems*, he chose this brief poem as the final access in his life-long dialogue with reality. The poem also completes the series of new poems added to the volume, which begins, significantly, with "An Old Man Asleep " and reaches a crescendo, after man's massive triumphs of " St. Armorer's " have been abandoned for " the chapel of breath," in the final celebrations of the cosmic poem and the creative flow of time—" The Planet on the Table " and " The River of Rivers." Following this opulence " Not Ideas about the Thing . . ." is a deliberate act of modesty and a conscious beginning again.

It marks, in a sense, a return to the old " comforts of the sun " and the bright wings of *Harmonium*. After the liberal pentameters of the late meditations, it marks a return to the experimental metrics of the earliest poems. But the title, and what becomes of it in the poem, displays a starkness and Stevens' perennial self-irony, a " cure " for his own pretensions. The title is bare in its matter-of-factness: a negative proposition. Apparently we have returned to an old quest: " We seek / The poem of pure reality, untouched / By trope or deviation " (*CP*, 471). We are promised an experience without the artist's " bravura," " not as in metaphor, but in our sense " of it (*CP*, 431). Yet here again the title submits to metamorphosis, as in " The Snow Man," who is neither object nor man but " an immaculate personage in nothingness " (*CP*, 434), and as in " The Course of a Particular," where the particle becomes not the expiring leaf but the immanently mortal poet.

In form, " Not Ideas about the Thing . . ." is an *aubade*, of sorts; but the poet is mute and it is his environment, the " weather," which at first seems to speak. The lyric voice is ambiguous, not the artist's, yet ultimately his. This last " aurora " of a March morning is far removed from the centrifugal wakings of Stevens' fellow " inquisitor of structures," Marcel Proust. For the poet must live in change, in constant alertness to the new sound from without, whereas the novelist seeks to counter the vertiginous awakening to time with an escape into the enclosed depths of self. For Stevens the past is hopelessly and cheerfully annihilated, with all its metaphors and memories, in the new light " as morning throws off stale moonlight and shabby sleep " (*CP*, 382) .

The project is familiar. The central poet is roused from the nothingness of sticky sleep to a new transparency, to new experience. But the winter cycle is almost ended, and the "rage to order" stirs with the early March wind. The possible source for the early exhalations of self and circumambient singing choir is paradoxical to say the least: Mallarmé's little *art poétique*, " Toute l'âme résumée . . ." Whereas the symbolist rigorously excludes " cheap reality " which abrades his " vague literature," Stevens choses once again to court reality. The " exhalation " has become an inhalation of the world and the weather.

The situation in the turning season and returning day is a moment of renewal " free from memory or artifice." Stevens uses his familiar private myth of the sun to announce this renewal of reality: "What is there here but weather, what spirit / Have I except it comes from the sun " (*CP*, 128) ? Like the warmth of the sun on Penelope's pillow, in " The World As Meditation," the mind wakens to " a planet's encouragement " (*CP*, 521) . The bird's cry is, at first, part of this great potency: "The sun is half the world, half everything" (*CP*, 481) : it is the first half, reality observed. But it becomes in the course of the poem the other half, the song of reality imagined.

In the first tercet, whose free, three-beat line recalls the metrics of " The Snow Man," the " scrawny cry " asserts itself " from outside" against the slackly colloquial simile: " seemed like a sound in his mind." The simile won't do: "He *knew* that he heard it ": and the cry on the early March wind repeats itself. The wind rises, and with it the earliest rays of the sun: " Il faut tenter de vivre! " The sun is itself, a world of air and light, and not a discarded and extravagant metaphor. ("Panache" recalls both the theatrical bravura of Mallarmé's shipwrecked Hamlet and a " rare " astronomer's word for a " solar protuberance.")

" It would have been outside," is deliberately ambiguous. "It " can refer to the bird's cry or to the total world of the sun, of which it is a part. " Would have been " is still tentative, pressing toward the complete assertion of the " outside " against the rejected metaphor of the mind. The points of suspension here, as in the succeeding stanza, mark the break between the " battered " and "faded" world of the mind on the one hand and the insistent sun on the other.

The negative predications continue. The experience is not the fabrication of the past, its tired poetry and discarded stage properties. It is not a feat of legerdemain or a parlor trick. Finally, the flat assertion: "The sun was coming from outside."

But now "that scrawny cry" describes a deflection familiar to Stevens' private dialogues. It becomes the "pure rhetoric of a language without words" (*CP*, 374): Unlike the leaves of the earlier poem, it "transcends itself"; the cry, again repeated, has become a song, although premature and partial, and the singer part of the universal choir like the red bird of "Le Monocle de Mon Oncle." The poem rouses to "poetry" in the line which sounds his note, a note which is part of the supreme fiction of "the inconceivable sun" in the mind.

> His self and the sun were one
> And his poems, although makings of his self,
> Were no less makings of the sun. (*CP*, 532)

The poem is rather a prelude to, and promise of, that song of which it is a part, distant, "Still far away."

The experience and the fiction are concentric. The translucent listener is surrounded by the sun and "its choral rings," and he is pierced by the rays of intentionality, illuminating with language the world newly won. The image of the ringing light and sound suggests another, grander experience of the threshold where Stevens' "master and commiserable man" prepares for the final fiction, "the ascent to heaven." "With every visible thing enlarged and yet / No more than a bed, a chair and moving nuns," the solemn sounds of Rome drift in on him

> In choruses and choirs of choruses,
> Unwilling that mercy should be a mystery
> Of silence, that any solitude of sense
> Should give you more than their peculiar chords
> And reverberations clinging to whisper still. (*CP*, 510)

"The thing itself" has become, in the final finding of the imagination, a surrogate for the poet. And, at last, the central man leaves bare statement behind and finds a simile which will suffice: "It was like / A new knowledge of reality."

5

Each of the three poems is a characteristic "winter-piece" in the weather of Stevens' imagination. The poet studies a chilly world from the "central hermitage." Each poem enacts a state of ultimate contraction and poverty and nakedness to experience. Each records that ultimate characteristic of modern life, the abandonment and vacancy of the *Entgötterung*, announced by Nietzsche and anatomized by Heidegger.[18] Yet each describes a different aspect of the negation at the heart of Stevens' poetic act: "The Snow Man," the successive "nothings" of perception; "The Course of a Particular," the "no one" who dies in human time; and "Not Ideas about the Thing . . . ," the same central man, roused from the nothing of sleep, living not in the thing itself but in the "nothing" of poetic transformation.

Stevens grounded his "Notes toward a Supreme Fiction" on three formidable axioms: "It Must Be Abstract"; "It Must Change"; and "It Must Give Pleasure." "The Snow Man" succinctly illustrates the "abstract," "invented" nature of his man of glass, who prefigures the heroic abstractions, the empty giants of his "major weather." In "The Course of a Particular," both the leaf and the listener live inexorably in change, and in the change from the life of the one particular to the existence of the other the poem finds its life. Finally, with "Not Ideas about the Thing . . . ," "Winter and spring, cold copulars, embrace / And forth the particulars of rapture come" (*CP*, 392); at the end of "winter's chastity" the bird's "scrawny cry" announces the delights of that "old chaos of the sun," the return of that fictive world whose pleasures are forever fading and forever fresh.

Each poem is true in its way to Stevens' dictum that "the greatest poverty is not to live / In a physical world" (*CP*, 325). Each experience, true to its weather, is "the marriage / Of flesh and air" (*CP*, 83). In his best poetry Stevens always gives a sense of the vividness of life—"the freshness of ourselves" (*CP*, 398). And yet the poet is always, like his version of Santayana, "living in two worlds" (*CP*, 509). One world is constantly

---

[18] Martin Heidegger, *Holzwege* (Frankfurt, 1950), pp. 69-70. Heidegger, like Stevens, sees in the rediscovery of *poiesis* the possibility for modern man, in the darkest night of his tradition, to restore the dimension of the *Heilige*. For Stevens, this means that the poet in "the mythology of modern death" can repair the loss of the gods and "the death of Satan, . . . a tragedy for the imagination" (*CP*, 314).

annihilating the other just as each poem systematically destroys its title. " The corporeal world exists as the common denominator of the incorporeal worlds of its inhabitants," he says in a lecture (*NA*, 118). Objects are given to be "decreated" by the imagination. The never-ending quixotic search for reality leads him to "Reality as a thing seen by the mind, / Not that which is but that which is apprehended" (*CP*, 468). The unity of the paradox is the poem. "Every image is the elaboration of a particular. . . . Every image is an intervention on the part of the image-maker" (*NA*, 127-28).

Paul Valéry, searching for an emblem to represent his crystalline ideal of a poem, the translation of a world of universal relativity into an absolute construction, came upon the craft of the diamond-cutter.

Diamant.—Sa beauté résulte, me dit-on, de la petitesse de l'angle de réflexion totale . . . Le tailleur de diamant en façonne les facettes de manière que le rayon qui pénètre dans la gemme par l'une d'elles ne peut en sortir que par la même—D'où le feu et l'éclat. Belle image de ce que je pense sur la poésie: retour du rayon spirituel aux mots d'entrée.[19]

The image of refraction corresponds to the way in which Stevens both freely accepts his world and simultaneously transforms it. It suggests the paradox which defines each poem and the ultimate reversal of each title. In the final simile of "Not Ideas about the Thing . . ." we see the title refracted back on itself and the saving powers of the imagination proclaimed, while the life work concludes with the evanescent word which Stevens in every season heroically sought to capture, to serve, to understand, and to celebrate: Reality.

[19] Paul Valéry, *Oeuvres*, I, 298.

XI

NUANCES OF A THEME BY STEVENS

BY DENIS DONOGHUE

The theme, from "Notes toward a Supreme Fiction":

A bench was his catalepsy, Theatre
Of Trope. He sat in the park. The water of
The lake was full of artificial things,

Like a page of music, like an upper air,
Like a momentary color, in which swans
Were seraphs, were saints, were changing essences.[1]

1

The occupant of the bench is the poet. Or rather the Poet: a generic figure, hardly to be distinguished too carefully at any moment. A flick of metaphor, even a second glance, will change him into the pensive man of "Connoisseur of Chaos," the pensive giant of "Notes toward a Supreme Fiction," the naked man of "Montrachet-le-Jardin." Depending on the weather and the make of the mind he will appear as the seeing man in "The Blue Buildings in the Summer Air," the "figure of capable imagination" in "Mrs. Alfred Uruguay," the dark blue king in "Extracts from Addresses to the Academy of Fine Ideas"; in several poems he is "the hero," sometimes "the fictive hero," sometimes "a man at the centre of men." And at dusk he is liable to become "major man" by an obstinate metamorphosis; under great pressure the very "idea of man." Stevens warns us, "Give him no names"; if we obey, we are then free to think of him in any one of a dozen roles. In "Of Modern Poetry" he is "a metaphysician in the dark" and something of an actor, a mime, acute in improvization. In "Asides on the Oboe" he is

The impossible possible philosophers' man,
The man who has had the time to think enough,

---

[1] *The Collected Poems of Wallace Stevens* (New York, 1954), p. 397. This book will hereafter be cited as *CP*.

The central man, the human globe, responsive
As a mirror with a voice, the man of glass,
Who in a million diamonds sums us up. (*CP*, 250)

Call him, then, the man of thought. At all cost not the man of
action, since we are reading Stevens and not another poet. The
best chance is that he is Stevens himself raised to the nth degree,
sua voluntate; metaStevens. But this is still a long way off. Meanwhile the man on the bench aspires to a condition of philosophic
rigor: he will, perhaps, wear the philosopher's hat.

But he will not be a mere philosopher. Stevens agreed with
Whitehead that "poetry and philosophy are akin," [2] and he allowed for the existence of men like Jean Wahl and George Santayana, poets and philosophers in high standing with both com-
munities.[3] But in his own behalf he said, "I am not a philosopher"
(*OP*, 195). And to push the matter a little further: "Nor are
we interested in philosophic poetry, as, for example, the poetry
of Lucretius, some of the poetry of Milton and some of the poetry
of Pope, and those pages of Wordsworth, which have done so much
to strengthen the critics of poetry in their attacks on the poetry
of thought." In short, a lot of philosophic verse is dull. And yet,
among the critics, Hegel tells us that this need not be so: in
Stevens' version, "A poem in which the poet has chosen for his
subject a philosophic theme should result in the poem of poems"
OP, 187). As against T. S. Eliot, who maintained that it is quite
possible for the great poet to do no "thinking" at all, Stevens
argued that "the greater the mind the greater the poet"; "the
evil of thinking as poetry is not the same thing as the good of
thinking in poetry" (*NA*, 165). And if you propose to think at
all, you are well advised to think along philosophic lines. Stevens
often condescended to the philosophers, as if they were second-
class citizens making the noise of "reason's click-clack" while
poets played the sweet music of the imagination. Philosophers
would give "the official view of being" (*NA*, 40), but the unofficial view contributed by poets is more exciting, more daring.
Since truth is unattainable in any form that would satisfy philosophers, those men must end in despair: "the philosopher comes

[2] *The Necessary Angel: Essays on Reality and the Imagination* (New York, 1951),
p. 30. This book will hereafter be cited as *NA*.
[3] *Opus Posthumous* (New York, 1957), pp. 183, 187. This book will hereafter be
cited as *OP*.

to nothing because he fails" (*NA*, 45). Meanwhile the poets live
dangerously in the life of the mind, improvident, wild gamblers
in casual exfoliations. When the deal comes through, they own
"the mundo of the imagination," a more vital possession than
"the gaunt world of the reason" (*NA*, 57-58). And yet the poets
do well to familiarize themselves with the world of the philosophers, because many of the concepts in that world are poetic.
Indeed, some philosophic ideas are the most beautiful materials
the poet will ever find. If they have the look of despair—we can
add this gloss—all the better: poets know this look, and know
how to deal with it.

2

Hence the man on the bench will use philosophic ideas in his
own way, as *materia poetica*, and he will entertain them not for
their truth or even for their beautifully desperate failure, but
for their "poetic" nature, their suggestiveness. He will feel that
some philosophic ideas are "inherently poetic"; the concept of
the infinity of the world, for instance. And the idea of God is
"the ultimate poetic idea" (*OP*, 183, 193). And if he offers any
philosophic or ethical observations on his own behalf, he will
ground them in an obstinate aesthetic. This will leave room for
difference, even for contradiction. If he attends with adequate
nobility and precision to the multitudinous seemings, he can let
the One Being look after itself: "let be be finale of seem," in
"The Emperor of Ice-Cream." After all, the most beautiful idea
in the world says that at some level of abstraction all things are
one; division sends us back to unity:

> It is the celestial ennui of apartments
> That sends us back to the first idea . . . . (*CP*, 381)

A wave is a force "and not the water of which it is composed,
which is never the same" (*NA*, 35). All things resemble one
another. The river of rivers in Connecticut is a force, "not to
be seen beneath the appearances / That tell of it" (*CP*, 533).
In "This Solitude of Cataracts" the flecked river flows through
many places "as if it stood still in one" (*CP*, 424). And, to crown
all seemings, in "A Primitive like an Orb" the lover, the believer,
and the poet conspire with earth and sky to celebrate "the central

poem " (*CP*, 441). Meanwhile the poet does what he can—writes poems: the central poem is the finale. He does this for a hundred reasons, but chiefly because he is devoted to the human imagination in its marvellous range, its plenitude, its manifold powers. One thing at a time. Let the fifteenth poem wait until the fourteenth is written. In any event, the true history of the human race —as Stevens calls upon Adams to testify—" is a history of its progressive mental states " (*NA*, 6). It is in the nature of things that one state should differ from another.

It is necessary to say these things because, in fact, the philosophic positions registered in Stevens' poems are severally in contradiction. If we were to list every variant reading in the argument of epistemology, for instance, we could quote a poem by Stevens in favor of each. To take only the extreme positions, realism and idealism: realism is endorsed in " Nuances of a Theme by Williams," "Study of Two Pears "—

> The pears are not seen
> As the observer wills. (*CP*, 197)—

in several parts of " The Comedian as the Letter C "—

> The words of things entangle and confuse.
> The plum survives its poems. . . . (*CP*, 41)—

and elsewhere, almost at random. (But it was not random. Stevens thought well enough of this mental state to give it in " About One of Marianne Moore's Poems " and to repeat it, word for word, in " On Poetic Truth ": " the sense that we can touch and feel a solid reality which does not wholly dissolve itself into the conceptions of our own minds " (*OP*, 236-37).[4] In " Sunday Morning " the woman laments that even in paradise we shall not find this objectivity, this *alteracion*: of the pear and the plum she says, " Alas, that they should wear our colors there " (*CP*, 69). For idealism, we could cite fifty poems, including " Another Weeping Woman "—

> The magnificent cause of being,
> The imagination, the one reality
> In this imagined world . . . (*CP*, 25)—

---

[4] Cf. *The Necessary Angel*, 96. " On Poetic Truth," however, is Stevens' collection of sentences and phrases from an essay of that title by H. D. Lewis. See Joseph Riddel, *Modern Language Notes*, LXXVI (1961), pp. 125-29.

parts of "Notes toward a Supreme Fiction," parts of "The Man with the Blue Guitar," "The Idea of Order at Key West," "Tea at the Palaz of Hoon"—

> I was the world in which I walked, and what I saw
> Or heard or felt came not but from myself. (*CP*, 65)

And for endorsing theory: Stevens quotes Joad, "Philosophy has long dismissed the notion of substance and modern physics has endorsed the dismissal. . . . How, then, does the world come to appear to us as a collection of solid, static objects extended in space? Because of the intellect, which presents us with a false view of it" (*NA*, 25). And Kant, who says that the objects of perception are conditioned by the nature of the mind as to their form; the phrasing is Stevens', in "The Figure of the Youth as Virile Poet" (*NA*, 56).

The happiest situation for Stevens, of course, is that reality and the imagination are equal and inseparable—a mutual tension, a fine acknowledgment of equals. And this credence is featured in many poems, such as "In the Carolinas," "Infanta Marina," "Montrachet-le-Jardin," and several others: for a motto, think of "a nature to its natives all / Beneficence" (*CP*, 442) or "the partaker partakes of that which changes him" (*CP*, 392). And the theory of this happiness is "The Noble Rider and the Sound of Words."

But it is necessary to say that these philosophic commitments are severally contradictory, not merely to repeat, as an apologia, that Stevens was not a philosopher, a systematic thinker. Stevens did not play with philosophic ideas: he was too scrupulous to frivol with the gravity of other men. Moment by moment, poem by poem, he committed himself to the "mental state" of the occasion, doing his best to make it lucid if nothing else. If it occurred to him that these local commitments were contradictory, he was not distressed, because he trusted that the work would conform to the nature of the worker, and no other conformity was required. Stevens' readers may yield him this courtesy; or they may refuse. (As a lay epistemologist I have my own position, and I am a little sullen when Stevens subverts it, either in verse or prose.) The principle of complementarity, which modern physicists espouse, would have been useful to Stevens and may be essential to his readers—the simultaneous presence of incompatibilities on the field of action. Among the philosophers and anthropologists, Joseph Campbell has recently used this principle to bring the consideration of symbolism to a high atmosphere. Starting at the easy level, he says: " According to one mode or aspect of our experience, all things—ourselves included—are implicated in a context of space-time determinants and are therefore bound; and yet according to the other mode of our experience (which is impossible to reconcile with the first) all things—ourselves included —are freely creating themselves all the time." But if we push the principle for what it is worth, contradictions wither: then, to cite one example, "Prometheus defying Zeus is not the free individual and social and cosmological order. Rather, Prometheus and Zeus, I and the Father, are one." [5] Stevens did not invoke this principle, so far as I recall; if we invoke it now, on our own behalf, it is to make our discussion civil, to fend off the brawling of yes and no, at least to ensure that we remain silent until the poems are heard. It was enough for Stevens, and it is enough for many of his readers, that the poems conform to the nature of the poet, to his "progressive mental states," and that that nature be handsome. (Aristotle allowed that a man may persuade in this way.)

3

Give him no names. Agreed; but we must work toward a description, at the least. His professional purpose is easily given in his own words: " It is very easy to imagine a poetry of ideas in which the particulars of reality would be shadows among the poem's disclosures " (OP, 187) . Since this note persists, we might call him an ideal poet; bring in Plato, who cannot be left out of Stevens; and remark an engaging link with the last plays of Shakespeare, which Northrop Frye calls "ideal comedies," bearing down with all necessary pressure upon the meaning of the adjective. And if we want a motto in Stevens' own words, there is the last paragraph of "Three Academic Pieces": " In short, metaphor has its aspect of the ideal. This aspect of it cannot be dismissed merely because we think that we have long since outlived the ideal. The truth is that we are constantly outliving it

[5] " The Symbol without Meaning," *Eranos*, Yearbook 1957, Vol. XXVI (Zurich, 1958) .

and yet the ideal itself remains alive with an enormous life"
(*NA*, 81-82).

Or we might call him a metaphysical poet, for the sufficient
reason that his themes are often metaphysical: appearance and
reality; the one and the many; being (as, specifically, in "Metaphor as Degeneration"); knowledge; image and idea; metamorphosis. But this would mean going against Stevens' wish. There
is a remarkable passage in "The Figure of the Youth as Virile
Poet"—a page of dear, gorgeous nonsense to rival Plato's—in
which Stevens says that when we find ourselves "in agreement
with reality" we "cease to be metaphysicians." In fact, we "do
not want to be metaphysicians." In the radiant and productive
atmosphere of poetry the virile poet sees metaphysicians in the
crowd around him, but he has his own sufficient reasons for being
himself—the poet, *ipse*.

Trying again: it would be possible and decent to think of
Stevens as a mythological poet, on the particular authority of that
passage in "The Comedian as the Letter C" in which he says,

> What counted was mythology of self,
> Blotched out beyond unblotching. . . . (*CP*, 28)

or that late poem in which he says that "a mythology reflects its
region" (*OP*, 118). And this, at the least, would be preferable
to the poverty of calling Stevens a symbolist poet; especially after
"This Solitude of Cataracts," in which the poet repudiates the
language of wild ducks or mountains that are not mountains.
But then we remark, with some embarrassment, that Stevens
also wrote "The Poem that Took the Place of a Mountain";
so we are advised to take another tack.

The last one: the man on the bench, "Theatre / Of Trope."
Call him, then, a tropical poet. Since this implicates Santayana's
The Realm of Matter—a crucial parallel text for Stevens—all the
better. By trope Santayana means the "essence of any event as
distinguished from that event itself." Tropes "belong to the
region of Platonic ideas: they are unitary patterns, distinguishable in the movement of things: they are no part of the moving
substance, executing those patterns and overflowing them."[6] This
is one way of putting it. Another way is Stevens':

---

[6] *The Realm of Matter* (London, 1930), pp. 101-2, 113.

> . . . To get at the thing
> Without gestures is to get at it as
> Idea. . . . (*CP*, 295)

And then there is, beside this, his famous law of abstraction.

We like this, or we do not. Stevens worked in this way because it was the nature of his mind to work in this way. One of his favorite sentences was Focillon's: "The chief characteristic of the mind is to be constantly describing itself" (*NA*, 46). And Stevens dramatized this in "The Man with the Blue Guitar":

> Or, at the least, a phrase, that phrase,
> A hawk of life, that latined phrase. (*CP*, 178)

When Renato Poggioli asked him what this meant, Stevens answered, "A hawk of life means one of those phrases that grips in its talons some aspect of life that it took a hawk's eye to see. To call a phrase a hawk of life is in itself an example."[7] Or, alternatively, "the image must be of the nature of its creator" (*OP*, 118): the act—our own gloss—must be of the nature of its agent.

My predicate runs somewhat on these lines. Stevens wrote his poems for a hundred reasons, including this one: to pass the time, to get through the evening. He wrote while waiting. For what? For the maximum disclosure of his own poetic powers. And because this is eight words he often reduced it to one, calling it God; or sometimes to three, calling it the human imagination. Hence and meanwhile there was something to be done. Good or bad, it would be better than its alternative—nothing, the ground zero. He had his own powers; and he had the language, in its dazzling resource. Put the two together, and you have a Theatre of Trope. Add the belief that the imagination is "the will, as a principle of the mind's being, striving to realize itself in knowing itself" (*NA*, 10).[8] And because this object is dauntingly far off, allow that the poet will push hard and live "on the verge of consciousness" (*NA*, 115).

He will push hard because "the imagination is the power of the mind over the possibilities of things" (*NA*, 136); it is "the will of things" (*CP*, 84); it must exert its mastery, reducing the monster (*CP*, 175). The pressure against it is often given as

[7] *Mattino Domenicale ed Altre Poesie* (Torino, 1954), p. 180.

[8] Cf. *Opus Posthumous*, p. 242.

the moon, " part of a supremacy always / Above him " (*CP*, 314) ;
and sometimes it is the direct pressure of reality, society, bourgeois triumph, war. Hence the war between the mind and sky
must continue because "the mind is the end and must be
satisfied":

> It cannot be half earth, half mind; half sun,
> Half thinking; until the mind has been satisfied,
> Until, for him, his mind is satisfied. (*CP*, 257)

Satisfied, assuaged, appeased; then "the vivid transparence that
you bring is peace" (*CP*, 380). In the Theatre of Trope the poet
is Prospero, commanding Ariel to devise revels, masques, con-
fections: poems all, at once "makings of the sun" and "makings
of his self" (*CP*, 532). Tropical poets are always Prosperos; all
they need is a little plot of ground, an ample language, and their
own imagination. Then the water of a lake fills itself with
imagined, artificial things; swans become seraphs, melting themselves in thin air, at the imagination's caprice. "The freshness
of transformation is / The freshness of a world" (*CP*, 397-98).
(But this is to anticipate.)

4

"The image must be of the nature of its creator": a Kantian
aphorism. Indeed, when we follow the man on the bench through
his progressive mental states, the way calls for description in
Kantian terms—somewhat as we trace a configuration and know
that at some late stage it will make a way of its own, denying
its paradigm, as Stevens does, at the end.

We should begin with Kant's term from the *Critique of Pure
Reason*, " empirical intuitions of sensibility." As he defines it, " The
capacity for receiving representations through the mode in which
we are affected by objects is entitled *sensibility*. Objects are given
to us by means of sensibility, and it alone yields us *intuitions*. . . .
The effect of an object upon the faculty of representation . . .
is sensation. That intuition which is in relation to the object
through sensation is entitled *empirical*." [9] This is Stevens' first

---

[9] The following, and all subsequent phrases from the *Critique* are taken from the
translation by Norman Kemp Smith (London, 1929), pp. 65, 93, 106, 308, 310-11,
550-51.

world, the world of *Harmonium* (except that *Harmonium* includes
a few poems, like "Sunday Morning," which point beyond that
world). The first poems celebrate many things which seem to
be "rankest trivia" but are in fact the *sensibilia* upon which so
much depends. They are the "arrant spices of the sun" (*CP*, 88),
the "immense dew of Florida" (*CP*, 95), "prickly and obdurate,
dense, harmonious" (*CP*, 35), "hallucinations in surfaces" (*CP*,
472). Stevens called them "*delectationes* of the senses" (*NA*,
166): Antonio Machado called them "the *Ole! Ole!* of things."[10]
When we think of this world in Stevens we call it, quite simply,
Florida; but this is to be a little too easy. More accurately, it
is the world evoked by words and phrases, some Stevens', some
not, like these: "gay is, gay was," (*CP*, 385), abundance, gallan-
try, elegance, epicure, euphrasy, regalia, panache, fastidious, swish,
vif, dizzle-dazzle.

Most poets begin and end in this world. It is a dense, sufficient
world as long as it remains so; or as long as the poet's mind is
satisfied with it. But Stevens moved on. He said farewell to
Florida and moved on and back to his "North of cold." Presumably he had his own sufficient reasons. But he would have had
to move in any event, as a good Kantian. The quotidian, he says,
saps philosophers (*CP*, 42); even the quotidian of Florida, presumably, has its attendant "malady" (*CP*, 96). But in any event
the Kantian's mind is never satisfied by sensibilia, however pro-
fuse: it always recognizes that there is a higher level of generalization, which must be possessed for the sufficient reason that it is
there. In Kant this world operates through "concepts of the
Understanding."

From the *Critique*: objects "are thought through the *understanding*, and from the understanding arise *concepts*. . . . The
Understanding is the mind's power of producing representations
from itself, the spontaneity of knowledge. . . . Insofar as imagination is spontaneity, I sometimes also entitle it the productive
imagination. . . . Concepts of understanding contain nothing more
than the unity of reflection upon appearances, insofar as these
appearances must necessarily belong to a possible empirical consciousness."

This is the world of *Ideas of Order*, though its first and greatest

[10] *Juan de Mairena*, edited and translated by Ben Belitt (Berkeley, Calif., 1963),
p. 44.

intimation is "Sunday Morning." Stevens speaks of it with
uncharacteristic directness: "Words add to the senses" (*CP*,
234). And again: "The eye sees less than the tongue says"
(*OP*, 170). In "A Collect of Philosophy" he says that poets and
philosophers are united in "the habit of forming concepts,"
probing for an integration (*OP*, 196). In "The Relations between
Poetry and Painting" he gives in his own words Kant's theory
of the productive imagination: the operative force is not the
sensibility, it is a constructive force which uses the offerings of
sensibility for its own new purposes. And its triumphs are "deliciae
of the spirit" (*NA*, 165-66). When we think of this world in
Stevens we think of words of a different order from those of *Harmonium*: words like resemblance, liaison, relation, integration,
humility, sentence, anatomy. The anatomy of summer is not the
same as summer. "A minimum of making in the mind" (*CP*,
473) is a late phrase, but it will serve our purpose if we take it
to mean a necessary minimum, altogether necessary and desirable;
as Stevens in an even later poem gives us two Romes, "the two
alike in the make of the mind" (*CP*, 508). Readers who love
Harmonium so much that they want Stevens to make his permanent poetic residence in Florida are never assuaged by his concepts of the understanding; in *Ideas of Order* they miss the poet's
gibberish, the zay-zay and rou-cou-cou of the venereal soil. If
Harmonium is a holiday poster, *Ideas of Order* is a lieder recital.
There is room for both. And the later book has, as its weather
and consistency, a sustained rhetoric, a high style, a sublime,
which the *vif* of intuition hardly allows—except as an occasional
grace note in poems like "Sunday Morning" and (in part) "The
Comedian as the Letter C." As in "Evening without Angels":

> ... Evening, when the measure skips a beat
> And then another, one by one, and all
> To a seething minor swiftly modulate.
> Bare night is best. Bare earth is best. Bare, bare,
> Except for our own houses, huddled low
> Beneath the arches and their spangled air,
> Beneath the rhapsodies of fire and fire,
> Where the voice that is in us makes a true response,
> Where the voice that is great within us rises up,
> As we stand gazing at the rounded moon. (*CP*, 137-38)

Most poets who achieve a grand rhetoric are satisfied: their
minds are satisfied. But Stevens was a good enough Kantian to

know that there was still one great resource of the mind lying
unpossessed: the powers of the imagination would have to take
one more country, or remain in part undisclosed. So he would
push toward a higher level of generalization, the Kantian-Hegelian
universal. In Kant's terms, ideas of reason. In the *Critique of
Pure Reason* he said that "in the domain of theology we must
view everything that can belong to the context of possible experience . . . as if the sum of all appearances (the sensible world
itself) had a single, highest, and all-sufficient ground beyond itself,
namely, a self-subsistent, original, creative reason." Stevens, of
course, will deal with this by calling it God and equating it with
the human imagination. Kant gives most of his thought by de-
fending Plato: he speaks of Plato's "flight from the ectypal mode
of reflecting upon the physical world-order to the architectonic
ordering of it according to ends, that is, according to ideas. . . ."
And again: "Plato knew that our reason naturally exalts itself
to forms of knowledge which so far transcend the bounds of experience that no given empirical object can ever coincide with them,
but which must nonetheless be recognized as having their own
reality, and which are by no means mere fictions of the brain."
The idea, in short, is an heuristic concept.

Stevens' way of announcing this is to invoke a supreme fiction
and say: *It Must Be Abstract.* Indeed, "Notes toward a Supreme
Fiction" is the culmination of Stevens' ideas of reason. For
motto: "This warmth in the blood-world for the pure idea"
(*CP*, 256). Sometimes Stevens will insist on having the idea in
all its purity, as in the second part of "The Owl in the Sarcophagus." At other times he will exert great pressure to reconcile
idea and image: when he enters the place of metamen and parathings, they must still be men though metamen, things though
parathings (*CP*, 448-49). In the second of the "Contrary Theses"
he will walk toward an abstract of which the sun, the dog, and
the boy are "contours": the abstract is the premise from which
all things are conclusions (*CP*, 270). In "The Noble Rider and
the Sound of Words" the measure of a poet is deemed to be "the
measure of his power to abstract himself, and to withdraw with
him into his abstraction the reality on which the lovers of truth
insist" (*NA*, 23). It is a hard saying, but Stevens will say it
again; notably in "Effects of Analogy," where he invokes "a world
that transcends the world and a life livable in that transcendence"

(*NA*, 130). And then there are moments in which the sensibilia, the contours, seem merely "crude compoundings," and the poet on the verge of consciousness demands that the real come because his need is so great:

> . . . To find the real,
> To be stripped of every fiction except one,
>
> The fiction of an absolute— . . . . (*CP*, 404)

When the going is as hard as this, Stevens often plays solitaire under the oaks, escapes to "principium" (*OP*, 111), reflecting— I assume—that major man is "abler / In the abstract than in his singular (*CP*, 388). And in such moments he always invokes Plato. Sometimes by loyal paraphrase: "The aim of our lives should be to draw ourselves away as much as possible from the unsubstantial fluctuating facts of the world about us and establish some communion with the objects which are apprehended by thought and not sense" (*OP*, 236). This is from "On Poetic Truth," and Stevens immediately protests that he, as a poet, is not prepared to dismiss "the individual and particular facts of experience as of no importance in themselves." But often, in the poetry, he escapes in precisely this way—sometimes by imagining a "person" who has escaped in his behalf:

> . . . If we propose
> A large-sculptured, platonic person, free from time,
> And imagine for him the speech he cannot speak,
>
> A form, then, protected from the battering, may
> Mature: A capable being may replace
> Dark horse and walker walking rapidly. (*CP*, 330)

The platonic person, the man on the bench in one of the extreme reaches of his imagination, composes structures of his mind; when a composition is complete, it has the composure and finality which Rilke found in Valéry's language. The structures are "stratagems / Of the spirit" (*CP*, 376), "academies" (*CP*, 386), "enclosures of hypotheses" (*CP*, 516). When we think of them, or—the same thing—when we think of their style, we say that the style is curial, doctrinal, exquisite, lofty, vertiginous. Stevens, like Santayana, is an inquisitor of structures, and he will test them as severely as he can. He knows as well as any other modern poet that one can be self-indulgent in words even more easily than in action or evasion. And he knows and does not need Elizabeth Sewell to tell him that words are a great defense of the mind against being possessed by thought: a defense and an ease of mind. Words alone are certain good, Yeats said, and only half-believed: the other half of the belief was taken up by Stevens, for whom the world had to issue in the word or declare itself redundant. As in " Description without Place ":

> Thus the theory of description matters most.
> It is the theory of the word for those
>
> For whom the word is the making of the world,
> The buzzing world and lisping firmament.
>
> It is a world of words to the end of it,
> In which nothing solid is its solid self.
>
> As, men make themselves their speech: the hard hidalgo
> Lives in the mountainous character of his speech. (*CP*, 345)

Everything is proved, justified, certified by the " acutest speech " which crowns it; and by that alone. Ideas of reason have no other ground than the nature of the imagination that constructs them. When Stevens confronted this fact, he sometimes construed it for his delight, and sometimes for his despair: the ground often was enough, but often not. And sometimes he protests too much.

This accounts for a characteristic sequence in many of Stevens' later poems: he will begin by positing a situation, often a loss, sometimes an " idea of reason " of some extremity; and then, whatever the situation, he will claim to rise above it because his imagination has encompassed it; and the claim sends him through the situation, through the poem. In " Notes toward a Supreme Fiction," for instance, he begins a sequence: "What am I to believe? " And then he posits an angel in a cloud, leaping down through evening's revelations and growing warm in flight. And then he asks: " Am I that imagine this angel less satisfied? " He answers this in his own favor: the poet, imagining this ease, possesses it. " I have not but I am and as I am, I am." (As he says in the *Adagia*: " Poetry is a purging of the world's poverty and change and evil and death. It is a present perfecting, a satisfaction in the irremediable poverty of life " [*OP*, 167].) And from the consoling refuge of this " structure of the mind "—this " academy "—he turns back to survey the quotidian world:

> These external regions, what do we fill them with
> Except reflections, the escapades of death,
> Cinderella fulfilling herself beneath the roof? (*CP*, 405)

Again, in "The Plain Sense of Things": when the leaves have fallen it feels like the end of everything, even the end of imagination. "The great structure has become a minor house." No *vif*, no romance, the malady of the quotidian. And yet, and yet, and yet:

> Yet the absence of the imagination had
> Itself to be imagined. . . . (*CP*, 503)

Hence . . . and so on.

The trouble in the great structures of the mind, of course, is that they are miles beyond verification. By conforming to the nature of the mind which invents them, they come into being, achieve their identity. But by conforming to nothing else, they achieve nothing else. They have no status in the world, except that which accrues from the prestige of their creator. At best, they are "supernatural preludes" (*CP*, 414) or "putative canzones" (*CP*, 420). If men are made out of words, then life does indeed consist of propositions about life (*CP*, 355). This is either true or false; if it is false, then we must write a poetry or (better) live a life to refute it. If it is true, then indeed "reality is a vacuum" (*OP*, 168). (And then we are reminded of Kant's great parable of the dove which, feeling the resistance of the wind, thought it would fly better in a vacuum.) In short, ideas of reason exist in a vacuum; they evade the resistances only too successfully. The man on the bench is poetically safe with his lakes and swans that change into seraphs; and he is still safe in the wilderness of essence and trope if he brings his own resistance, his scruple. If not, not. The third phase of Stevens' poems invites description in these terms: the ease of mind, freedom of trope, resistances entirely adequate or not quite adequate, air or vacuum. But the story is not finished; there is still *The Rock,* and beside it there are several resistant poems in *The Auroras of Autumn.*

5

We posit for our man on the bench a certain scruple. He will quickly become dissatisfied if his ease of mind is too easy, and he will construe the cause with some severity. In the wilderness of essence one moves, presumably, with miraculous freedom; there are no obstacles of sensibility or understanding; the burdens of the past drop from us. And so on. But there is a passage in " The Figure of the Youth as Virile Poet" that makes us ponder. Stevens has been thinking of the past, and the several images it throws before us. And he imagines a young man emerging from one of these backgrounds; he represents " the intelligence that endures." He is the son, still bearing the burden of the father: Aeneas, carrying Anchises. " It is the clear intelligence of the young man still bearing the burden of the obscurities of the intelligence of the old. It is the spirit out of its own self, not out of some surrounding myth, delineating with accurate speech the complications of which it is composed " (*NA*, 53). This is the poet's program for resistance. When the wilderness palls in its ease, Stevens—I speak now mostly of *The Rock*—brings resistance in the form of contingency, fact, appearance, even " familiar things " (*CP*, 338).

This is not a return to *Harmonium*, a senior citizen's retirement to Florida. It is not even a repudiation of Kant and Hegel and all the old immortals. Rather, in these great last poems Stevens is gathering all his resources, disowning nothing, and laying them all at the feet of humanity. He doesn't need a theory for this; besides, he has done his homework, he has been to school at the philosophers and aestheticians. If there is any theory behind these poems, it is Croce's Oxford lecture of 1933 in which the philosopher invoked an image of " the whole man: the man who thinks and wills, and loves, and hates " (*NA*, 16). Stevens quoted a few sentences in " The Noble Rider and the Sound of Words " and returned to expand them in one of his last essays. The expansion has a certain interest, short of the highest interest, and it includes a sentence by Whitehead that Stevens quotes now (1955) and that he would not have quoted but for a radical change in his whole bearing. The sentence from Whitehead reads: " Who shall say that to live kindly and graciously and meet one's problems bravely from day to day is not a great art, or that those who can do it are not great artists." And—for good measure— the next one reads: " Aesthetics are understood in too restricted a sense " (*OP*, 230). That these sentences were quoted and en- dorsed by Stevens is fantastic—Stevens, who asked, " What is there in life except one's ideas? " and thought of " the world as word." But there it is. This is his final yes, to other people, other lives. His new text of the world is " a scribble of fret and fear and fate " (*CP*, 494) ; and as if to deny to himself—the man on the bench—the pleasure of changing swans into seraphs, he says now:

> . . . We seek
> The poem of pure reality, untouched
> By trope or deviation, straight to the word,
> Straight to the transfixing object, to the object
>
> At the exactest point at which it is itself,
> Transfixing by being purely what it is. (*CP*, 471)

Hence the rock itself. " The rock cannot be broken. It is the truth " (*CP*, 375) . And again:

> The rock is the gray particular of man's life,
> The stone from which he rises, up—and—ho,
> The step to the bleaker depths of his descents . . . . (*CP*, 528)

The last word in the *Collected Poems* is " reality "; its proof, its illustration is a bird's cry heard—heard, not posited or dreamed—in March.

Most of the evidence is in. If we try to trace the source of this new feeling in Stevens—the feeling for humanity that gets into the poems of the last nine or ten years of his writing life—the signs are thin on the ground. But there is, for one thing, his strange praise of " the ignorant man ": praise common enough in Yeats, Synge, Williams, Eliot, but nonetheless strange when Stevens gives it.

> You must become an ignorant man again
> And see the sun again with an ignorant eye

he said in the first moments of " Notes toward a Supreme Fiction." And there is his tone in " In a Bad Time ":

> But the beggar gazes on calamity
> And thereafter he belongs to it, to bread
> Hard found, and water tasting of misery. (*CP*, 426)

This is one thing. And another is Stevens' response to particular lives. Santayana is only an extreme instance, who prompts us to see that *The Rock* is more densely populated than any other book by Stevens; it is the only collection of Stevens' poems that one would invoke in a discussion of personalism, dialogue, *I and Thou*, Gabriel Marcel, Camus. For the first time Stevens has written a book which says *Thou*.

6

And now we may think of the man on the bench coming out of
his trance, his catalepsy, and asking himself, a little dazzled by
the Theatre of Trope:

> I wonder, have I lived a skeleton's life,
> As a questioner about reality. (*OP*, 89) [11]

And the wondering at once testifies to his scruple and enlarges
it. This is 1947; for the remaining years of his life he will pay
less devotion to the rhetorical handbook than to the "handbook
of heartbreak" (*CP*, 507): he will be touched by other lives,
Santayana, an old man asleep, "strong peasants in a peasant
world" (*CP*, 530), even Ulysses and Penelope. He will listen
to "the cry of leaves that do not transcend themselves, / In the
absence of fantasia" (*OP*, 96-97). He will look at ponds that
do not reflect him (*CP*, 503), and facts that proclaim his failure
(*CP*, 502-3). There is still the imagination, and it still works by
analogy, resemblance, metaphor, metamorphosis:

> A flick which added to what was real and its vocabulary,
> The way some first thing coming into Northern trees
> Adds to them the whole vocabulary of the South,
> The way the earliest single light in the evening sky, in spring,
> Creates a fresh universe out of nothingness by adding itself,
> The way a look or a touch reveals its unexpected magnitudes.
> (*CP*, 517)

But his acknowledgment of other people, of the quotidian in all
its malady, imposes a resistance never felt in the wilderness of
trope. Its symbol now is still the candle, the light of the imagination, but in "To an Old Philosopher in Rome" it is

> A light on the candle tearing against the wick
> To join a hovering excellence, to escape
> From fire and be part only of that of which
> Fire is the symbol: the celestial possible. (*CP*, 509)

And the saving grace is in the tearing, the wick, the sensible fire:
so much so, that even at the end when every visible thing is
enlarged it is "no more than a bed, a chair and moving nuns";

[11] Cf. *Opus Posthumous,* p. 117.

these, at the last, are the props and *personae* of " the immensest theatre "—no longer a Theatre of Trope. It comes to this: the imagination lives even in a quiet normal life:

> There was no fury in transcendent forms.
> But his actual candle blazed with artifice. (*CP*, 523)

Desdemona understood a fury in the words, but not the words. Yeats invoked an artifice of eternity. In Stevens, " artifice " is a word for " imagined "—nothing more—the humanist imagination, in time and place. This is the imagination of " The World as Meditation," Long and Sluggish Lines," " Final Soliloquy of the Interior Paramour," " The Rock," " St. Armorer's Church from the Outside," " The River of Rivers in Connecticut," and " The Course of a Particular." It is a kind of total grandeur at the end.

XII

THE CONTOURS OF STEVENS CRITICISM

BY JOSEPH N. RIDDEL

1

There is not yet a Wallace Stevens "industry." But Stevens' rise in critical esteem since his death in 1955 portends one. What once seemed a solid but esoteric achievement must now be acclaimed one of the established canons of modern poetry. Where once Stevens was thought the dandy among a select group of coterie "romantics," he now appears destined for a literary peerage with Eliot, if not with Yeats. There is more to Stevens' growing eminence, happily, than the fortunes of criticism's Bourse. The Stevens revival has nothing about it of frantic (or commercial) "rediscovery"; on the contrary, his poetry never suffered from critical inattention. There were, of course, what the late Hi Simons called his "vicissitudes of reputation," occasions when his poetry and its age seemed at a loss to recognize each other. But he was never lost to the critical eye. One may even assert that in the carpet of Stevens criticism there is a revealing figure of our twentieth-century literary, and cultural, history. In any event, there has developed in the last decade an increasing opinion that Stevens rather than Eliot speaks most authentically for modern American man (or for modern man), which has stimulated a formidable revaluation of his poetry. The significance of this revaluation involves a great deal more than the fluctuation of one poet's reputation.

A few months before Stevens' death, Randall Jarrell vouchsafed his triumph: "If someone had predicted to Pound, when he was beginning his war on the iambic foot; to Eliot, when he was first casting a cold eye on post-Jacobean blank verse; to both, when they were first condemning generalization in poetry, that in forty or fifty years the chief—sometimes, I think in despair, the only—influence on younger American poets would be this generalizing, masterful, scannable verse of Stevens', wouldn't both have laughed is confident disbelief?" (*Yale Review*, March, 1955)[1] Echoing

[1] A minimal bibliographical reference is included in the text of this essay, and in the

Jarrell, the late Theodore Roethke published at nearly the same time his jaunty "A Rouse for Stevens," subtitled "To be Sung in a Young Poet's Saloon" and concluding with this lusty impiety:

> Roar 'em, whore 'em, cockalorum,
> The muses, they must *all* adore him!
> Wallace Stevens,—are we *for* him?
> Brother, he's our father!   (*7 Arts,* 1955)

Stevens' influence on a younger generation of poets is more than incidentally related to his increasing stature among critics; or better, the two are opposite but complementary. Despite the enthusiastic reception of his *Collected Poems,* and the more recent Vintage paperback selections, Stevens' popular reputation, if it can be called that, rests almost exclusively upon a handful of early poems, mostly from *Harmonium.* His later verse, despite much recent attention, is far better known in name than in fact. Stevens, in short, is still popularly identified by his anthology pieces, and the elegance of his early style. This is a poet's poetry, a highly polished sport of the imagination. But within the panoply, we see in retrospect, are those "recessive elements" of the self seeking self-definition which Louis Martz finds to be the flower of greatness in the later poems (*Yale Review,* June, 1958).

Stevens' rise to Parnassus has occurred only after some vigorous and persistent acclamations for his later work, those meditative capstones which continue to haunt exegetes, bemuse professors, and alienate fellow poets who consider what Stevens called the "life" of the imagination a retreat willy-nilly from the stuff of life. The task ahead, as Roy Harvey Pearce has reminded critics, is to penetrate Stevens' late poems, to visit upon them the kind of "preliminary exegesis which even their most enthusiastic readers on the whole so far have declined to give them" (*The Continuity of American Poetry* [Princeton, 1961]). Pearce was pointing to the fact that Stevens' work, except for a few choice pieces, has not enjoyed Eliot's *succès d'estime.* The later Stevens remains an enigma of sorts, but the growing conviction is that the earlier hedonist will not be understood until we know the "inquisitor of structures."

---

footnotes. Readers are referred to the substantial bibliography contained in *Wallace Stevens Checklist and Bibliography of Stevens Criticism* (Denver, 1963), by Samuel French Morse, Jackson Bryer, and Joseph Riddel. In every case, only the first appearance of the essay is noted in the text, unless it is more familiarly available in one of the author's books.

The labors of "preliminary exegesis" had begun, however, even
before Pearce wrote, and now are beginning to submit those first
tentative perspectives which will eventually bring the Stevens
canon into clear focus. This promises to be an exhausting, and
even acrimonious labor: this "placing" of Stevens, this reading
into and out of and beyond his extraordinarily complex poems.
Already sides are forming, attitudes hardening. Soon there will
be platforms and dogmas. This is in one sense the expense of
greatness; in another, a deserved tribute. For Stevens, his popular
reputation notwithstanding, has become the unofficial preceptor
of the modern romantic self, except possibly to the isolated cult
of neo-primitivism, best exemplified perhaps in the separate
criticisms of Karl Shapiro and Kenneth Rexroth.

The import of this present revaluation of Stevens is manifest
in a number of recent studies which have found his poetry a culmination of the Romantic tradition. Set beside individual examina-
tions of his work, these reassessments of Romanticism, its tradition, and its contemporary issue have virtually resurrected
Stevens from the limbo of artists who stood autonomously
outside traditions and movements. Frank Kermode's *Romantic
Image* (London, 1957) used Stevens briefly to confirm certain
post-Romantic attitudes of the artist toward his own role in a
secular and alien world. Kermode's informative introduction to
Stevens (*Wallace Stevens* [Edinburgh, 1960]), though it does not
ride a hobby-horse, is soundly based on the earlier book. More
recently, Harold Bloom's reading of the English Romantics as a
Visionary Company makes extensive reference to Stevens as the
modern culmination of the Romantic poet's search for a myth of
self. One feels occasionally in reading Bloom that without Stevens'
radical modernism the critic would have no focus on his traditional
company. Morse Peckham, James Benziger, and Edwin Honig
in his redefinition of allegory as a cardinal literary trope, have
found Stevens an essential modern voice in the Romantic and
Romance tradition. Roy Harvey Pearce's view of the "continuity"
of American poetry retrieves Stevens from the French Symbolist
tradition, in which criticism a decade or so ago most easily placed
him, and evinces his Americanness, particularly the import of his
"egocentric" affirmation of the creative self as the ultimate expression of our native idealist temper. Now, Professor Pearce is
at work on a briefer study, tentatively entitled *The Final Yes*,

that appraises Stevens as "father" of a new humanism in our poetry of the last two decades. (A part of that book is published in this collection.) Frederick Hoffman's impressive study of death and modern literature, *The Mortal No*, takes its title from the Stevens who Hoffman believes is a representative modern imagination, one who by accepting the rule of self and denying the traditional consolations of immortality most vividly expresses the conatus of secular man to live, in Stevens' words, "without belief, beyond belief." These last two titles, drawn from related passages in Stevens to preface studies of vastly different conviction, speak eloquently of Stevens' increasing hold upon the modern intellect. The list might be extended. But my purpose is to lay the ground for a few observations on the what and why of the criticism behind Stevens' flourishing reputation, and its significance not only for literary history but for the understanding of the modern self. The phases of Stevens' critical reception constitute one part of the story; the more recent criticism, and the uses to which the poetry has been put, another. And lastly, there is the question of whither Stevens criticism, if not whither the modern imagination.

2

Stevens' reputation in the little magazines preceded the first critical regard of his work by a few years.[2] Indeed, as Hi Simons later pointed out, the earliest criticisms of Stevens are to be found in various reviews of collections in which his work appeared, particularly the *Others* anthologies.[3] But the first noticeable, if not notable, criticism belongs appropriately to that tireless entre-

---

[2] There were some appreciative critical notices of Stevens' Harvard juvenilia published in the *Harvard Crimson* from March through June in 1900. The first known mention of his maturer poetry, for which I thank Robert Buttel, appeared in a magazine called *Minaret* (Feb. 16, 1916), 26, which used Stevens' "Phases" as an example of the "nauseating" war realism being printed in *Poetry*. This notice precedes Hi Simons' discovery of a review by George Soule, of the *Anthology of Magazine Verse*, in *The New Republic* (Mar. 25, 1916).

[3] See "Vicissitudes of Reputation, 1914-1940," *Harvard Advocate* (Dec., 1940), pp. 8-10, 34-44. Simons' essay provides a generally full account of Stevens' reception, in reviews and in avant-grade literary chatter, up to 1940. He mentions the Aiken-Untermeyer spat, and categorizes the conflicting opinions of reviewers, colleagues, and antagonists of Stevens. But his purpose, unlike mine, was to present the reputation in and for itself, and not within the larger context of modern criticism and Stevens' development.

preneur, Louis Untermeyer, whose *New Era in American Poetry* (New York, 1919) presumed to establish its own hierarchy of American literary values. Stevens was little more than a minor foil in Untermeyer's scheme, which set forth pugnaciously the qualities of an "American" as opposed to a "pure" poetry. Conrad Aiken, reviewing the volume, defined its irritations very well as repugnant to poetry, thereby setting off a dogmatic spat (see *Scepticisms* [New York, 1919]). The Aiken-Untermeyer dispute originated in *The New Republic* (May, 1919). A minor skirmish as these things go, it used Stevens as merely a symptom. Untermeyer had categorized Stevens as an impressionistic *precieux*, not one of the roughs. Aiken's defense scoffed at Untermeyer's crude values. All this is pretty common knowledge. What is significant is that Aiken more or less accepted Untermeyer's Stevens, rarely mentioning him except in conjunction with Kreymborg, Bodenheim, and the impressionist "gang" of *Others*. In matters of taste, Aiken implied, to like Stevens was to opt for poetry rather than homily. Untermeyer's opinion would ordinarily be of little note had it not instigated one prevailing view of Stevens in the twenties. Four years later, in his *American Poetry Since 1900*, Untermeyer found a place for Stevens: he is a "pointillist rather than an impressionist"—this after relegating him to the larger category "Impressionist" along with others of this ilk, Adelaide Crapsey and Alter Brody! If nothing else, this provided the obliquely fulsome vocabulary by which early Stevens would be known: aesthete, hedonist, dandy, Impressionist. In a final say, reviewing *Harmonium* for the *Yale Review* (Oct., 1924), Untermeyer rebuked the fetish of "determined obscurity," calling Stevens a word-painter interested only in "sound-values" (no pun intended): "For the most part," he opined, "this conscious aesthete 'at war with reality' achieves little beyond an amusing preciosity."

There were two apparent ways to read *Harmonium*, and both from our present vantage seem questionable. One is manifest in Harriet Monroe's ecstasy, which deserves quoting as an example of her persistent etherealizing of Stevens: "Others may criticize and complain, may long for more perfect worlds or search subliminal mysteries—for him it is enough to watch the iridescent fall of sunlight on blue sea-water and pink parasols, and meditate on the blessed incongruities which break into rainbow colors this earth of ours and the beings who people it" (*Poets and Their*

Art [New York, 1932]).[4] This familiar pastiche of Stevens' titles and imagery became commonplace for those for whom poetry was "essential gaudiness." Those more knowledgeable of literary history and influence soon identified his unique mode as Symbolistic, that is, *Symboliste*. Within the first group there were two persuasions: represented by Miss Monroe's levitations on the one hand, and on the other by the more stringent critiques of Stevens' escapism, hedonism, and wholesale moral anarchy, which were to culminate in Yvor Winters' noted censure. Though the tremulous-aesthete view of Stevens was short-lived, the reviews of the hedonist, dandy, and Symbolist continue today, if with increased subtlety and penetration. The development of these lines alone shapes the larger contours of Stevens criticism until 1945 at least.

William Van O'Connor has called Stevens' early reputation a "legend," that is, a myth which grew out of the poet's private life and attached itself to his poetic self (*The Shaping Spirit* [Chicago, 1950]). The "legend" is, at least in part, a canard, compounded of Stevens' stylistic lucubrations and a personal manner that seemed to prompt his friends to myth-making. O'Connor's account of the "legend" is a semi-accurate summation of the stories that collected around poet and poetry, but appears otherwise to over-emphasize their significance. Stevens apparently had a facility for wearing the poses of his verse. Hence, those stories recorded by compeers and later perpetuated as a badge of literary identity tend to stress an eccentricity which is in turn read into the poetry.[5] And, indeed, the image of the shy, jovial, impish man

---

[4] Llewelyn Powys surely takes uncontested honors for this kind of rhetoric: Listening to his poetry is like listening to the humming cadences of an inspired daddy long-legs akimbo in sunset light against the colored panes of a sanct window above a cathedral altar " (*Dial*, July, 1924).

[5] O'Connor's "legend" is a composite of the stories by Alfred Kreymborg (*Troubadour* [New York, 1925]; *Our Singing Strength* [New York, 1929]), Harriet Monroe (*Poets and Their Art; A Poet's Life* [New York, 1938]), Amy Lowell ("A Critical Fable," 1922), and later articles and interviews by Charles Henri Ford (*View*, Sept., 1940) and Will Vance (*Saturday Review of Literature*, Mar. 23, 1946), as well as remarks by William Carlos Williams and other friends of Stevens'. See also Simons, "Vicissitudes of Reputation." There is a great dearth of accurate biographical information, and but a small part of this is in print. An interested reader might look at essays by Jerold Hatfield (*Trinity Review*, May, 1954), Byron Vazakas (*Historical Review of Berks Co.*, July, 1938), Michael Lafferty (*Historical Review of Berks Co.*, Fall, 1959), and Morse's introductions to *Opus Posthumous* (New York, 1957) and *Poems by Wallace Stevens* (New York, 1959). But until the publication of Professor Morse's critical biography even this evidence must be used with care.

that emerges from so many reports reflects his strategy of masking emotion in comic-ironic postures, of de-personalizing the personal. But promoters of this image did little more than call attention to the surfaces of the poetry, as Amy Lowell's doggerel reveals:

> He has published no book and adopts this as pose
> But its rather more likely, I think, to suppose
> The particular gift he's received from the Muses
> Is a tufted green field under whose grass there oozes
> A seeping of poetry, like wind through a cloister . . .
>   ("A Critical Fable," 1922)

This myth of Stevens' slight productivity persisted until well into the 1940's, when it became apparent that he was hardly the least prolific of modern poets. But it is the other myth, of the cloistered, ethereal self, which drew attention away from *Harmonium*, or, focusing attention upon it, called down upon it moralistic ire. Marianne Moore, reviewing the volume for *Dial* (Jan., 1924), cautioned the reader that here was seriousness *con brio*. Yet, her own unmatched genius for fixing upon the elegancies of sound and unique particulars pointed away from the "ferocity" she found there. She was not alone is discovering Stevens' "violence"; Paul Rosenfeld in *Men Seen* (New York, 1925) spoke of his "concentrated violence . . . almost naturalistic." But the consensus was that within this stylistic elegance, precision, and wit, the "ferocity" was merely verbal, pointing away from, not toward, the wasteland. Even the title of John Gould Fletcher's half-laudatory review (*Freeman*, Dec., 1923) reserved its praise: "The Revival of Aestheticism." Fletcher qualified his admiration of style and wit in words very close to Edmund Wilson's (*The New Republic*, March 19, 1924), insisting that Stevens must "either expand his range to take in more human experience, or give up writing altogether." Wilson more bluntly called Stevens "impervious to life."

Untermeyer could safely be ignored, for his chauvinist fervor dismissed alike Eliot and Stevens, and thus two primary modes of the new poetry. But Stevens' occasionally crystal-pure surfaces and detached sophistication disturbed too many consciences. Few critics could swallow with Llewelyn Powys a poetry "beyond good and evil, beyond hope and despair" (*Dial*, July, 1924). In the end, those who like Wilson and Fletcher opted for the poet of "life" and "human experience" offered firm demurrers against

Stevens' gaudium. Gorham Munson's essay in *Dial* (Nov., 1925), following as it did Powys', is the most influential of the moral critiques before Winters', combining the usual blandishments for style—"adding elegance to correctness"—with excoriations of Stevens' "temperate romanticism." Munson performed an adroit critical maneuver by taking away with one hand what he had not really offered with the other, admitting Stevens' precise (but effete) music while thwacking him for using it as a transport to ease: "Mr. Stevens . . . appears to sit comfortably in the age, to enjoy a sense of security, to be conscious of no need for fighting the times." This is a call for a crisis literature and moral firmness, an attack on the tranquil acceptance of things as they are by a "New World Romantic" who has deserted the vigorous revolt of the unrepentent "Old World Romantic." Denying Stevens' "ferocity," Munson concluded that he represented the American syndrome which "drives passionately toward comfort."

Harmonium, then, verified the fragmentary impression of Stevens that formed from his uncollected works: like "Peter Quince," and the shorter "Sunday Morning," and such eye-catching *tours de force* as "Bantams in Pine Woods." Almost every critic found the style impeccable, but in the especial sense of its elegance, purity, and gaudiness—terms which seemed alien to Pound's and Eliot's war on Romantic effusion. Stevens was occasionally associated with the Imagists, though nearly always recognized as an innovator. But more than anything else, it was his affinity with French poetics which attracted comment. Some two decades later Hi Simons noted that of 195 critical essays (he must have included parts of essays) on Stevens, "the poet had been compared with, or said to have been influenced by, Gautier, Baudelaire, Verlaine, Mallarmé, Rimbaud, and Valéry; but the variety of resemblances between his writing and Jules Laforgue's have attracted most attention" (*Modern Philology*, May, 1946). Simons points to the most influential as Rene Taupin's *L'Influence du Symbolisme Française sur la Poésie Américaine* (1929), which quotes a letter from Stevens stating his immense regard for French poetics. There is no doubt of Stevens' knowledge of Laforgue, if only through his repeated contacts with the *Others* group, among whom Walter Arensberg and Maxwell Bodenheim were enthusiastic Laforgueans. Paul Rosenfeld in *Men Seen* stressed his point about world-weariness and violence in Stevens by calling the poet Pierrot.[6] Munson's essay supported its estimate of Stevens' dandyism with a parallel to Baudelaire, pointing out explicitly that whereas Baudelaire's dandyism led to disaffection, melancholy, and finally bitter denunciation of the social order, Stevens' led only to acceptance. Indeed, it was on this point of dandyism that Munson contrasted Stevens and Eliot, a dubious argument even then, but one which helps explain why Stevens' dandyism, as opposed to Eliot's, was thought to be out of touch with its age.

If anything distinguished the popular criticism of Stevens it is this insistence that his poetry was disengaged from reality, was, in Powys' phrase, "hermetic art." Eliot, critics like Wilson recognized, was a dandy, a wit, a professed admirer of Laforgue and Baudelaire; and his poetry achieved, like theirs, a tone which brought the age into critical focus even as it detached the poetic self from the age's chaos. Stevens' hedonism, invading language, made such beautiful music that it destroyed meaning. This withdrawal of self into the imagination's finery, it appeared, denied him the privilege of facing the age objectively and critically. His detachment took the form of irresponsible escape. He became to many critics virtually the voice of his poems: he was " Crispin," and " Hoon," and " mon oncle." Eliot's poignant, his tragic irony—they are Wilson's words—apparently disengaged him from Prufrock, and surely from Sweeney. When in 1929 Allen Tate remarked that Stevens, who had not published anything for five years, was " the most finished poet of his age," it was the Parnassian he praised (*Bookman*, Jan., 1929). And it must have seemed then kindly praise indeed, for aestheticism was going out of style.

3

The 1931 edition of *Harmonium*, with its fourteen new poems (three of the original were dropped), inspired some important revisionary criticism. Morton Zabel, reviewing it in *Poetry* (Dec., 1931), addressed himself directly to Munson's attack, rebuking

---

[6] The influence of Laforgue was given added currency by H. R. Hays's " Laforgue and Wallace Stevens " (*Romantic Review*, July-Sept., 1934), and has been revived in a number of recent studies of Stevens' comic masks. Michel Benamou, however, has offered several serious qualifications to the familiar view of Stevens' Laforgueanism (*Romantic Review*, Apr., 1959). His and other recent attitudes towards Stevens' symbolism are discussed later in this essay.

the latter's version of the comfortable dandy: "Mr. Stevens never urged the idea of denying danger by opposing it, or of disguising reality by order. Order is ultimately for him, the product of the 'will of things.'" Zabel stressed the precision of style, its disciplined moral intelligence. He even hinted at an intellectual content, and prophetically isolated Stevens' preoccupation in the coming decade with "order." But it was R. P. Blackmur who supplied the first great apology for Stevens (*Hound & Horn*, Winter, 1932). Blackmur's essay remains today one of the three or four most notable introductions to Stevens, if only because it meticulously presented him as the poet of a precisely expressed interior life. It is a landmark, too, in the development of the "new criticism," which would have so much to do with the shift of literary values in the next two decades. With an impressive variety of examples and cross-references, Blackmur showed that Stevens' apparent "ornamental use of words" was to the contrary "the establishment of interior experience by the construction of its tone in words." Anticipating his subsequent interest in Jamesian ambiguity, Blackmur praised Stevens as the modern poet who has created a "new sensibility" in his marriage of "what is felt with the senses and what is thought in the mind." Blackmur's is a valuable document in reaffirming the significance of self in Stevens' poetry, just to the degree it marks a turning away from the "humanistic," rational criticism of the twenties. Yet, its stress on the subjective was not the thing to make Stevens appear a poet of great moment. Following Blackmur's definition, critics in the thirties could dismiss Stevens as they did James, since the era of the unique self (even if it posed as a humanistic self in search of its humanity) was vanquished. Before Blackmur's essay appeared, Stevens had begun to publish again: poems which, though clothed in familiar ornaments, revealed the distress of the times. William Carlos Williams commenced a review of *The Man with the Blue Guitar and Other Poems* (*The New Republic*, Nov. 17, 1937) by averring that Stevens "of late has turned definitely to the left." There was to say the least some question about this. The most famous of Stevens' literary skirmishes had occurred two years previous, the result of Stanley Burnshaw's somewhat intemperate review of *Ideas of Order* (*New Masses*, Oct. 1, 1935). Any student of Stevens knows the story: that Burnshaw approached Stevens' new volume by first reproaching the subjectivism of

Harmonium—"the kind of verse that people concerned with the murderous world collapse can hardly swallow today except in tiny doses"—a fault, he added, Stevens tried subsequently to correct and failed: "*Ideas of Order* is the record of a man who, having lost his footing, now scrambles to stand up and keep his balance." The review is famous for provoking Stevens' personal reply in a long poem that became the second part of the original "Owl's Clover," entitled "Mr. Burnshaw and the Statue."[7] Though an incidental piece of Leftist rhetoric, and for that matter not wholly wrong in judgment, Burnshaw's attack echoed the sentiments of its age. It became for Stevens the paradigm of ideological error, the reduction of poetry into partisan rhetoric, and the doctrinaire assertion of "one idea" as the sum of human truth. What it pointed up, nevertheless, was Stevens' resistance to, even as he acknowledged, the demands for a social panacea. The tenor of criticism like this, however, drew attention away from Stevens' effort to preserve poetry (thus, the individual self) from affairs that were anti-humanist and perhaps ephemeral. But his poetry in the thirties had in the end to acknowledge what Stevens called the "antipoetic," or "things as they are," as the given of a democratic, secular world. Hence, Stevens' alertness to the political crisis, his attempt to define poetry's responsibility to the human polity yet to preserve the self against the immediate and temporal, necessarily involved him in some curious and inelegant defensiveness.

The reviews of this poetry were divided. Critics as acute as Theodore Roethke (*The New Republic*, July 15, 1936) and Dorothy Van Ghent (*New Masses*, Jan. 11, 1938) regretted his turning away from the "present-day world" and his absorption with the "decaying imagination." Those who would praise spoke very little of the rhetorical subject-matter, and lauded a new strength of style. F. O. Matthiessen, rising as he consistently did above his Marxist persuasion, extolled *Ideas of Order* for its integrity in expressing the will of the individual confronted by social (and moral) anonymity. Surprisingly, he thought it better on the whole

---

[7] In all fairness to Burnshaw, one must acknowledge his explanation of the motives and the occasion that led to this review (see *Sewanee Review*, Summer, 1961). The review was not, as he says, as momentous as the *éclat* it provoked. Burnshaw takes full blame for the youthful pride and passion with which he engaged his task. But he speaks also of the awe in which he held Stevens. The whole affair is truly a significant footnote to the history of poetry and criticism in the thirties.

than *Harmonium*, more "robustly integrated" and the year's only book of poetry "that would lend great distinction to a Pulitzer Prize"; ironically, his review devastated the propaganda of Burnshaw's own volume of poems, *The Iron Land*. At decade's end, surveying Stevens' achievement, Matthiessen again had occasion to praise the sophistication with which Stevens expressed "his deepening preoccupation with the problems of social order," his "many sided awareness of disruption and breakdown" (*Harvard Advocate*, Dec., 1940).

On the whole, however, Stevens' poetry in the thirties suffered unfavorable comparison to *Harmonium*. Dr. Williams bemoaned Stevens' movement toward a poetry of ideas, and blamed it on the pentameter line. Williams approved "The Man with the Blue Guitar" because its swift moving tetrameters came close to his idea of "a meter discovering itself in language" as opposed to the turgid "five beats" that make the modern poet "think he wants to think." The object of Williams' scorn was "Owl's Clover," the poem which caused Stevens no end of concern because of its defensive tone and its bow to affairs of the moment. It was a very personal bow, however, and if its subject was, as one critic said, "the decline of the west," the decline had everything to do with the failures of poetry, the disintegration of the modern imagination, and the general rout of the self. The mutations of Stevens' style called attention to his changing subject matter, revealing a latent tendency toward the oracular and philosophical that was not obvious in *Harmonium*. But when Yvor Winters came in 1943 to assess Stevens' decadence, it had become clearer that this laureate of imagination had been concerning himself not so much with the crisis of the social order as with what Winters called the fortuitous "severance between the rational understanding and the poetic imagination" (*The Anatomy of Nonsense* [Norfolk, Conn., 1943]).

Stevens said of "Owl's Clover" that his purpose was "to isolate poetry," by way of maintaining it as a human activity in the face of systems which denied the human and coerced poetry into ideology. In *Harmonium*, style alone had sufficed to define the self and authenticate the reality of poetry; in times of social distress, this style was almost self-mocking, when it did not give way altogether to a defensive rhetoric. Still, critics no longer refer to this phase as an interlude of social conscience, but tend rather to accept Roy Harvey Pearce's view that "Stevens, meaning not to forego but to subsume politics, the socio-economic, even the ordinary run of experience, in the end intended no less than to show how man, by the exercise of his strictly human imagination, could resolve the proximate into the ultimate" (*The Continuity of American Poetry*). Few critics today agree with O'Connor that "Owl's Clover" is Stevens' "finest long poem and undoubtedly one of the best long poems in English published during the first half of the twentieth century" (*The Shaping Spirit*). O'Connor's view of Stevens' "Politics of Order" has a strangely misplaced emphasis on the doctrinaire argument for a future state, albeit poetic, ruled by imagination. For O'Connor neither distinguishes adequately the relation of this poem to its period, nor its difference from subsequent poems it makes way for. Both Louis Martz (*Yale Review*, June, 1958) and Samuel French Morse (*Origin V*, Spring, 1952) have been clearer about this, the former pointing out Stevens' movement from a momentary confrontation of the mid-thirties turmoil in *Ideas of Order* toward some mystique of an enduring, "semi-Jungian" self in the "subman" of "Owl's Clover" and beyond to a new poetry of the idea of man, in "Blue Guitar," which apotheosizes the self as sole creator and center of poetry and hence life. To state it thus is to blur Martz's fine distinctions and careful readings, but it does emphasize his discovery of the continuity within Stevens' poetry during this period, and the way in which the interlude becomes integral to the greater canon.

This phase of Stevens, then, repays critical attention, not only for what it forecasts of his subsequent development but as a chapter in the historical struggle of poetry and poetics to survive as a humanity. Whatever there is of a broadening social awareness, we now see that Stevens' subject was poetry, and by extension the destiny of man's conative will to maintain his selfhood, to define the authority of his own fictions as against the abstract promises of ideology and the dying forms of religion. The poems seen in this light are what Stevens later called acts of the mind seeking "what will suffice," with the emphasis on "act" as a process of steadily defining the amplitude of the self living in the face of collective anonymity (see my essay in *NEQ*, Sept., 1961). In that respect, Stevens' flirtation with the "subman" in "Owl's Clover" is at once a revealing and dubious rationale for the imagination, in contrast to any ideology, as the unique power binding together and defining man: "Night and the imagination being one," "Owl's Clover" concludes, thus emphasizing the poet's need to separate his unique self from political or religious definitions of man, and to plunge back into the self (a collective subconscious), there to rediscover the ground of his humanity, the universal imagination. That universal imagination, he suggests, explains man's need of social and religious forms, and subsumes the individual imaginations that create these forms.

This impetuous need to establish a universal imagination to oppose universal (collective) ideologies explains, I think, the ponderous tone of "Owl's Clover." That Stevens was alert to this rhetoric, enough so as to reject the poem, helps one to understand what he discovered in the process of writing "Blue Guitar," in which turning more directly to the "act" of poetry and away from argument, he articulates the conjunctioning between the self and the conditions within which it must create. The recent increase of critical attention to "Blue Guitar" would seem to indicate its centrality not only to Stevens' movement toward the late phase, but to the formulation of his aesthetic law that poetry and life are one.[8] It is, I would suggest, one of the great political poems of its age—political in the sense that it begins at the foundation of politics, the adjustment of the individual to the conditions which surround him and threaten his selfhood.

4

Though his poetry of the thirties impressed but few, Stevens by 1940 had a considerable reputation, primarily among fellow poets and fledgling "new" critics. The *Harvard Advocate* in a Special

[8] "Blue Guitar," at the same time one of Stevens' most praised and most blamed poems, has had only a modest amount of attention in essays and books, though certain poems of the sequence have been repeatedly isolated and discussed as basic to Stevens' whole work: particularly the one beginning "Poetry is the subject of the poem," and the one concluding "Poetry/ . . . must take the place / Of empty heaven and its hymns." But this one poem, like no others of Stevens', has been the subject of two doctoral dissertations: one a linguistic study by Mac Sawyer Hammond (Harvard, 1962) and the other a study of semantics and poetry, by John Logan (Texas, 1962). One of the few lengthy treatments of it in essay is Merle E. Brown's (*American Literature*, May, 1962), which unfortunately fails to take account of Stevens' own extensive commentary on the poem in *Mattino Domenicale ed Altre Poesie,* trans. Renato Poggioli (Torino, 1954).

Number (Dec., 1940) paid homage to an old alumnus who at sixty-one had proved himself; it was impossible to realize then that Stevens was only, so to speak, in mid-career. About this time Hi Simons published the first of his series of distinguished essays intended as a future book on Stevens. But two other essays of the period—by Horace Gregory and Yvor Winters—more clearly underscore Stevens' "vicissitudes of reputation." [9] Gregory's "An Examination of Stevens in Time of War " (*Accent*, Autumn, 1942) summarizes the critical disaffection that greeted *Parts of a World*, measuring Stevens' recent work unfavorably against the earlier. Later, in the Gregory-Zaturenska *History of American Poetry*,

[9] Perhaps one should add a third, Julian Symons' in *Life and Letters Today* (Sept., 1940). Symons' essay is important for two negative reasons. Presuming to "introduce" a neglected writer to a British audience, it set some kind of record for condescension. And it established a tone of disparagement that characterized most English criticism of Stevens up to Kermode. Symons' was an old and fulsome song: "An unfriendly criticism of Stevens would conclude that he has not much to say, but an unusual felicity in saying it." Symons, however, can be even more unfriendly, speaking as he does from his dogmatic position developed in *Twentieth Century Verse* that the poet must become a legislator of values for his society. Thus, he beards Stevens' "fribble of taste," his lack of an "objective view of life." British criticism after Symons seldom failed to point up this deficiency of "life." G. S. Fraser is most notable: Stevens lacks "human grasp," "human contact"; he has made, alas, the "matter of mind" a substitute for the "matter of life" (*Vision and Rhetoric* [New York, 1960]). Even A. Alvarez's complimentary essay in *Stewards of Excellence* (New York, 1958), which takes Stevens as a "Platonic Poet," concludes with reservations that his poetry is always departing life for "a voyage into abstraction." Anthony Hartley's recent essay (*Twentieth Century*, June, 1960) has great respect for Stevens, but the same reservations about his solipsism. Kermode has long since dismissed this problem by indicating just where Stevens stands in the Romantic tradition, though it is a tradition Kermode finds to be moving toward sterility (*Romantic Image*). And Geoffrey Moore's contribution to *The Great Experiment in American Literature* (New York, 1961) does much to reject Fraser's attitude, at the same time making an effort to see Stevens as a central figure in an American tradition of poetry.

My nomination for the greatest English animadversion of them all is Fraser's condescending jab at Stevens' mindlessness in a review of *Opus Posthumous*. It is entitled "Mind All Alone " (*New Statesman*, London, Jan. 9, 1960), and it quotes extensively from an essay included in *Opus Posthumous*, " On Poetic Truth," as a grand example of Stevens', and in general the American poets', intellectual silliness. The essay, so much the worse for Fraser, is not Stevens' at all. Stevens culled it, mainly the topic sentences, from an essay of the same title by an English academician, H. D. Lewis, used it liberally in an essay on Marianne Moore, citing Lewis, and left the compilation in longhand among his posthumous papers. Morse, who could not have known it was not Stevens', published it in the posthumous collection (see J. N. Riddel, in *Modern Language Notes*, Feb., 1961). The British view of Stevens as aesthete has flared up again in the columns of the *Times Literary Supplement* of Aug. 20, 1964, in which was reviewed the Ashley Brown and Robert S. Haller collection of essays, *The Achievement of Wallace Stevens*. The controversy continued subsequently in the letters to the editor column of late September numbers.

1900-1940, Stevens' contribution was defined almost exclusively in terms of *Harmonium*. He was the "Whistler of American Poetry," a lightweight American post-Symbolist, which to Gregory, of course, was praise.

If anything, the reception of Stevens' poetry in the forties was even colder than in the previous ten years. First *Parts of a World*, then "Notes," then "Esthétique du Mal," then *Transport to Summer*, recorded Stevens' evolution toward a discursive, meditative, even dialectical verse, which took poetry as its own best subject. *Parts of a World* impressed almost no one. Blackmur, discovering "Notes," detected a philosophical toughness and cogency (*Partisan Review*, May-June, 1943), as if to refute Gregory's earlier charge that "Mr. Stevens is one of those who were kept in mind when poets were excluded from the ideal republic." But with some little disagreement, the greater number of reviewers seemed in sympathy with Peter Viereck who, setting *Transport* beside the reissued *Harmonium*, could only say of the former, "an invidious comparison insists on being made" (*Kenyon Review*, Winter, 1948). Stevens' fellow poets especially were at a loss to explain the decline of *brio*. But Yvor Winters had already brought the severest indictment against Stevens, explaining not only the causes of loss but the moral degeneration it implied. As Frank Kermode has put it, "Just as you need to have an answer for Dr. Johnson if you are to admire *Lycidas*, so you need to deal with Winters if you claim that Stevens wrote even better verse after 'Sunday Morning'" (*Wallace Stevens*).

The history of Winters' regard for Stevens is fascinating. Having barely entered his majority, Winters was already sure enough of his judgment to call Stevens the greatest practicing American poet (*Poetry*, Feb., 1922). His consistent praise of "Sunday Morning" as the apogee of our modern poetry is well known, and, in fact, is the key to his later disaffection with Stevens. Stevens' malady, as Winters anatomized it over the years, was his "cultivation of the emotions as an end in itself." As early as *Primitivism and Decadence* (New York, 1937), Winters associated Stevens with the moral evasions of romantic irony, that "opposition and cancellation" of two moods which denies the poem resolution and confuses both mind and emotions. The symptoms of this illness were disintegration of style into verbosity, self-parody, and fragile elegance. There was too much of this "affectation" in *Harmoni-*

um, though in poems like "Sunday Morning" and "Le Monocle de Mon Oncle," which either avoid irony or transcend it, "he is probably the greatest poet of his generation." Louis Martz has said of Winters that he "made a brilliant diagnosis of the malady; but he underestimated the patient's will to live." And it is true that Winters had some powerful evidence of Stevens' wrestling with self-doubt, and protecting himself with an irony that dissipates or confuses the emotion of the subject. This very problem lies at the heart of so much critical disagreement about "The Comedian as the Letter C," in which jubilee and self-mockery sport freely together. There is in the poem that sense of a farewell to poetry noted by Winters, who concluded that Stevens did not have the courage of his convictions. And it is true that the poem, in hedging its attitude toward the Romantic will, does occasionally blur the focus of its irony. Yet, as more than one critic has recently shown, comedy may cut several ways at once without losing its ironic clarity, and Romantic irony is not necessarily self-pitying. It is this vitality, rather than exhaustion, that makes the poem fascinating as a spiritual autobiography not of Stevens alone but of the modern poetic self.[10]

More questionable is Winters' Procrustean bed of rational paraphrase. His interpretation of "Anecdote of the Jar" is a case in point, in which the jar, forcibly equated with intellect, is made to appear in the role of nature's corrupter. One has only to set this over against Kermode's reading in *Romantic Image,* or any of several essays which find this a central poem for early Stevens, to understand the ruthless instrument Winters' paraphrase can be.[11] Similarly, his dismissal of Romantic irony tempts him to

---

[10] Of all Stevens' poems, "The Comedian as the Letter C" has proved most perplexing, largely because of its association with the author's poetic, if not autobiographical, image of himself and his age. It has, on the whole, satisfied very few critics, but it has seldom failed to attract comment. Besides Professor Morse's new interpretation, published in this collection, the following will offer any interested reader a bewildering diversity of opinions: Blackmur (*Hound & Horn,* Jan.-Mar., 1932); Guy Davenport (*Perspective,* Autumn, 1954); J. V. Cunningham (*Tradition and Poetic Structure,* 1960); John J. Enck (*Texas Studies in Literature and Language,* Autumn, 1961); Daniel Fuchs (*The Comic Spirit of Wallace Stevens* [Durham, N. C., 1963]); and Francis Murphy (*Wisconsin Studies in Contemporary Literature,* Spring-Summer, 1962). Pearce's *The Continuity of American Poetry* offers some interesting observations on the possible connections between "Comedian" and Eliot's *The Waste Land.*

[11] Daniel Fuchs deserves quoting on this aspect of Winters' humanism: "Winters should lament, not the self-destructive quality of this irony, but its effectiveness in destroying the values which he does not like to see disturbed. In reality, it is not

slight those occasions when the poet's voice speaks through the irony and resolves it: Winters' grudging admiration of "Le Monocle" seems to grasp this voice, just as it misses the humanistic tension of "Anecdote of the Jar." The unfortunate thing about Winters' criticism, however, is that his intransigence—a man of "one idea / In a world of ideas," Stevens might have said—has estranged critics who could have benefited from such things as his acute sense of style.[12] But having buried Stevens, Winters would not stop to praise, finding nothing but an occasional gem among the "detritus of doctrine" in late Stevens (see the "Postscript" to "The Hedonist's Progress," *On Modern Poets* [New York, 1959]). Stevens' nominalist theory of imagination, says Winters, is simply another form of hedonism, living off the fat of one's own abstractions. What disturbs Winters is not that Stevens seems to have become a poet of ideas, but that his ideas violate Winters' severe decorum of mind.

Despite Winters, or perhaps because of him, Stevens' poetry of the forties, for all its difficulty, began to earn him regard in academe. It was another triumph of the "new criticism." There is in this criticism a number of historically discernible patterns: among them the fact that as fellow poets grew disenchanted with Stevens' abstractness, critic-scholars were attracted to his brilliant marriage of structures and textures. Hi Simons' series of essays provided a number of intelligent points of departure, most notably giving substance to his alleged *Symboliste* roots and affirming in opposition to Winters a vital humanism: "a humanism with an aesthetic instead of a moralistic bias, more yea-saying and better humored than the humanism of Babbitt and More that went flat" (*Sewanee Review*, Autumn, 1945). What, one asks, could have been more upsetting to the older humanists than to find their -*ism* married with that of a Symbolistic, subjective poet? Louis Martz, reviewing *Transport* (*Yale Review*, Dec.,

'careless feeling,' much less 'careless writing,' which irritates Winters, but the jarring moral and aesthetic dissonance created by bold and original minds who dare disturb the universe. For the universe has disturbed them" (*The Comic Spirit of Wallace Stevens*). "Anecdote of the Jar" is a favorite target of humanists (see Stanley P. Chase's "Dionysus in Dismay," in Norman Foerster (ed.), *Humanism and America* [New York, 1930]).

[12] J. V. Cunningham, one of Winters' protégés, has proved the value of Winters' observation that in much of *Harmonium* there is "traditional seriousness and a traditional rhetoric cognate with that attitude," in his essay frst published in *Poetry* (Dec., 1949), then revised for his *Tradition and Poetic Structure* (Denver, 1960).

1947), offered his first tentative observations on Stevens' development of a meditative mode. *Transport* was even reviewed (favor-
ably) in the *Journal of Philosophy* (Feb. 26, 1948), which affords
an interesting footnote to Oscar Cargill's version of Stevens' anti-
intellectualism in *Intellectual America* (New York, 1941). With the
publication of *The Auroras of Autumn* (1950) it was evident that
Stevens had not only survived hedonism, but that his early mode
must now be reassessed from later perspectives. There was by no
means unanimous agreement about this survival: attitudes ranged
from Randall Jarrell's eloquent dispatch of *Auroras* (*Partisan
Review*, May-June, 1951) to Marius Bewley's finely-toned judgment of Stevens' development toward *Transport to Summer*, " undoubtedly his best volume " (*Partisan Review*, Sept., 1949).

Jarrell and Bewley appropriately typify the divided attitudes
toward Stevens in the forties; moreover, they anticipate the directions of subsequent criticism. It is unfair to Jarrell to identify
him with those who cannot abide the later Stevens, if only because
four years after his first essay, he returned to Stevens' last poems
contrite and admiring (*Yale Review*, March, 1955). Nevertheless,
Jarrell's vendetta against the poetry of abstraction, and especially
Stevens' " generalizations of an unprecedentedly low order," is
representative, establishing as it does an image of this poetry as a
series of half-articulated statements about poetry and half-formu-
lated ideas about the relevance of poetry to life. What Jarrell
denied Stevens was the poet's earlier trust in the primacy of the
concrete. It is instructive to place Jarrell's second essay beside
the first, not to vindicate the critic but to discover just how much
concentration the last poems demand. In retrospect, Jarrell still
senses a cold monotony in *Auroras*, but he has discovered magic
in *The Rock*: " As we read the poems we are so continually
aware of Stevens observing, meditating, creating, that we feel like
saying that the process of creating the poem is the poem." Something like this lies in Bewley's discovery of the evolution of
Stevens' style, its " deeper explorations and wider applications."
Neither Bewley nor Jarrell, however, was in a position to do more
than tentatively assert the late greatness. But never again could
a balanced assessment of Stevens be made without attention to his
development, without seeing the early in the light of the later.
Moreover, Stevens' flourish of prose essays had brought full attention to his " theory of poetry " and its apotheosis of the single,

separate creative self. It was in this atmosphere that Roy Harvey Pearce's longish essay in *PMLA* (Sept., 1951) appeared, with the first attempt to formulate the significance of Stevens' development. What had occurred, we can now see, is that Stevens and poetry had weathered three decades of Eliot's broadsides against romanticism, and had gone about its business creating a new secular (and humanistic) poetry out of the vestiges of a routed Romantic style.

5

The only uniform agreement among his recent critics is that Stevens is a considerable poet. Beyond that, a great many fits and starts toward "preliminary exegesis" and several tentative and contradictory theories about the import of the canon.[13] There have been a number of attempts to preserve the image of his purism, to deny his "thought" by way of saving him for poetry. Increased attention has turned likewise to the implications of his comic-ironic manner, now seen to be less an escape than a genuine poetic strategy for carrying out his engagement with reality. The intensest energy, however, has been directed at reviewing the complete consort, which once seemed to stand on its individual parts and now appears to be more substantially whole and historically central than was thought a decade ago. Furthermore, the emphasis on his development has helped to accentuate his intrinsic Americanness and to redress the image of his isolation from modern reality. But a great deal of criticism appears settled upon old assumptions. Of the four other books now in print on Stevens (at this writing), only Kermode's has found it advantageous to approach the poetry chronologically. The most recent, Daniel Fuchs's *The Comic Spirit of Wallace Stevens*, even contends that "the problems in Stevens criticism now are . . . likely

[13] It is impossible in an essay of this kind to include studies of individual poems, unless these poems and these studies are used to throw light on the whole of Stevens, or unless the essays offer in their commentary a radical departure in Stevens criticism. I have not, for instance, been able to fit Sister Mary Bernetta Quinn's most deserving essay (*The Metamorphic Tradition in Modern Poetry* [New Brunswick, N. J., 1955]) into my developing argument, though it is surely one of the most helpful studies of Stevens. The reader is referred to the bibliography listed in footnote one for essays on individual poems. Stevens has been and remains a favorite subject for exegetes; for example, there have been to this date at least twenty-six pieces on his poetry in *Explicator*.

to concern what he is saying rather than how he has developed or changed," assuming that Stevens *says* the same thing in the later poetry as in the early. O'Connor's study, the first (1950), and Robert Pack's (1957) approach Stevens in terms of various but interrelated themes, implying a similar consistency of thought from first to last. William York Tindall's little essay in the Minnesota Pamphlet series creates a universe of its own.

This point about approach is hardly moot, for the established view of Stevens as hedonist does not admit of a significant development, just changes in the texture of one long argument. Richard Eberhart, reviewing *Transport to Summer* (*Accent*, Summer, 1947), claimed that Stevens "has shown no major change in growth, so that his late poems partake of the same type of sensibility as his earlier ones."[14] What Eberhart meant, it would appear, is that seen from a remove the same general situation, and the poetic resolution of it, characterizes the poetry from first to last. But this, first Bewley, then Pearce, then Jarrell, then Martz, then many others were to point out, is expressed as the experience of a changing sensibility, a growing self. Both reality and imagination change in degree, and even kind, though their conjunctioning may remain as a general formula. But the great change is a change in growth of the self, indicative of a self-perpetuating imagination.

The misologists, to the contrary, see everything through the prism of *Harmonium*. There are still a few echoes of Powys' view of Stevens, and Harriet Monroe's, now less subjective but no less intent on saving poetry from intellect, or on identifying it with

[14] This point of whether Stevens matured is largely, it seems, a point of what is emphasized. Like Eberhart, A. Alvarez says that "though Stevens' poetry changed a little, it hardly matured" (*Stewards of Excellence*). Marianne Moore once noted the remarkable organic consistency of Stevens' development (*Kenyon Review*, Winter, 1943), emphasizing not so much his repetitions as the way one phase of his poetry grew out of the previous. The significance of Stevens' development has been stressed in two different ways: by William Van O'Connor as "a turning from subjects for poetry to a consideration of poetry itself as it relates to the role of imagination in a world of shifting values" (*The Shaping Spirit*); and by Roy Harvey Pearce: "Stevens began by looking directly at our experience of the reality in which we are bound, and has most recently been exploring the general implications of the predicament. . . . He began by looking directly at the world which limits belief, continued by examining the possibilities of belief and commitment in the face of that possibility, and has most recently been exploring the nature of possible belief" (*PMLA*, Sept., 1951). Seen thus, Stevens' organic changes are not simply variations on a theme, but a "major change in growth."

spontaneity and joy. For Dr. Williams, for instance, Stevens' drift into abstraction had resulted in a forfeiture of vitality—and vitality was the soul of poetry (*Poetry*, Jan., 1956). Lionel Abel's "In the Sacred Park" (*Partisan Review*, Winter, 1958) performed the neat and unique trick of reclaiming Stevens as the last great aesthete. It is difficult to conceive of an essay in the past decade calling Stevens an "amateur poet" "whose spiritual problem is to choose between alternatives of sensuous enjoyment," an essay which snipes at Blackmur for talking of Stevens' precise meanings while insisting on his "taste for preciosity" first and last. This is, of course, extreme, but it reflects the attitude of many who would save Stevens from his "ideas."

In this regard Tindall's essay has its Pyrrhic triumph. Urbane and stylishly clever, Tindall sets out to correct those who take Stevens' thought seriously. But Tindall wants the best of two worlds: Stevens as *élégant*, Stevens as burgher; French stylist, American bourgeois. Denying any consistency (or what is worse, any meaning) to Stevens' "thought," asserting that one can make anything one wishes from his essays, Tindall surely proves this to be possible with the poetry. His method suggests that the ablest introduction to Stevens is a prose that emulates the poem's coruscations. This is a severe indictment of an essay which has been praised for its witty *aperçus*. But it is an essay, for all its worth, which egregiously distorts the significance of Stevens' fun, and very often the poems: it violates contexts, confuses continuity, and runs amuck with puns at the expense of Stevens' more relevant ambiguities. Compared with Kermode's, Tindall's remarks on Stevens' intellectual and literary sources are inconsistent if not careless; especially so are his many attributed parallels between Stevens and the French Symbolists. Tindall's real thesis, however, is that Stevens in his late poetry did not write philosophy: "Nothing here approaches systematic thought. Rather, it is a meditation and a drama of thought in progress with all its hesitations, failures, and triumphs." Few critics have said otherwise; Northrop Frye, in fact, had argued that Stevens was a philosophical poet on these very grounds, that a poem is a "secondary imitation of thought," that it is concerned "with forms of thought rather than specific proposition" (*Hudson Review*, Autumn, 1957). But Stevens, says Tindall, is true to "himself alone and to pure form." Tindall's pamphlet, in brief, would not be a significant piece of criticism did it not reassert in public the image of an euphoric dabbler in precious objects and fine feelings.

There is really only a point of emphasis (major, however) separating Tindall from critics of the intellectual persuasion. What Tindall denies to Stevens' long poems is their "philosophical" substance. ("Not his statements but their composite shape is the point of this poem," he says of "An Ordinary Evening in New Haven." The evocative word "shape" is Tindall's favorite for a poem which does not *mean* or *plea*.) In this sense Tindall is on the side of the Muses. But he errs in thinking that critics who would relate Stevens' "thought" to modern philosophical currents find only formula in the poems, though he does isolate one of the major problems in judging late Stevens. A poem which *is,* as Tindall says, the *process* or *act* of mind necessarily contains the *matter* of mind we call thought, even as it may mock the limitations of its matter. Putting his emphasis on Stevens' comic-ironic persona, however, Tindall ends with a gross distortion of the canon. He concludes his deceptively proleptic essay by finding Stevens an uninhibitedly joyous, "persona of summer," looking past the poems of "autumn" and the "rock" to offer us a poet whose composure is less sublime than conspicuous.

The persistence of the hedonist view has done much, however, to emphasize the essential seriousness of Stevens' gaiety. Fuchs's study, which suggests Tindall's influence in its focus on the comic-ironic masks, indicates how closely Stevens' irony was to the temper of the twenties, and discusses the translation of dandyism into an American and a post-war context. Claiming as he does that what Stevens says is more important than how he developed, Fuchs shows nonetheless that the "comic spirit" is a method and a style, which in Stevens was capable of extraordinary variety. There is some question, to my mind, about the depth of Fuchs's sketch of this phase of our cultural history, but it provides him with a framework by which to define Stevens' early exuberance and even diffidence. But the "comic spirit," though given to profundity as Fuchs proves, does not serve so well as a focus on the later poems, which must come to terms with an "esthétique du mal." Fuchs is hampered too by a rather thin argument for the French (especially Baudelaire and Laforgue) influence, and what it meant to the revival of poetry in this century. The degree of Stevens' Symbolistic debts has been, in fact, a troublesome one for critics. It was from the beginning so common-place to associate

Stevens with Laforgue, Baudelaire, Mallarmé, and Verlaine—as previously indicated—that the burden of recent criticism has been to dissociate him from them. Hi Simons' study of "Wallace Stevens and Mallarmé" (*Modern Philology*, May, 1946) synthesized the prevailing opinion that Stevens was a Frenchman *manqué* by pointing convincingly to numerous parallels between the two. It was several years before critics began to put Simons' analogies back into their respective contexts where they proved to be anything but parallel. Many subsequent essays—ignoring Blackmur's caution that "he is not a symbolist . . . : the iconography of his mind was immediate and self-explanatory *within* his vocabulary" (*Kenyon Review*, Winter, 1955) —accepted the Symbolist identification without much investigation, remaining satisfied with obvious similarities of symbols, metaphors, techniques. But closer examination invariably shows, as Michel Benamou has proved, that in nearly every way but a mutual recourse to art for order and self-identity Stevens stands opposed to the Symbolists' and post-Symbolists' poetics, even as he has absorbed much of value from their techniques, and even though some of his poems in the 1940's, especially "The Pure Good of Theory," come very close to echoing Valéry and his predecessors.[15]

In the first of three penetrating essays, Benamou re-examined the apparent Laforguean parallels, finding that Stevens' irony was the very antithesis of Laforgue's and that Stevens' clownish mask could only be related superficially to the Pierrot (*Romanic Review*, April, 1959). Stevens' irony, while preserving him from the world's chaos, moves toward an appointment with reality

[15] Tindall says, for instance, that although Stevens was in the French tradition he was not in the Symbolist tradition. Most critics can no longer square Stevens' devotion to the physical world with the Symbolist's transcendental longing. Thus Pearce on *Harmonium*: "These are not 'symbolist' poems—since the data which compose the experiences of their protagonists 'correspond' to nothing outside the closed systems of meaning which are the poems" (*The Continuity of American Poetry*). But, one should add, though Stevens is not technically a Symbolist, he does reflect many of the Symbolistic mannerisms, as described by Kermode in *Romantic Image*, or even by Charles Feidelson in his *Symbolism and American Literature* (Chicago, 1953): particularly, as both Feidelson and Kermode note, the tendency to make poetry its own best subject, the one reality in an imagined world. Pearce argues in his book, though, that Stevens in the end was not wholly satisfied with poetry, and in several ways looked beyond it to some "ultimate poem." This in itself has some of the symptoms of Symbolistic vision. The problem remains one of definition, for modern poetics, including Stevens', have amalgamated the Romantic and Symbolist traditions in so many different ways that it is often easy to note in poets like Stevens Symbolistic qualities which lead to anti-Symbolistic conclusions.

rather than a withdrawal into the melancholic self. In subsequent essays Benamou has been at pains to differentiate between Stevens and the purer Symbolists on specific points of their poetics and styles. His "Sur le Pretendu 'Symbolisme' de Wallace Stevens" (*Critique* [Paris, Dec., 1961]), which he translated and revised for this collection, submits detailed evidence of Stevens' anti-symbolism: for example, his humanist embrace of the world's body in the form of the "Fat girl" as opposed to the bodiless (ideal) veiled ladies of Symbolist worship. Benamou's essays not only bring into question the basic assumptions about Stevens' Symbolist heritage, but point toward further investigations of just what Stevens found of value in French poets of the last century, and French poetics of this one. In the interim between *Symbolisme* and Stevens, as between Whitman and Stevens, a great many transcendental faiths had been disposed of, leaving forms without substance and man alone at the center of his own reality in an all-too-physical world.

Much of the tentativeness in recent Stevens criticism results from incomplete knowledge of the man himself. Until Morse's biography is published, and until there is an ample edition of letters, Stevens' intellectual sources and sympathies will, with certain exceptions, remain foggy. The paucity of this information has, so far, tempted critics to impute to Stevens an intellectual tradition of sorts, and has motivated several essays which, confining him to one set of ideas or another, restrict the import of his poetics. The earliest studies of his poetics stressed the obvious connection of his imagination with Coleridge's, and by association with German idealism. Such parallels, however, besides pointing to the continuity from the English to the French to the modern Romantic tradition, have never really clarified Stevens' theory of imagination, much less defined it in terms applicable to a thoroughly secular, humanistic poetics. One exception is Newton P. Stallknecht's "Absence in Reality: A Study in the Epistemology of the Blue Guitar," (*Kenyon Review*, Autumn, 1959), which even as it argues too intently for Stevens' traditional romanticism, is cautious about what occurs when the imagination takes on modern dress and loses much of its transcendental origins. O'Connor's book said something about this but did not pursue the philosophical grounds; so has J. V. Cunningham (see note 12), and James Benziger in his *Images of Eternity* (Carbondale, Ill., 1962), stressing Stevens' relation to traditional Romantic forms of thought. But what has been lacking is a route from Coleridge to the modern imagination. It is the post-Romantic Stevens with his radical modernism, it seems, which has recommended him to recent students of the Romantic tradition, and has, moreover, created the enthusiasm for the historical "role" of his poetry.[16]

There is reluctance, however, even among Stevens' more perceptive critics to attribute to him intellectual sophistication. Morse himself has cast some doubt about how thoroughly his biography will examine Stevens' learning, or even his "ideas": "As for his 'ideas' they had their source much less often in the work of Plato or Henri Focillon or Santayana than in his own experience and imagination. In this respect he was a provincial, not a cosmopolitan. . . . In this respect, too, he was not an intellectual poet or a symbolist poet, although he was a man of intellectual principle and much given to speculative thought about the sound and color of life" ("Introduction," *Poems by Wallace Stevens*). Evidence proves the contrary, if only in the case of Santayana, whose influence on Stevens' thought has motivated at least two doctoral dissertations and numerous shorter commentaries in essays and book.[17] Morse's remarks, however, deny only that Stevens, in contrast say to Eliot, approached his learning systematically and used it with intellectual scrupulosity. With this no

[16] Hi Simons once suggested, too, parallels between Stevens and the English Metaphysical poets (*Sewanee Review*, Autumn, 1945), as did O'Connor in *The Shaping Spirit*, the latter concluding that Stevens like other moderns had deftly assimilated the Symbolist and Metaphysical modes. Neither of these points has been pursued very far in more recent essays, an indication that Stevens was not so intensely absorbed by Metaphysical poetry as were many of his contemporaries. Perhaps the best connection between Stevens and seventeenth-century poetry is made by Louis Martz in his *The Poetry of Meditation* (New Haven, Conn., 1954), and in his excellent essay on Stevens, in which he makes valuable distinctions between the secular and religious modes of meditative poetry.

[17] C. Roland Wagner's "The Savage Transparence," a Ph. D. dissertation in philosophy at Yale (1952), gave individual chapters to Stevens and to Santayana. The Stevens chapter culminated the essay, Stevens providing the example of the move from an aesthetic philosophy to a philosophical aesthetic and poetry. More recently, William Burney's dissertation at Iowa (1962), entitled "Wallace Stevens and George Santayana," has treated the subject more from Stevens' point of view, though Burney is often unaware of previous criticism. The dissertations of Daniel John Schneider (Northwestern, 1957), and Joseph N. Riddel (Wisconsin, 1960), add extensive commentary, as does Kermode's book, and most notably, essays by Guy Davenport (*Perspective*, Autumn, 1954), and Stallknecht (*Kenyon Review*, Autumn, 1959). See also Norman Holmes Pearson on "Wallace Stevens and 'Old Higgs'" (*Trinity Review*, May, 1954); Riddel (*PMLA*, Sept., 1962), and Frank Doggett (*Criticism*, Winter, 1960; *Chicago Review*, Summer-Autumn, 1962). This by no means exhausts the essays which mention Stevens-Santayana parallels.

critic disagrees, though to accuse Stevens of provincialism is at best questionable. Parochial, maybe—in that he reduced ideas into aesthetics—but only by way of affirming the larger humanity of art. Morse's position shows that the great schism among Stevens critics is more a matter of definition than anything else. Kermode, for instance, indicates the fruitfulness of examining Stevens' philosophical heritage, if one keeps in mind that a poet's "philosophy" is not a fabric of categorical ideas. Stevens himself laid stress upon the idea of the poem which in turn is clothed with the "poetry of the idea." Better to say, then, that those who concentrate on Stevens' "thought," or aesthetic, are looking for his place in the context of modern literature, looking that is for his modes of thought, not for his *Biographia Literaria*.

Kermode's claims for the explicit parallels between Santayana's aesthetic and Stevens', and his comments on Bergson's theory of flux and the falsification of abstraction as they are absorbed into the oppositions of Stevens' poetics, prove less that Stevens was a conscientious student of Romantic and post-Romantic philosophy than that he in a way similar to Wordsworth absorbed the currents of modern thought, synthesized them experientially, and projected them into expressions uniquely relevant to modern man's conception of himself. Kermode, along with Frank Doggett and others,[18] have through studies of the intellectual contexts and parallels of Stevens' poetics pointed up his essential modernism, while in no way confusing him with Santayana or Bergson or Whitehead. They account for his current popularity, then, as spokesman for the era of man, the minimal god in an otherwise godless world. One of the unhappy consequences of O'Connor's book is that it describes Stevens' thought as a frail imitation of the flimsiest romanticisms, stressing as it does Stevens' exploitation of the irrational to the point of confirming Winters' worst fears. Robert Pack's study, on the other hand, has failed to be influ-

[18] Among Doggett's several essays on Stevens are three which go at length into the intellectual and philosophical analogies in Stevens' poetry and theory: see *Criticism* (Winter, 1960); *New England Quarterly* (Sept., 1958); and *Chicago Review* (Summer-Autumn, 1962). There are mentions also in his essays on "Notes toward a Supreme Fiction" and on the late poems: in *ELH* (Sept., 1961; reprinted in this book) and *ELH* (June, 1958), respectively. The problem with Doggett's essays is that they provide analogies without too much concern for proven sources so that in many cases the accumulation of parallels blurs Stevens' own use of the ideas, or gratuitously adds dimensions to his thought that are at best questionable. Nevertheless, Doggett, even without specific evidence of Stevens' education, indicates how fully Stevens sits in the currents of modern thought, rather than in the backwash of aestheticism.

ential just to the degree that it systematized Stevens' themes, turning the poems as it were into footnotes to certain categories of thought. Pack, taking Stevens' essays at face value, reads the canon in terms of his abstract poetics. O'Connor skims the intellectual surface, and leaves the image of Stevens as a dabbler in outmoded forms of subjectivism. Perhaps the point should be made again that what the most illuminating studies have assumed is that the poems are processes, acts of the mind caught, as Randall Jarrell said, in the act of *being*. This at least is what James Baird implied when he associated Stevens' theory of imagination with the existential phenomenology of mind (*Studies in Honor of John C. Hodges and Alwin Thaler*, Tennessee Studies in English, 1961). And in another sense, it is what Northrop Frye identified as the social activity of Stevens' imagination engaged in the unending war of experience: "arresting the flow of perceptions without and of impressions within" (*Hudson Review*, Autumn, 1957).

Baird, it seems to me, is nearer to Stevens' theory of imagination (with its emphasis on the incessant decreation and recreation of the mental act producing the phenomena of consciousness) than is Frye, who in making Stevens' imagination an extension of Coleridge's sees it in terms of his own theory of a universal human intelligence expressing itself through archetypes, or Aristotelian Forms. There remains, however, an important similarity in approach, each critic discovering in Stevens a uniquely modern mode of consciousness, Baird more so than Frye for whom all forms are traditional. The significant thing, however, is that these are essays which could not have been written without the perspectives of the later poetry. This is precisely the import of Louis Martz's "Wallace Stevens: The World as Meditation," which made the first sustained attempt to account for the deeper continuity in Stevens' development. Martz, though somewhat over-critical of the early hedonist, has provided the most cogent essay yet on the evolution of Stevens' style, and its significance not only for the poetry but the poet. His definition of the later poetry as secular meditations brilliantly reaffirms Stevens' own attitude toward poetry as an "act of the mind." Just why Martz agrees with Winters that the poetry of *Harmonium* was inherently self-destructive is not clear, unless one takes it in the un-Winters sense that Stevens, having discovered the diminished self that emerges from *Harmonium*, could never be satisfied with remaining detached and static in a world of change. Martz does not elaborate, but he implies this last when he discovers in the poetry of the thirties Stevens' anguished struggle to escape the anachronism that was Crispin, yet retain the "idea of man" as the only viable ideology. The remainder of Martz's essay is a formidably succinct account of Stevens' "rebuilding," and the way the secular (as opposed to religious) meditation expands consciousness, refines and regroups experience, and reorients the self to a physical world.

Martz's greatest contribution, then, is the frame of reference within which the later Stevens can be comprehended, not as a poet promulgating aesthetic doctrine but as one in the act of creating and sustaining himself through poetry. *Harmonium* in this light is a first act of self-definition, which, however momentarily adequate, had for the sake of poetry and the self to be outlived. The "philosophy" of Stevens becomes not a decadent aestheticism but a reaffirmation of mind (of consciousness, and thus man) which he passionately celebrated with the synthetic term of "imagination." Imagination implies a potential unity of self in time rather than a fragmentation. But this unity is achievable only with the greatest expenditure of imagination in its never-ending meditation of the real, of change and otherness and finally death. The movement, I might suggest, is upward from Emerson's "mean egotism" toward Thoreau's cabin on the frontiers of thought.

Critics who maintain that Stevens' stylistic changes are simply new jars for old moonshine sacrifice much of his substance in order to attain their own coherent view of the late poems. The expense of this has been exposed by Roy Harvey Pearce in *The Continuity of American Poetry*. If Pearce had done nothing else, his contribution to the theory of Stevens' development would be a critical landmark. As it is, he provides a rationale for Stevens' breakthrough to the poetics of the future. Drawing together his earlier *PMLA* essay and a subsequent examination of the later poems (*International Literary Annual, No. 2*, 1959), Pearce sets them down in the greater context of an American tradition. But he adds to his "historical" view of Stevens a striking thesis. Picking up Stevens' phrase, "modern reality is a reality of decreation," Pearce applies it to the later Stevens' "act of the mind," claiming that his search for an "ultimate poem" (or ultimate reality) constituted an act of imaginatively breaking down the commonsense structures of reality by way of possessing a reality within reality, a pure abstraction. This is a difficult idea to conceive. It does not, for instance, claim this ultimate reality to be a Lockean substance, nor God, nor an Emersonian supernature (oversoul). It is rather a transempirical and imaginatively conceivable truth, which man can desire and work toward possessing simply because he has the power of mind to conceive and " blood " abstractions. In other words, those late difficult poems of Stevens, as Pearce sees them, are processes of decreating the structure of things perceived, subjecting experience to a process of imaginative abstraction which pushes towards a grasp of the "thing itself," an ultimate reality. Stevens represents for Pearce the culmination of an American tradition of egocentric poetry whose great preoccupation has been to define man by the nature of his ability to create himself, and his world.[19]

Perhaps Pearce's theory is best summed up in the half-title of a dissertation by one of his students, Mrs. Georgianna Lord: " The Annihilation of Art," (Ohio State Univ., 1962). Surely there was this problem in late Stevens, this desire to get beyond the forms of art, or any mediate forms whatever, to a "pediment of appearance," to attain to the pure abstraction, or even become one with it. (One real flaw in Frye's essay is that he denies this in Stevens; his system forces the denial.) There was the desire, then, to get beyond *Harmonium*, and even to a truth beyond the truths of metaphor or poetry he had celebrated as the necessary fictions of life. But there was the equal compulsion, as Mrs. Lord's dissertation details it, to accept the earth and one's human place on it,

---

[19] The number of comments on Stevens' Americanness has increased extensively in recent years. Other than Pearce's, the most important is Samuel French Morse's " The Native Element " (*Kenyon Review*, Summer, 1958). Much of the earlier criticism, like that of Julian Symons for example, spoke of Stevens as trying to escape the confines of a crude bourgeois world by affecting continental airs, thus branding himself as the American artist encaged in the very weakness he would escape. Now we tend to see his poetry as a central expression of the modern (and American) artist, honestly confronting the diminished condition of the self and the diminished dignity of poetry. Blackmur and Simons had seen evidence of this in their consideration of " The Comedian as the Letter C." Bewley tried to make a case for Stevens' rising above his American provincialism on the wings of an international sophistication. And Geoffrey Moore has recently contributed the one firm English view of Stevens as in the American tradition (in *The Great Experiment in American Literature*). In my " Walt Whitman and Wallace Stevens: Functions of a 'Literatus'" (*South Atlantic Quarterly*, Autumn, 1962), I have offered some tentative comparisons and contrasts between two kinds of personalism in poetry.

including an acceptance of poetry and a less than supreme fiction. There is truth in the "evasions" of metaphor, human and fictive truths; but they are only human, imaginative, not supreme or transcendental. Indeed, much of Stevens' poetry from 1937 on is concerned with just this paradox of the truth and the falsifications of metaphor, with the uncomfortable knowledge that everything we know as truth comes to us in forms shaped by the mind. We are consciously aware that the mind shapes not the "thing itself" but an "evasion." Still, the imagination is capable of touching not ideas about the thing but the thing itself—of conceiving, that is, an ultimate reality beyond all forms. This was not simply an epistemological debate. On the contrary, it had everything to do with defining man in his own *mean* form, in his consciousness of the paradox of consciousness. It is in response to this problem, as Pearce sees it, that Stevens grew, and evolved his later style—the "basic style" of a new humanism.

There is a point where other critics may assume that Professor Pearce's theory has abstracted itself from poetry altogether. But what Pearce has done is establish in a philosophical (and historical) framework the assumptions Stevens' poetry makes in terms of Stevens' own imaginative experience, the experience of a representative "separate" self contemplating in poetry the very ground of selfhood, contemplating human possibility and human limitation. Pearce's view of the extreme thrust of late Stevens is, to my mind, in itself extreme. Even though this last poetry evidences the wish to get beneath appearances to a thing-itself, even though its own style seems intent on pulverizing the metaphors and myths by which mind clothes reality, even though it occasionally asserts that the self must push itself toward the purity of the ultimate abstraction—even though all these are given voice, what remains vital in this poetry is the tension, pointed out by Mrs. Lord, between what is desired and what is finally accepted as possible. Stevens' final composure, then, need not be explained as achieving what it willed (to "know" the "thing itself"). Rather, it would seem to be a final affirmation of the power of the self to *be,* to conceive and meditate a reality other than that which ordinary experience affords, and to find its *being* in the act of the mind that can create abstractions. I have argued, somewhat in opposition to Pearce, that Stevens' "thing itself" becomes at last the process of poetry, that his discovery of an "ultimate" reality is his discovery that only in the "act of the mind" is there any such experience of reality (*PMLA*, Sept., 1962). Reality, then, would reside in that incessant movement of imagination between the world of change and the ultimate abstraction (the "supreme fiction" become the "rock") which the mind can conceive because it can abstract from change. Here at last for Stevens poetry and life became one, poetry and life being "good" even in their limitation, even in their dependence on the mind's being able to conceive a reality beyond form, and thus to conceive a reality that is a negation of poetry and life.

It is right here that Pearce's view of Stevens adds a new dimension. By defining the extreme aspiration of Stevens' poetry as a radical humanistic desire to make man the sole arbiter of the real, Pearce has made it possible to see these late poems as progressive and profoundly continuous acts of self-creation. Like Whitman's *Leaves of Grass*, but in a modern, non-transcendental context, Stevens' canon becomes something else again than a collection of separate poems, and his development something other than casual changes of style. Similarly, this view calls for a revaluation of the poems of *Harmonium*. Rather than seeing them as variations on a constant theme, or as radically separate from late Stevens, Pearce would make them the initial acts of the self introducing itself to the "sensuously flowing aspects of reality," to the physical world itself. From this initial birth of self-consciousness, there develops the struggle to define men's being as it is affected by ever-changing reality (social and intellectual) which mocks formulas of belief and self-definition, until at last one comes upon the ultimate questions, of "final belief." If one accepts this organic view of the canon as a whole greater than its parts, whether or not he accepts this as viable or healthy for poetry, he can understand something of Stevens' radical reconceiving of poetics. And Stevens' poetry may then be seen as something more than a casual collection of expressions—but rather as a central act in modern man's struggle to know himself.

I do not end by suggesting that Pearce's Stevens (and certainly not mine) is a final definition. Such systematized perspectives may do little more than provide a context within which this difficult poetry can be understood in and for itself. Perhaps Louis Martz has provided the best framework so far, in that his view of the poems as meditations allows one to see the later poems

as poems first, answering the requirements of a traditionally coherent and public poetic form. Pearce, on the other hand, points
up the fallacy of judging Stevens' late poems in the light of
Harmonium rather than the reading of *Harmonium* in terms of
the greater consort. To do this, he shows, is to distort Stevens'
particular relevance to the modern imagination, if not to the
history of modern poetry itself. Pearce raised the question in his
study about whether Stevens' last poems were poems at all and
not just attempts to define the province within which a poetry
could be written today. Whether relevant or not—and it seems
to me that above all Stevens was constantly trying to realize his
life of the mind in recognizable poetic form—the very fact that
this question can be raised makes the development of Stevens
criticism more than peripheral in our literary history. Most of the
criticisms of Stevens, of course, accept without reservation that
the poems are poems, of a man speaking to men, or speaking of
himself by way of speaking for man. As Martz implies, these are
modern poems, yet traditional. This does not, however, reject the
view of Stevens' role within his greater culture, as one intent on
establishing poetry as a living human act, perhaps the only one
remaining to verify man's nobility of self. It might be better to
say, then, that Stevens' development was a continuous search
for the analogies of belief to which a secular self could attach
himself, a search which discovered that belief in a time denying
transcendental reality lies in the very "act" of searching. But a
thesis like Pearce's, even if it antagonizes those who like their
poetry purified of metaphysics and returned to the common
emotions, established a frame in which these poems cannot be
denied "life." One can still read *Harmonium* as a collection of
nearly pure lyrics if he wishes; he can no longer dismiss the late
meditations as an idle toying with ideas which in a literal sense
take poetry to be the better part of life. The unresolved critical
problem would now seem to be how these poems, which on the
surface reflect so much conventional Romantic doctrine, add new
dimensions to the experience of the modern self—not as doctrine
but as poems of the life of the mind. Pearce stresses Stevens'
new humanism; Martz the forms through which he worked, and
worked beyond. But the intrinsic worth of the later poems remains to be discovered, and with it the worth of the entire canon.
It may well require the industry of an "industry." The only

unanimous agreement among Stevens devotees is that his poems deserve the effort, and are durable enough to survive it.[20]

[20] Since this essay first appeared, one year ago in *ELH*, two full-length studies of Stevens have appeared. John J. Enck's *Wallace Stevens, Images and Judgments*, the first extensive chronological look at Stevens' development, except for Kermode's, attempts to define Stevens' achievement in terms of his unique Imagism. Enck argues generally that Stevens' later poetry can be seen in relation to the early most clearly in the proliferations and enlargements of basic images, and that the total corpus is the record of maturing judgments. Implicitly, Enck rejects the kind of development I have suggested in this essay, which is to say, he sees Stevens' development only in terms of changing perspectives upon experiences very nearly alike.

Enck begins with the rather peevish (and inaccurate) charge that "irresponsible historians have drawn few lines between him and the rest [of the Imagists]." I am not sure how one can be irresponsible unless he has drawn the lines wrongly instead of not at all. But then few "historians" (Mr. Enck's "irresponsibles" are, he assumes, self-evident) have drawn the lines of influence and association so narrowly and exclusively as Enck, except those who early found Stevens almost exclusively a Symbolist. The thing is, Enck's "irresponsibles" play straw-men to his "truth." They are those who (1) try to see any consistent system of thought or lines of development in Stevens, and (2) impute to his ideas any philosophical relevance at all. Enck's overview of Stevens is summed up in his own tentatively formulated view that Stevens is a kind of "synchronistic connoisseur," fusing images out of perceptions, whose imagistic range can be best described in terms of the Chinese oracles, *I Ching or the Book of Changes*. It is, to say the least, a rare theory, especially in view of Enck's own curious remarks on the history and meaning of Imagism and Stevens' relation to that style. Enck does offer several new, interesting, and provocative interpretations. Few of them, however, can go unchallenged. And his whole argument is wrapped in a style that speaks more often for itself than for Stevens. The following are exemplary: "Prolifically as resemblances exfoliate, how determinedly to push the parts into a whole remains an unsolved enigma, which threatens rigidity or shambles"; or, "Often Stevens probes his values by rhetoric, and, if they can keep their pedestals when decked in the highest flattery, then, presumably, he judges them companionable for the hearth." It is a little hard to pin down the Stevens Enck presents. And if it is the author's purpose to deny that Stevens can be pinned down, then we might protest that a critical style need not imitate its purpose. In the end Enck joins with those who would save Stevens from his ideas; and no less from his critics—except, of course, one.

Henry Wells's *Introduction to Wallace Stevens* is, however, a far less satisfactory book, perhaps the least reliable and least informative full-length study of Stevens. Wells's approach is thematic, a general, appreciative overview, an introduction in the most elementary sense of the word. Assuming that Stevens is summed up in two important poems, "Owl's Clover" and "Esthétique du Mal," Wells mixes lengthy exegeses of these poems with eleven chapters on general themes, on style, and on ideas. There is nothing new in the book, nothing indeed that was not said or suggested in O'Connor's and Pack's studies. As for Wells's readings of the poems, they seldom explore deeply; similarly his scattered remarks on Stevens' thought. Wells is best on style, but totally ignores the implications of the changes in that style.

A third book, a collection of essays in the Twentieth Century Views series, edited by Marie Borroff, contains several of the essays discussed here (most notably those of Pearce, Frye, and Martz), a previously unpublished study of "Notes toward a Supreme Fiction" by Harold Bloom, and a substantial introduction by the editor.

NOTES ON CONTRIBUTORS

BERNARD HERINGMAN teaches at Baldwin-Wallace College in Berea, Ohio, and has written a number of articles on Wallace Stevens.

FRANK DOGGETT is principal of the high school in Jacksonville Beach, Florida, and is the author of many essays on Stevens.

ROBERT BUTTEL teaches at Temple University and has written on the early work of Stevens.

SAMUEL FRENCH MORSE is Wallace Stevens' literary executor and the editor of *Opus Posthumous* and *Poems by Wallace Stevens*.

MICHEL BENAMOU is in the Department of Romance Languages at the University of Michigan. His dissertation for the Sorbonne is on Wallace Stevens.

ROY HARVEY PEARCE is the author of *The Continuity of American Poetry*. He is chairman of the Department of Literature at the University of California, San Diego.

J. HILLIS MILLER teaches at Johns Hopkins. He is the author of *The Disappearance of God*.

HELEN HENNESSY VENDLER is the author of *Yeats's Vision and the Later Plays*. She teaches at Smith College.

MAC HAMMOND teaches at the State University of New York at Buffalo. He wrote a dissertation at Harvard on " The Man with the Blue Guitar."

RICHARD A. MACKSEY teaches in the Writing Seminars at Johns Hopkins and has written several articles on modern literature.

DENIS DONOGHUE is the author of *The Third Voice*. He teaches at University College, Dublin.

JOSEPH N. RIDDEL teaches at the University of California at Riverside. His book on Wallace Stevens is in press.

A NOTE ON THE ESSAYS

Eight of the twelve essays in this volume have been previously published in *ELH: A Journal of English Literary History*. Bernard Heringman's essay was published in 1949; Frank Doggett's in 1961; Robert Buttel's in 1961. The essays by Samuel French Morse, Michel Benamou, Roy Harvey Pearce, J. Hillis Miller, and Joseph N. Riddel were published in March, 1964, in a special Stevens issue of *ELH*. The essays by Helen Hennessy Vendler, Mac Hammond, Richard A. Macksey, and Denis Donoghue are published here for the first time.

INDEX

[This index is divided into two sections: I. The Writings of Wallace Stevens (poems cited in the text by volume and page number are indexed by poem titles); and II. General Index of Names.]

I. THE WRITINGS OF WALLACE STEVENS

II. GENERAL INDEX OF NAMES

THE ACT OF THE MIND
Essays on the Poetry of Wallace Stevens
edited by
ROY HARVEY PEARCE AND J. HILLIS MILLER

designer:	Edward King
compositor:	J. H. Furst Co.
typefaces:	Scotch and Caslon Openface
printer:	J. H. Furst Co.
paper:	Perkins and Squier GM
binder:	Moore & Co.
cover material:	Columbia Milbank Linen